SOMERSET CRICKETERS REVISITED

New Discoveries

BARRY PHILLIPS

Best wishes
Barry Phillips

First published in 2023

ISBN 978-1-3999-4872-2

LEISURESOLVE PUBLISHERS
BEECH HOUSE, HOLTON, OXFORD OX33 1QF

PRINTED AND BOUND BY: P2D BOOKS LTD.

Special thanks to:

- David Wood of the Somerset Cricket Museum for valued support
- Hannah Wilmshurst for her design and typesetting skills
- My wife, Wendy Gillard, for her understanding

Also available from Halsgrove and the Somerset County Sports Shop, Cooper Associates County Ground:

Somerset Cricketers 1882-1914 by Stephen Hill with additional research by Barry Phillips (VOL.1)

Somerset Cricketers 1919-1939 by Stephen Hill and Barry Phillips (VOL.2)

Somerset Cricketers 1946-1970 by Stephen Hill and Barry Phillips (VOL.3)

Somerset Cricketers 1971-2000 by Stephen Hill with additional research by Julian Wyatt (VOL.4)

A fifth volume was published privately in 2021:

Somerset Cricketers 1876-1890 – The rise to First-Class Status by Stephen Hill and Barry Phillips (VOL.5) published as a limited edition of 110 copies in 2021 (all copies sold)

This book, *Somerset Cricketers Revisited*, refers to the five previous books as volumes in the abbreviated form shown in brackets above

Contents

New Discoveries – Other

Somerset v Long Ashton, Ashton Court, 10 August 1881:
Standing L-R: J.J. Cross, S.C. Newton [23], J.B. Challen [41], A.J. Fothergill [11], H.E. Winter [48]; seated L-R: H.G. Fuller, H.F. Reed [20], W. Massey [13], C.H.R. Stock [VOL.5], J.A. Winter [40], F.W. Terry, [18] TU Cross

Foreword

It is only a matter of time after publishing a work of history before fresh discoveries cause consternation and regret. It happened when I wrote *ARTHUR WELLARD: No mere slogger*. The most important fact about my hero's life was the unusual circumstances in which he came to play for Somerset having rejected Kent's advances during a match between Bexley CC and the Kent Club and Ground. As it occurred more than seventy years before publishing the biography, who was going to challenge my account anyway? I was confident I had the full story, but shortly after publication I received a letter from octogenarian George Lovegrove who was Bexley's scorer that day and overheard Arthur telling Gerry Weigall, the Kent coach, to stick his contract up his arse! Fortunately, the gist of the story was correct except that George told me the exchange had happened in 1929 *not* 1928 as recorded in the book. It still vexes me that I missed George's first-hand account of the confrontation. George reckoned that, in clean bowling Weigall that day, he had never seen Arthur bowl faster.

The first volume of the *Somerset Cricketers* series was published in 2016, the fifth volume in 2021 and these will be referred to in this book as VOL.I through to VOL.5. Over the passage of these seven years, mistakes have been found and new material unearthed, and as these have grown, so has the need for a supplement to the series.

The one discovery that finally tipped the balance was the team photograph that features on the front cover of this book and the opposite page. This superb photograph was taken at Ashton Court, home of Long Ashton CC, on 10 August 1881. And it is a historic find because it was taken some six years before the acknowledged earliest Somerset team photograph (the 1887 team photograph used on the dust wrapper of VOL.5 and here on page 32). Furthermore, it offers clear images of players from VOL.1 whom we had to reluctantly accept had no known image. Of the 227 players covered by VOL.1, we were unable to find images for seventeen of them, and now three of this number - both Winter brothers and one of the Reed brothers – can be revealed for the first time. It is particularly pleasing to find an image of John Winter as he is the reason that Somerset are based at the Cooper Associates County Ground.

The Long Ashton match was one of twenty-one friendly fixtures played against local clubs and district sides between 1878 and 1881 They were arranged with the intention of promoting the new county club, taking a county cricket team to all parts of Somerset, but they were not always representative of a typical Somerset team. And they were generally against weaker opponents often comprising fifteen or sixteen players to make it a more even contest. In this match, it was a contest between twelve of Somerset and thirteen of Long Ashton CC, but it does not diminish the importance of this photograph as in this match the line-up was typically representative of the sides that played in 1881. It deserves the accolade of earliest known Somerset team image. Three of the Somerset cricketers in the Long Ashton photograph only played in this match and therefore have not been included in any previous volume. To complete the picture of the players in this photograph, biographies of these three gentlemen have been included in Appendix 1.

I have drawn on the archives provided by the subscription website run by CricketArchive and have found this source invaluable. There are however various corrections to be made to the database in due course. I have generally referred to the Somerset County Cricket Club as 'Somerset' or occasionally as 'Somerset CCC' and to the Somerset Cricket Museum as the 'Cricket Museum'. For ease of reference, the name of a cricketer (when not referred to informally by first name) is followed by the unique appearance number used in the first four volumes, for example, H.E. Winter **[48]**, or in the case of the fifth volume where no number exists, by reference to the volume and page number, for example, E.J.P. Cassan **[VOL.5, page 16]**.

Stephen Hill has been engaged on other literary projects and was unable to devote his energies to this book, but he has supported me all the way and proved an excellent guide and proof reader. I am grateful to the Trustees of the Cricket Museum and especially to David Wood who has given me his customary assistance and access to the Museum's collections. I would also like to thank David Ashworth, Alan Collier, Jill Cowles, Guy Curry, Duncan Davies, Andrew Dawson, Lesley Edwards, Suzanne Foster, Roger Gibbons, Chris Gore, Phil Hill, Hilary Lucier, Roger Mann, Richard Miller, Phil Nichols, Jerry Rudman, Hedley Stroud, and Keith Walmsley.

All the images used in this book are mine or are held by the Cricket Museum unless otherwise attributed in the text.

Barry Phillips
Beech House, Holton, Oxford (bpwg@sky.com)

New Discoveries – Players

HARRY GEORGE TATE [3]

Over the course of six seasons since formation in 1876, Somerset had earned the right to be recognised as the club to represent the whole of the county, based in the county town. Somerset played Hampshire (twice), Gloucestershire (twice), Kent and MCC during the 1881 season. All three counties had first-class status. Somerset were held back by the lack of a permanent home venue but that was about to change. At the meeting of county secretaries at Lord's in December 1881, E. Western **[27]**, was able to announce that the County Ground would be available for first-class cricket in 1882. And he persuaded his fellow county secretaries to grant Somerset two matches against prestigious Lancashire while retaining the Hampshire and Gloucestershire fixtures.

Given the importance of Somerset's inaugural first-class match, which was against Lancashire at Old Trafford beginning 8 June 1882, it might be presumed that the club was well prepared for such a challenging encounter. But Somerset were missing key players. F. Reed **[19]**, H.F. Reed **[20]**, S.C. Newton **[23]**, and A.H. Evans **[30]** had teaching commitments, while R.C. Ramsey **[14]** and W.N. Roe **[26]** had examinations at Cambridge. D.D. Pontifex **[12]** also withdrew at the last minute. It left Somerset scrambling to form a side and when the team was announced in the newspapers, the relatively unknown name of H.G. Tate was included in the XI.

Harry George Tate who preferred to be called George was born in East Knoyle, Wiltshire on 18 July 1862, the son of a GWR railway guard. On his sixteenth birthday, he joined his deceased father's employer as a 'lad clerk' in the goods section at Taunton station and was soon making a reputation for himself as a promising all-rounder for Taunton CC. George was selected to play for a

Somerset Colts XV against a Somerset XI in the first ever cricket match played at the County Ground, on Whit Monday, 29 May 1882. The grand opening was very poorly attended, the locals preferring cheap day railway excursions to the seaside resorts of Devon and North Somerset. Admission to the ground was one shilling (5p) plus an extra sixpence (2.5p) for viewing the fireworks. The pyrotechnics received better support than the cricket, the finale cleverly crafting the words 'SUCCESS TO SOMERSET CRICKETERS' writ large in letters of fire.

The cricket match was effectively a trial for the fixture against Lancashire starting ten days later and George played well for the Colts, captained by the influential Edward Western. He opened the innings with a top score of 45 runs, took two catches and bowled 8 overs for a meagre 18 runs. It was more than enough to warrant his selection in a makeshift side that would be trounced by the Lancastrians. Somerset were dismissed for 29 in the first innings and 51 in the second, losing by an innings and 157 runs. George scarcely enhanced his reputation, out for a duck in both innings and not asked to bowl, but he was far from alone in this embarrassing one-sided contest. The openers, W.H. Fowler **[1]** and E. Sainsbury **[2]**, made 53 of the 80 runs scored by Somerset and 11 of the remainder came from extras.

George would surely have had other opportunities to add to his single first-class appearance had it not been for his imminent posting to Reading station during the summer of 1882. This became a permanent transfer in February 1883. It was Somerset's loss but Reading CC's gain as he would become an outstanding performer for Reading throughout the 1880s. Despite considerable effort, no image of George was found for VOL.1. This can now be rectified with this splendid image courtesy of George's granddaughter, Ms Pam Tate. It is from a team photograph featuring Christ Church CC in the Reading and District Challenge Cup Final of 1889. He had

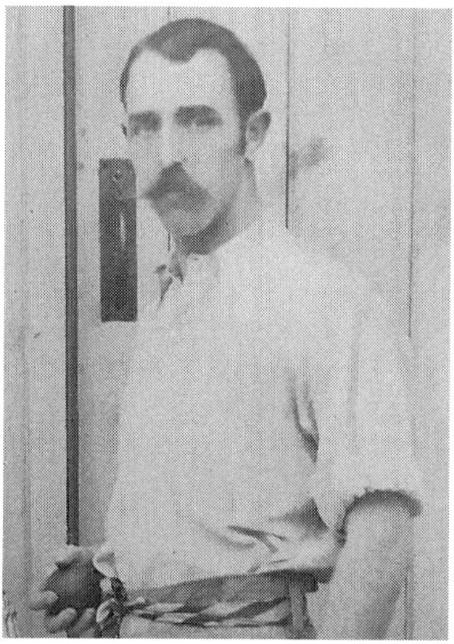

just completed a successful season for Reading, topping the averages with bat and ball (his 38 wickets came at 5.50 runs apiece), but Reading was not allowed to play in the Challenge Cup, so George played for his local team, Christ Church. He was the outstanding player in the final, scoring 57 runs and taking 5 wickets to restrict the opposition to a modest score of 69. He played in several other cup finals for Christ Church over the years. After Reading CC, George had equal success playing for Caversham CC until leaving the area with his wife Eliza (née Southwood) and their three children to take up an appointment as a cashier in the goods section at Birkenhead station.
George remained at GWR Birkenhead until his retirement and the family then returned to Taunton where his wife Eliza had been born (her family were the owners of land in Comeytrowe around the area on which the post office now stands and the family name is enshrined in nearby Southwood Grove). George and Eliza made Bishops Hull their home. Eliza died there in 1947, and George joined her two years later, on 9 March 1949, aged eighty-six.

ARNOLD JAMES FOTHERGILL [5]

The 1881 Long Ashton photograph offers a fine early image of Arnold. He was not the first Somerset professional. That was H. Scott **[11]**, against Dorset at Sherborne School in 1879, but he was the most successful during Somerset's early years. He first played in 1880 when he combined or alternated with Scott and another professional A.J. Brookes **[VOL.5, page 157]**. In the first-class years from 1882 to 1885, he played sixteen matches for Somerset taking 57 wickets at 21.05. By 1889, he had also taken well over a hundred wickets in Somerset's other matches.
He is credited as Somerset's first Test player having gone on Major R.G.

Warton's MCC tour of South Africa in 1888/89 although technically he shares that honour with R.B. Stewart **[VOL.5, page 8]** who was playing for South Africa. Cricket historians have challenged the status of this match, but it remains a Test Match in the records. Arnold was a ground bowler at Lord's all the time he was at Somerset, and it is how he came to be on this MCC tour. In fact, he played more first-class matches for MCC and the South at Lord's than he did for Somerset. In a typical illustration of Somerset's treatment of professionals, the AGM in December 1888 reported that the club would be better off by £40 to £50 because he had broken his qualification 'by going off to the Cape'. But in 1889, the club realised they needed him more than he needed them, and he played the first four matches of the season. These were his last for the county.

Arnold only came south for the summer. His home was in Newcastle where he was born on 26 August 1854. During the winter he worked as a clerk, at one point for his uncle in the offices of the Beaumont Lead Mines. He married a local lass and had the first six of his ten children there. It was only while coaching at Repton School between 1893 and the mid-1900s that the family moved with him. He then returned to clerical employment in Newcastle.

The only blemish on his Geordie credentials was a move to Sunderland in 1929 when he needed to be close to one of his married daughters. He died there on 1 August 1932 aged seventy-seven. He had not been well for some time and, a fortnight earlier, he broke an arm falling over in his garden and never recovered from the fall. In an odd coincidence, his daughter Vera married Reginald Foster who was in the Harrow XI that played Eton at Lord's in 1903. Reginald became a noted racehorse owner and Vera had a horse (Faux Pas) in the 1951 Derby. Arnold would have enjoyed that occasion!

HENRY GEORGE HAMLET HALL [10]

Hamlet's younger brother Ernest (H.E. Hall **[43]**) disliked his first name Horatio and preferred to use Ernest or Ernie. Some match reports give Hamlet his full set of initials, and others refer to him as plain 'H. Hall'. Reports related to Ernest use a single initial or a combination of both initials but not in a consistent order. This has naturally caused confusion. Hamlet has always been credited with playing in Somerset's inaugural first-class match at Old Trafford on 8 June 1882, but after careful consideration it is concluded that it was Ernest *not* Hamlet who played. Fortunately, it has a limited effect on numbering, but it does mean that Ernest should be numbered **[10]** and Hamlet should be **[41]**. J.B. Challen becomes **[42]** and T. Robinson becomes **[43]**. Reasons to support this conclusion are given in Ernest's updated biography on page 41.

WILLIAM MASSEY [13]

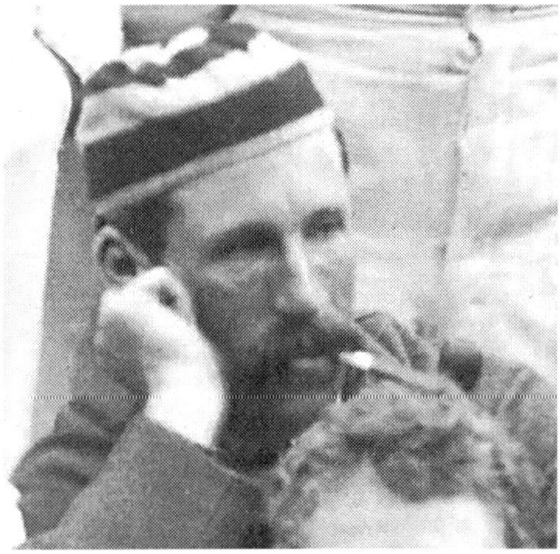

No other image of William has been found except in the less than clear photograph of the Staten Island team (shown on page 20)

William Massey added the middle initial 'N' or 'M' and caused a hundred years of confusion for cricket historians who believed him to be William Morton Massey of Canadian heritage. The plain William Massey came from a strict Methodist family much nearer home. He was born on 11 April 1850 in Ardwick, a suburb of Manchester a mile or so from the city centre. His father, William Massey snr was a cotton buyer and hosier manufacturer who was in business with Charles Lings, the owner of several spinning mills in the area. The men were also connected personally (there were three marriages between their children), and all the family members lived close by in the fashionable Burnage suburb of Manchester. William Massey was an outstanding athlete. Described as a 'giant' he was strikingly tall and built like a barn door, but this was no obstacle to regularly proving himself to be the fastest sprinter at athletic meetings. No wonder then, that he played rugby for three leading counties as a full-back and place kicker, two of which he captained. Or that he represented three counties as a hard-hitting batsman, making first-class appearances for two of them.

Details about William's early life were hard to find for VOL.1, but further research has traced his secondary education to the Wesley College in Sheffield where he was a gifted track and field athlete and rugby player. After College he returned to Burnage Lane and was expected to work in the family business alongside his younger brother Herbert. Both brothers played their rugby for Free Wanderers, one of the foremost rugby clubs in Lancashire whose annual fixtures included the likes of Sale and Manchester.

And they both competed successfully in the regular athletics meetings that took place around the country, often in five or six events in a single day. In William's case he would run or hurdle over any distance up to a mile, compete in the long and high jump events, and throw objects such as the cricket ball, hammer, and a 33lb 'weight'. His large and powerful frame also helped with his cricket, played for Didsbury CC, and it gained him a reputation for hard but sporadic hitting.

William's father indulged him in his sporting pursuits but sensing that his son, now twenty-four, was all play and no work, sent him off to the West Country to help run the Town Mill in Ottery St Mary, a silk mill established in the 1820s which employed three hundred men, women, and children from the town. Its owners, J.C. Newbery & Co., needed an injection of cash and perhaps some Manchester expertise from the Massey/Lings cotton dynasty. And William was the solution. He moved to Ottery in the spring of 1874 to become a co-partner with John Colin Newbery, but it is questionable whether William had much time to devote to the task of running a mill judging by the amount of sport he played. He was immediately in demand from the Ottery cricket club where John Newbery was a key member. That did not stop him playing for the cricket clubs of Axminster, Axe Vale, Budleigh Salterton, Chard, Cullompton, Corfe, East Devon Wanderers, Fullands and Sidmouth among others during the next couple of seasons. His batting was inconsistent, but he was a regular wicket-taker at this level of club cricket.

Within months of arriving, he seems to have gained so much popularity in the town that his name was put forward for election to the Ottery School Board. Given his chapel background, it is no surprise that he stood as a 'Dissenter' (Nonconformist) and Liberal on a platform of shaking up the Church of England's conservative hegemony over the manner and content of school teaching. It was the talk of Ottery at the time and the election caused a heated debate over the relative merits of the nine candidates for five Board member positions.

The church candidates set about questioning William's fitness to serve, calling him 'almost a stranger'. William spoke of correcting the injustice of the church seeking to exert unopposed control of the School Board and said he was firmly against the teaching of creeds and catechisms. His message clearly resounded with the large chapel following in this sleepy little East Devonshire town. In November 1874, he topped the poll with 354 votes compared to the next highest candidate's 270 votes. Fellow dissenter Mr Newton from the Town Mill was also elected, much to the annoyance of the church. All subsequent reporting suggests that William served the Board diligently and both he and Mr Newton were re-elected at the triennial elections in 1877.

His School Board and Town Mill duties were not so arduous as to preclude enthusiastic participation in a full season of rugby during his first winter in Ottery. He joined Exeter rugby club, and this became his main club for the next three seasons though other clubs such as Paignton and Plymouth were very happy to make use of William's services, soon to be regarded as the outstanding full-back in the county. He even appeared as a half-back for Taunton in December 1874 with J.A. Winter **[40]** partnered at full back. By 1876 he was captaining the Devon XV. His cricket was on a less dramatic upward path though he could often be relied upon to provide quick runs such as for the Gentlemen of Devon v Dorset in 1876 where he was said to have hit 63 'very finely'.

It is noticeable that as the decade progressed his allegiances gradually switched towards Somerset, no doubt encouraged by the likes of the Rev F. Reed **[19]**, H. Fox **[8]**, W.B. Marke **[VOL.5, page 74]**, and J.J.E. Willmott **[VOL.5, page 84]** who were his regular teammates and opponents in both rugby and cricket matches. By 1878, his main rugby club was Weston-super-Mare although he would still return to play the occasional match for Exeter and Plymouth including a match for the latter in 1879 under floodlights and watched by several thousand spectators. And as late as 1879, he turned out for the Devon XV against Somerset where he was still listed as 'W. Massey (Exeter)'. This did not stop him playing for the Lancashire XV against Northumberland and Durham in the same year while, at cricket, he managed to play for the Gentlemen of Devon, the Gentlemen of Somerset, and a Somerset XI against MCC. His club cricket was equally peripatetic with appearances for Fullands, Weston-super-Mare, and Taunton, among others.

None of this activity could have been conducive to running a business and it is not surprising that a creditors' petition for bankruptcy was heard in Manchester in January 1880 against William and ratified in the London Bankruptcy Court. The Court was told that William had liabilities of £19,360 (£1.63 million in today's money) and assets of £150. News of William's downfall must have been met with incredulity locally when reported in the *Exeter and Plymouth Gazette* on 16 January 1880. This larger-than-life Mancunian who had become a prominent and popular resident of the Town must have overnight become *persona non grata* on the streets of Ottery St Mary. No wonder he removed himself to a temporary residence in The Strand, London while the bankruptcy proceedings progressed. In the liquidation proceedings that followed later in the year, William's meagre offer to creditors of four shillings in the pound was accepted. It was no doubt negotiated by the Massey family lawyers and financed by his father.

Such small matters of business did not affect his cricket that summer. He managed a match for Somerset at the beginning of July 1880, against Sussex at Bath, which was to firmly establish his reputation as a hard hitter. His knock of 120 not out (in a team innings of 227) probably contained many lofty sixes, but sadly, the page in the Somerset scorebook is missing. However, the newspapers do record one such hit as soaring over the Combe Park pavilion and out of the ground. Peter Roebuck in *From Sammy to Jimmy* had this game taking place three years earlier in 1877 and consequently claimed incorrectly that William was Somerset's first centurion (this accolade belongs to E.W.M. Lloyd **[VOL.5, page 21]**, who scored 110 against Dorset in 1877). William followed up his appearance at Bath with two matches for Devon later in the month and five two-day matches for Somerset in August.

In the circumstances, William might have been expected to return to the North West, but in 1881 he can be found lodging with Edward Western, still the honorary secretary of Somerset CCC, and playing a full season's cricket for Somerset including the match against Long Ashton CC in which he is photographed. He played a single first-class match for Somerset against Gloucestershire in 1882, out for a duck in the first innings and tellingly stumped (a regular dismissal for William) for 4 runs in the second. A return to Manchester was inevitable and no doubt commanded by his hitherto tolerant father, but he would continue to play rugby for Somerset as late as the 1882/83 season, except now he was referred to as 'W.M. Massey (Manchester Free Wanderers)'.

Back in Manchester he played his cricket occasionally for St Helens CC but mainly for Manchester CC where in 1883 he played 14 matches and topped the batting averages with 37.3. In 1884 he played a further 23 matches, averaging 17.3 with the bat. In May 1883, he scored a century for Manchester against Longsight and the *Manchester Courier* records 'Mr Massey was in rare form, making 113 by brilliant hitting, three drives going clean out of the ground for six' (hitting out of the ground was the only means of achieving six runs at this time). It was this century plus another that same month which earned him a first-class appearance for Lancashire in June 1883. However, it didn't go well, being out for scores of 5 and 1, and he was not selected again.

Meanwhile, after playing his rugby football for Manchester he made the switch from the handling game to the dribbling game playing association football as a goalkeeper for Manchester Wanderers. Such was his ability and athleticism that the *Sporting Chronicle* was soon calling him 'the best goal-keeper in the North' and others were speculating on an international call-up. Manchester Wanderers later became Manchester Association FC, and their closest rivals were Newton Heath FC, later to become Manchester United. William then moved to Darwen FC which was famous for being the first Northern club to achieve any success in the F.A. Cup reaching the quarter finals in 1879 and going one better in 1881.

But William's sporting dalliances were about to end as the family was running out of patience with him. William's brother Herbert had taken over the Massey side of the combined business and his brothers-in-law, James Scott Lings, and George Scott Lings, were running the Reddish Spinning Company which had woollen and cotton mills in the Burnage and Didsbury areas. James had married William's sister Mary and George had married William's sister Edith. George was overseeing the import/export side of business from his base in New York and was in the process of setting up a new mill at Fall River Massachusetts. No doubt the Massey and Scott Lings families were growing tired of the amount of time William devoted to playing sport to the detriment of the family business. William was now thirty-five years old, and it was time for him to pull his weight. In November 1885, William was duly sent to assist George in New York. An *Athletics News* reporter carried the following mention of his departure:

Mr W. Massey, another well-known gentleman who has played a prominent part in Manchester cricket and football has departed for America. Ten or twelve years ago he was a prominent member of Free Wanderers when the team could hold its own against the strongest opponents. I have seen him keep goal at the Association game in a manner that could not be beaten. As a cricketer Mr Massey was known for his tremendous hard hitting and rattled up some big scores with a speed which few batsmen have excelled.

But if the family had reckoned his sporting days were over, they were wrong. In June 1886, the *Athletic News* reported 'William Massey is showing good cricket with the Riverside Club, New York. A fortnight ago he practically won them the match scoring 23 and taking 4 wickets'. The newspaper described him as a 'tremendous hitter'. The Riverside Club had to share his skills with Kings County CC and Staten Island CC that year. A New York newspaper suggested that Staten Island Cricket Club would be strengthened in 1886 by his inclusion. This was the same year that Staten Island were in the process of moving to a new ground at Livingstone on the Island (the club's ground to this day) and the inaugural match was fixed for Independence Day, 4 July 1886. The match was between the American and the British contingents within the club. A photograph of this occasion is shown below, courtesy of the Staten Island Historical Society:

William Massey can be found in the back row, fifth from the right, with his best friend C.J. Wilson **[VOL.5, page 33]** next to him fourth from the right. Cyril Wilson is mentioned later in this book (page 205).
William also played for Staten Island against two touring teams, the first against

the West Indians and the second against an E.J. Sanders' XI. Ned Sanders had been a teammate of William's for Devon CC and Exeter RFC. Another old teammate from those days, F.T. Welman **[4]**, kept wicket for the English XI. William would periodically play for Staten Island until 1895 when into his mid-forties. And in that year, he was the captain and secretary of Incognito, an exclusive section of the club that played against the Staten Island 1st XI and proceeded to tour the United States as 'Incognito of Brooklyn'. He appears to have given up playing after 1895, retiring to his Florida residence where he had set up home with his Canadian wife, Elizabeth McLain Saunders. It is surprising to note that, four years later, this most active and athletic man died suddenly, on 17 April 1899, aged just forty-nine, while on a business trip to New York.

N.B. VOL.1 included a quote from Peter Roebuck in *From Sammy to Jimmy*, which suggested that William, after scoring 1,998 runs one season, had arranged another match to score the two more runs needed, only to score two ducks. This tale, which may in any event be apocryphal, should not have been attributed to William. It is a story which relates to the Canadian born and bred cricketer, William Morton Massey, whom Roebuck had understandably confused with William 'M' Massey from Manchester.

FRANCIS WILLIAM TERRY [18]

VOL.1 relied on various source documents which have since proved incorrect. Firstly, it was stated that Francis, usually known as Frank, was born in Wells on 26 October 1860. While his date of birth is correct, further research shows that he was born in Mells *not* Wells. The village of Mells is near Frome and some eleven miles from Wells.

Secondly, it was stated that he worked at the Mimico Asylum, part of the Ontario Hospital of Senility in Toronto, providing pastoral care to the mentally ill. This was far from correct because it is now clear that Frank was a patient at the Asylum, *not* a member of staff.

'IS TERRY INSANE?' reads a headline in *The Miner* (Nelson, British Columbia) on 9 December 1893. It reported that 'The Canadian cricket captain and star batsman has just been readmitted to an asylum in London, Ontario'. It was neither his first nor his last spell as a patient at Mimico.

VOL.1 contained a famous and well-used image of Frank taken from a later

period of his life after his emigration to Canada. It was the only image that could be found which makes the discovery of him in the 1881 Long Ashton photograph even more important to historians.

Frank was educated at St Edward's School, Oxford where, as a forceful batsman and wicketkeeper, he captained the cricket 1st XI. From there he went to Merton College, Oxford, a short stroll away along the Woodstock Road to the City centre. He did not make the University XI at any time during his studies at Oxford and must have known from the outset how difficult it would be to break into the team. In the two freshmen trials of 1881, he was placed in the same team as M.C. Kemp, who was preferred as wicketkeeper and who would gain his blue over four consecutive years. As will be seen later (on page 49), Kemp also kept the Somerset wicketkeeper A.E. Newton **[63]** out of the University XI.

Frank scored some runs in the trials, but they were not enough, and it was much the same in the following years. *Athletic News* in 1884, noted that 'he never [did] justice to himself' in trial matches. It is interesting to note that when Frank and Arthur Newton appeared in the 1883 trial for the 'Next XVI' against the University XI (captained by M.C. Kemp) they were joined by another Somerset man E.W. Bastard **[35]**. Edward Bastard did do 'justice to himself' taking nine wickets in the match including a hat-trick with Kemp as his third victim. He was the only one of the three Somerset men to play for the University and obtain his blue that year.

Merton did not award Frank his BA until 1886 due to a persistent failure to complete the studies set for him and to show evidence of satisfactory academic work. It does suggest that his priorities lay elsewhere and that he was spending too much time on the playing fields of Oxford, though early signs of mental health issues cannot be ruled out. He certainly had an insatiable appetite for cricket. C.J.M. Godfrey of Sussex, who was also in the Next XVI trial match of 1883, was interviewed by W.A. Bettesworth for his *Chats on a Cricket Field* series. Godfrey recalled Frank making six centuries on consecutive days, beginning on a Monday, playing for a wandering team at Oxford. Godfrey, who describes Frank as a magnificent cricketer, ends the recollection with the words "on Cowley Marsh too!". This remark was intended to emphasise the magnitude of the achievement as the wickets at Cowley Marsh were not conducive to good batsmanship. It makes this story more than apocryphal because Godfrey was a contemporary of Frank at schoolboy and university level.

It is unfortunate that Frank was at Oxford the same time as Kemp because he was a more than capable wicketkeeper. The local reporter in the match against Long Ashton in 1881 refers to 'Mr Terry's wicket-keeping being particularly noticeable'. This was not his first match for Somerset. That had been against Hampshire at Combe Park, Bath the previous month and he also featured in the return match at Southampton in late August where his 29 not out in a low scoring game caught the eye. Frank was only available for ten first-class matches over the course of four seasons 1882 to 1885. During this time, he would average 32.47 with the bat. He began brightly with a score of 77 not out in the first year, but this was eclipsed in 1883 when he scored 121 against Hampshire. It was his only first-class century (a later one for Canada was not first-class). The following season, Hampshire were again subjected to a Terry onslaught when his sparkling innings of 51 included twelve fours. Frank kept wicket in most but not all his appearances for Somerset.

During his time at Oxford, he also played cricket for Wellingborough Grammar School in the summer term of 1884. It is not clear whether he was appearing at the invitation of J. B. Challen **[41]**, who played alongside him, or whether he was in a temporary teaching role at the school. He went on to train for the priesthood at Wells Theological College and in 1886 was appointed to the role of assistant curate in Horsham. He had two whole seasons playing for Horsham CC where he was the mainstay of the club's batting. In 1886 his batting average was above 50. But the demands of the curacy proved too much for him, and by December 1887, the *West Sussex County Times* was reporting that 'Rev F. W. Terry has been obliged, owing to overwork and anxiety, to leave Horsham for a short time, in order to get some change and rest'. Shortly after this newspaper report, on Christmas Day, Frank was admitted to Bailbrook House in Bath which also had the words 'lunatic asylum' in its title. It seems an odd day for an admission and his father George Terry, who was the medical officer for the Frome area, must surely have been involved. The records show that Frank was discharged on the 21 February 1888, and it can surely be no coincidence that his father died two days later at his home, Bilboa House in Mells, from the head injury sustained from falling off his horse a few weeks previously.

Frank never returned to Horsham, although he recovered sufficiently to be appointed on a temporary basis as curate at Buckland St Mary in September 1888. His tenure there was short-lived, and in 1891 he left for Canada, initially to seek solace and professional help at the London (later Mimico) Asylum, before he was due to take up a teaching post at the Upper Canada College for boys in Toronto, in October of the same year.

He was soon making headlines as 'a scintillating batsman and an alert and clever wicket-keeper', but mental health issues were never far from the surface. To his credit (and that of staff at the asylum), he kept trying to carve out a career for himself beyond the hospital walls. It no doubt helped his job prospects that he was widely regarded as the jewel in the crown of Canadian cricket (captaining the national side and registering the country's first century against their local rivals, the USA). In 1893, he was appointed to the role of minister at the newly founded church of St Luke at Red Deer, Calgary.

On leaving Toronto, he was presented with the bat with which he had scored his century for Canada and the ball he smote to all parts of the ground, both with engraved silver plaques. The new challenge in Calgary proved too much and during one episode the Mounties had to take him into custody for his own protection. A later summary of the history of the church at Red Deer confirms that 'Rev F. W. Terry, a man of excellent education, a very pleasant manner, and a great cricketer … commenced his duties on November 1, but shortly after suffered a recurrence of a mental disorder that necessitated him being taken back to London, Ontario, for treatment'.

Perhaps Frank Terry was as bewildered as his adoring public about why a man who revelled in the spotlight whether entertaining the crowds with bat in hand, or singing solos heartily at musical concerts, or preaching lustily from the pulpit, could be so beset by demons. The newspapers were now openly describing the country's cricket captain as 'insane'. There was still no doubting his all-round abilities as a batsman/wicketkeeper but also as a bowler. At least one reporter, sharing his thoughts in *Toronto Saturday Night*, was of the view that the skipper should be shedding the gloves more often and turning his arm more. He wrote:

He bowls a lightning round-arm, delivered low and continuing low, [with] an emphatic in-break of six inches, and so true that almost every ball, unless played, would knock down the outside stump of the right-hand batsman. It is unusual to find a round-armed bowler who finds the exact spot so invariably... He should not let his modesty deter him from trying a few overs when the enemy are making a stand.

After another spell at the asylum, he accepted a coaching role with Clinton CC in Ontario and was mentally strong enough to plan a tour against three USA teams. There followed a spell as a coach at McGill University, Montreal between 1898 and 1899, but by the following year, he was back home, reviving his Church of England career with a temporary curacy at Madron. The parish records and the local press reports reveal that he was busy both as a curate and a cricketer, bringing Madron CC unexpected success. He also played for Penzance and was invited to play for Cornwall (an invitation he declined). In February 1901, at the Madron CC AGM, he was appointed team captain, but he was gone before the start of the season. In May 1901, the *Cornishman* reported:

FROM Madron great lament comes, as the club was looking forward to such a successful season under the leadership of Rev F.W. Terry. His serious illness has indeed been a great blow to the club, and one bears the utmost sympathy expressed for the reverend gentleman, on all sides, and many hope that he may speedily be restored to health.

The 'serious illness' obliged him to return to Mimico Asylum in October 1901. He was in his forties by then and, inevitably, his cricketing prowess had begun to wane. He played cricket for another two decades and was still representing Canada as late as 1907 but he must have needed stays at Mimico during this time. He continued to play for Mimico Asylum, one of the strongest teams in Canada able to call on five Canadian internationals, and it is believed he played his last match for them in 1919.

This rare image is of the London Asylum team (1903), courtesy of the Canadian national Library. Frank is seated in front row, third from the right:

Frank died in the Mimico Asylum (by then Ontario Hospital) on 6 October 1936, at the age of seventy-five. This was after a final stay at the institution of a little over five years, during which he was diagnosed as suffering from 'senile psychosis'. By then, Canadian interest in the sparkling career of one of its founding fathers had waned and his death went unreported.

HERBERT FARRANT REED [20]

Herbert was the son of William Reed snr who was the proprietor and headmaster of Fullands School. William snr ran this very successful school as a family business with his brother George, his first wife Eleanor Morris née Farrant, known as Ellen, and her younger sister Emma who was employed as an assistant teacher. The two sisters were members of a Sidmouth family which had seen its fair share of tragedy. They had witnessed the deaths of both parents and three of their four siblings all within the space of a dozen years.

Ellen had three children with William snr after their marriage in Sidmouth in 1845. William jnr came first, followed by Frank (F. Reed **[19]**) and Rose. And then her family's bad luck returned when she herself died of tuberculosis in 1851, aged just twenty-six. It was therefore understandable that Ellen's sister would take on responsibility for her nephews and niece, all under the age of four, and three years later become William's second wife. Emma bore William another six daughters and one son, Herbert Farrant Reed, born in Wilton, Taunton on 10 September 1865.

VOL.1 has no image of Herbert but his youthful looks in the 1881 Long Ashton photograph (he was a month short of his sixteenth birthday at the time) makes for an easy identification. He was still a pupil at Fullands School when this match was played but was clearly able to hold his own in this level of company. He bowled throughout the Long Ashton first innings finishing with impressive figures of 29 overs, 9 maidens, 4 for 36.

Herbert's half-brother William jnr also played for Somerset on occasions but only in minor matches during the non-first-class years of the 1880s. A year before the Long Ashton match, Herbert and William had played for Emeriti against a Somerset team which contained the third brother Frank. Frank was arguably the best cricketer of the three, especially with the ball in hand. All three brothers were well-known in local cricket circles, ever-present for Fullands CC where they would often encounter their Somerset contemporaries. William jnr and Frank both taught at Fullands and a few months before this photograph was

taken, William jnr, as the eldest son, had become proprietor and headmaster of the school on the death of their father. Herbert would remain at the school in a pupil/teacher role until he went up to Queens' College, Cambridge in 1883. Herbert played one match for Somerset in 1882 and a further six matches for the club during the seasons 1883-1885 (seven in total, not eight as stated in VOL.1). For some unaccountable reason five of Herbert's seven matches were against Hampshire, four of them in Southampton. He was arguably never given the chance to blossom as a bowler. Used sparingly, he took just two wickets at 30.50. He never had much of an opportunity with the bat either, coming in at lower-middle order, but he still managed a batting average in double figures. And this was a young man who regularly opened the innings for Fullands CC and scored 133 against the Wesleyan College in 1885. He was valued more for his energetic fielding than anything else and his athleticism was also appreciated on the rugby field for Taunton and Somerset. He played his rugby as a forward which is somewhat surprising judging by what appears to be his slight build in the above image.
By the time Somerset had been reinstated as a first-class county in 1891, Herbert had left the West Country permanently, taking a succession of teaching jobs before suffering several acute illnesses in later life. He endured a painful death in the British Home for Incurable Diseases, Streatham, on 9 March 1911, aged forty-five.

CLEVELAND EDMUND GREENWAY [22]

Cleveland's father, John, married his first cousin Martha Greenway in Clifton in 1853 and moved to Buenos Aires where John had set up business as a merchant broker and where Cleveland, their only child, was born on 29 October 1864. John died there in 1877, but Martha remained in Argentina, never remarried, and only returned to live with her son in the early 1900s. Buenos Aires was no place for a child where typhoid and yellow fever were endemic, and he was sent to the UK when he was five years old. He was cared for by his aunt Georgiana and her husband the Rev George Wright, in Bilton, Warwickshire. George was the proprietor of Overlands School in Rugby and Cleveland was taught there before he became a boarder at Cheltenham College. Cleveland was in the 1st XI and 1st XV at cricket and rugby during his last two years at Cheltenham. In his last year, 1882, he had a successful season captaining the cricket XI and opening the batting. It included several individual performances with the bat including a century against Liverpool and 39 not out against Marlborough College (out of a team score of 58).

An early image of Cleveland found too late to be published in VOL.1

Cleveland does not appear to have had any prior connection with Somerset. He did have relatives in the Clifton and Yeovil area and may have been staying with one of his mother's many sisters. And there is evidence that he was opening the batting and taking wickets for North Perrott CC during the summer after leaving College. Perhaps this was what earned him his only appearance for Somerset against MCC at Lord's in 1882. He was seventeen years old, but he was already a powerfully built young man, six feet two inches tall, who had earned a reputation as a hard-hitting batsman (years later he was given the nickname 'the leather mover'). Somerset must have had confidence in his ability because he was sent in against MCC first-wicket-down when the score was on nought. This quickly became 3 for 4 with the three dismissed batsmen all making ducks. He was clearly not overawed by being at the home of cricket and chose to hit out. He was stumped on 18 and was one of only three batsmen to reach double figures in Somerset's first innings. He scored just a single run in the second and was not asked to bowl.

It is perhaps no surprise that someone with no close family ties who had experienced such a regimented upbringing should choose to join the British Army on leaving college. It marked the end of any possible further connection with Somerset. He joined the 3rd Bedfordshire Regiment as a lieutenant before being posted to India with the King's (Liverpool) Regiment where he was aide de camp to two lieutenant governors of Bengal. Later he fought in the Third Anglo-Burmese War before returning to duty as a major with the Auxiliary Forces in the UK. Cricket was very much a part of his life. He travelled with

George Vernon's team to Ceylon and India in 1889/90 scoring an unbeaten 130 in the opening match against Calcutta. And he often turned out for MCC including a first-class match against Essex in 1895.

He was at one time attached to the Northumberland Fusiliers and played for Northumberland. VOL.1 had stated that these matches occurred between 1900 and 1902 but a recently acquired photograph shows that he was playing for Northumberland in July 1898. He is standing far right in this photograph:

Cleveland married Maud Mary Sykes, in 1894 and they had one son, Thomas Cleveland Greenway, the following year. He was promoted to Lieutenant Colonel, later Honorary Colonel, in charge of the 5th battalion of the Rifle Brigade in 1907 stepping down in 1913 after the customary six years of command. That same year aged forty-eight and accompanied by his wife Maud, he captained an Incogniti tour of North America. During the First World War he was briefly in France before commanding the regimental depot of the East Surrey Regiment at Kingston-upon-Thames. After the war he lived out his retirement at 'Hatchlands' in East Liss, Hampshire before making the final move of many in his life to Kensington. He died in the Royal Bethlem Hospital, Beckenham on 17 June 1934, aged sixty-nine.

STEPHEN COX NEWTON [23]

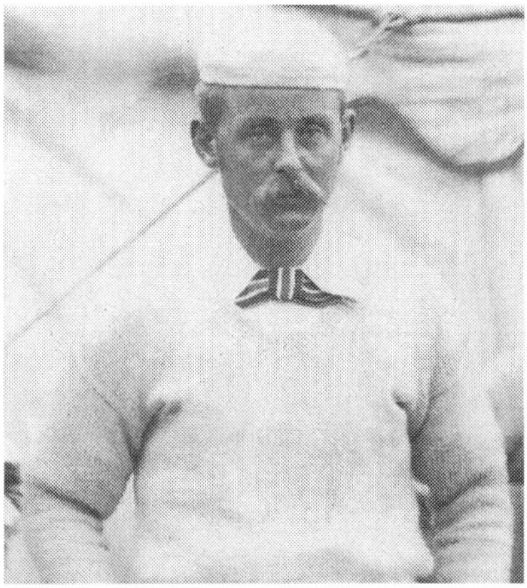

When Stephen appeared in the Long Ashton match of 1881, he was teaching at Highgate School and spending his summer holidays with his father Robert in Wraxall on the outskirts of Nailsea. By 1881, he was the biggest employer for miles around with forty employees in his businesses as a builder, timber merchant and farmer. Robert specialised in public building works and there are many examples of his work in the local area such as Christ Church Nailsea, Walton Church near Clevedon, All Saints Church Wraxall, Failand Church Wraxall, Four Oaks School in Nailsea, and the pagoda-like Market Hall in Clevedon.

Robert married Elizabeth Catherine Cox in 1840 and they had eight children; the last born, Elizabeth, named in honour of her mother who died nine days after her daughter was born in 1859. Five of the children (including Stephen who was born in Nailsea on 21 April 1853) were under the age of eleven and Robert enlisted the help of his sister to look after them. Two of the older children were sent to Germany to be educated and others like Stephen were sent to Jersey for the same purpose. Robert had been planning to take his family to Australia before Elizabeth died, and although the plan was aborted, his two eldest boys – Fred, an Anglican minister, and Walter, a farmer – both emigrated to Australia. A third son Arthur (A.G. Newton **[VOL.5, page 46]**), who played four matches for Somerset in 1876 and 1877, was left to run the family businesses when Robert died in 1884.

Stephen was the last of the four sons to be born. He attended Victoria College, Jersey where on 21 June 1871 he set the current school record for throwing a cricket ball 120 yards (109.73 metres). It is still celebrated as an annual event, known as the "Newton Toss", with the winner receiving the Newton Cup. He had been in the 1st XI at Victoria College, but appears to have played little senior cricket on going up to Corpus Christi College, Cambridge in 1872 until his last year in 1876 when he obtained his cricket blue. He was awarded a 2nd class BA degree in the classical tripos but remained at his college as a scholar while also teaching at Highgate School. During that summer, he appeared in the four principal matches played by Somerset and most principal matches in 1877 and 1878 when matches were played during the month of August. But as the county's fixture list grew, Stephen was unavailable for matches played during term time. He played in fifteen first-class matches between 1882 and 1884, captaining the side on each occasion. He married Sophia Catherine Bell in August 1883 at St Michaels Church, Highgate, and the following year left Highgate School but continued to live in London.

Stephen played no cricket for Somerset in 1885 or 1886 (although he did turn out in first-class matches for MCC and Middlesex). He returned in 1887 to play Hampshire (twice) and Gloucestershire at Cheltenham. This is the team photograph from the match at Cheltenham:

Standing L-R: T. Knight (scorer), G.B. Nichols, H.T. Hewett, H.F. Fox, H.E. Murray-Anderdon (Hon. Sec.), T. Spencer (Asst. Sec.);
seated L-R: A.J. Fothergill, J.B. Challen, W.N. Roe, E. Sainsbury, ***S.C. Newton****, A.E. Newton, S.M.J. Woods;*
seated on ground: E.W. Bastard

After 1887, Stephen made one further appearance for Somerset before the pressure of running his own school restricted his summer vacations to the West Country. It was against Hampshire in August 1890 and although his batting failed in both innings his fielding was as sharp as ever, taking five catches in the match. T. Robinson **[42]**, who played with Stephen on many occasions, reckoned that he was one of the finest cover points in England.

Stephen had opened his own private school called Loudoun House School in 1888, based a few hundred yards from Lord's. It is still a school to this day, now known as Arnold House School. Stephen is recorded as living there in the 1911 census by which time there is just one boarding pupil, outnumbered by an assistant schoolmaster, a matron, and three domestics. His wife had died in 1906 and they had no children. Sometime after 1911 he retired to the Vines, Yoxford, Suffolk, which had been Stephen and Sophia's holiday getaway and the reason he played three minor county matches for Suffolk in 1905. He died on 18 August 1916 at an Ipswich Nursing Home, aged sixty-three.

EDWARD WESTERN [27]

Edward, brought up in the care of two elderly spinsters from Brislington, was known to have been born on 12 May 1845 and VOL.1 speculated that Mary Western, the young servant of a Bristol accountant, may have been the mother. Beyond that, nothing was known about his birth because it appeared to have never been registered, at least not under the surname of Western. But it is now possible to clarify some of the circumstances of his birth. Applicants for the civil service unable to provide a birth certificate were required to provide an affidavit as proof of age. Edward must have had thoughts of being a civil servant because his affidavit has been found. Sworn in front of a magistrate, it reads like a plot from a novel by Charles Dickens. It is partly reproduced here:

I have been informed and believe that the said Edward Western was born on the twelfth day of May 1845 at Polton in the County of Wiltshire On the night of the birth of the said Edward Western he was removed from his mother and conveyed to Bristol since which time he has not been known to his said mother The father of the said Edward Western is now residing in Canada From the circumstances connected with the birth of the said Edward Western I believe that it was never registered The said Edward Western has been brought up in the neighbourhood of Bristol I have constantly seen him and can identify him as the infant who was brought to Polton on the night of the twelfth of May 1845

Despite the incorrect spelling, the affidavit does establish that Edward was born in Poulton, then in Wiltshire, now in Gloucestershire (some databases, including Wikipedia, still have him born in Paulton). The affidavit was provided by George Frederick Fox who clearly knew more about Edward's birth than he needed to reveal. George Fox was a solicitor practicing in Corn Street, Bristol and it suggests that he was acting for and/or acquainted with Edward's father who may well have been providing Edward with financial support. It would explain how a child from an impoverished background came to receive a private education at Fullands School in Taunton.

Edward took full advantage of the opportunity. He obtained a double first-class education certificate and remained at Fullands as an assistant schoolteacher qualifying as a Member of the College of Preceptors. It was through his association with Fullands, playing for the school's cricket XI and the Gentlemen of Somerset that he became Somerset's first honorary secretary. He was captaining the Gentlemen at Sidmouth in August 1875 and it was Edward who drafted the three resolutions which formed the modern club. Edward, a cricketer of modest ability, played 38 matches for Somerset during the non-first-class years 1876-1881, either against minor opposition or as a lower-order batsman in county matches when he struggled to form a team. He played two first-class matches for Somerset in 1882 and 1884, making up the numbers and scoring 6 runs at an average of 3.00. He also played in another first-class match for MCC against Somerset at Taunton when the opposition turned up with just eight men. Edward made up the numbers along with H.F. Reed **[20]** summoned from Fullands, and a young Taunton CC and occasional Somerset club and ground player by the name of Clement Star Pavey. This was the latter's single first-class appearance. Edward made his highest first-class score of 19 in this match, but it was a flat and docile wicket on which the under-representative MCC still managed to score 506 runs.

Edward resigned as secretary at a special meeting of members in September 1885 after what was described as a disastrous season, and the resignation came as no surprise. Henry Murray-Anderdon had already been lined up as a replacement and the job had long since become too much for Edward, especially after his appointment as headmaster of Langport Grammar School in 1883. Prior to accepting the headship and on leaving Fullands towards the end of the 1870s, he had run a small preparatory school in Weston-super-Mare with support from his friend W. Massey **[13]**. Edward was at Langport for

nine years, then returned to private tutoring before moving to Alcombe, near Dunster, in 1897 where he took on the headship of Alcombe School.
A year later, on 1 August 1898, he married Mabilla Chanter of Millslade, Brendon, in North Devon, the daughter of the late Reverend J.M. Chanter of Ilfracombe. Mabilla's mother was Charlotte Kingsley. Her brother Charles found fame writing *The Water Babies*, her brothers Henry and George were respectively a novelist and travel writer. But Charlotte also wrote (including the novel *Over the Cliffs* in 1861) and will be remembered for starting the Victorian fad for collecting ferns having written *Ferny Combes* in 1856.
Mabilla was a forty-three-year-old spinster when they married. They remained at Alcombe until the summer term of 1905 when they moved to 28 The Parks, Minehead opening a small preparatory school on the premises with assistance from Mabilla's spinster sister Kathleen. Edward was still described as a teacher in the 1911 census, at the age of sixty-five, and spent his leisure time on the links of Minehead and West Somerset golf club. He was an excellent golfer playing off a single-figure handicap and winning several cups. After Edward died on 16 October 1919, aged seventy-four, the two sisters remained at the Parks for the rest of their lives; Mabilla was the last to die in 1945, aged ninety.

JAMES JOHN ALEXANDER PARFITT [36]

James was born in Brecon on 23 December 1857, the last of five children born to James and Rebecca Parfitt. His mother was from Brecon, but his father was from a large Roman Catholic family which was long-established in the Bruton and Bath areas of North Somerset. His uncle Charles was Monsignor Parfitt who was the resident confessor and chaplain to the family which owned Midford Castle near Bath. The Monsignor achieved notoriety when he was left the entire estate and extensive landholdings on the death of the owner, a Mrs Connolly, much to the annoyance of her natural heirs. Court cases followed but the Monsignor retained most of the legacy and set up home in the Castle where he died in 1886.
James's father worked as a legal clerk in Brecon and died there, aged forty-five, when James was just nine years old. Soon after, Rebecca left Wales and moved with her children firstly to Westbury-on-Trym and later to Bath. James had one brother, Thomas, and they were both sent to be educated at the Roman

Catholic school, Prior Park College near Bath, where the Canon of Clifton, the previously mentioned Monsignor Parfitt, was an influential figure. James was in the College 1st XI from 1873 to 1876. Very tall and a lively fast bowler, he did particularly well against a strong Lansdown XI in his last year at Prior Park taking nine of the ten wickets that fell for 130 runs. S.C. Voules **[VOL.5, page 36]** and E. Sainsbury **[2]** were among the Lansdown batsmen.
James was at the University of London before he taught at Cardinal Newman's School in Edgbaston for three years while studying for the bar exams. He was called to the bar in 1887. By this time, he had represented Surrey eight times and Somerset six, with a first-class batting average of 9.25 and 38 wickets at 24.52 apiece.
After forging a career as King's Counsel, he later became a well-respected county court judge famed for his use of cricket analogies in his summations. VOL.1 stated that James died on 15 May 1926, which is the date recorded in CricketArchive. This is *not* his correct date of death. He died two days later, at 2am on Monday, 17 May 1926. He died from a heart attack after a short illness suffering from pleurisy.
In the absence of any early image of James, VOL.1 resorted to a photograph of Judge James sporting a wig and gown. This carte de visite photograph of the Prior Park 2nd XI of 1871 has since become available:

Although James and his older brother Charles are listed on the back of the card, no order is given. It is tantalisingly close to offering an image of him in cricket attire. By comparison with his later bewigged self, it is tempting to suggest that Charles is seated far left and James seated far right, but this is no more than an educated guess.

JOHN ARUNDELL WINTER [40]

John was born at one of his family's many estates, Ash Priors, on 28 July 1851. His family had accumulated wealth and property through generations of well-connected individuals. Sir William Winter was one of Queen Elizabeth's admirals at the Spanish Amada and his son John was second-in-command on Sir Francis Drake's voyage around the world. A later ancestor, Charles Winter, was responsible for building Watts House in Bishops Lydeard, which is now known as Cedar Falls Health Spa. John inherited Watts House, as the eldest of four sons, after his father died in 1873.

VOL.1 did a disservice to John in understating his cricketing ability as further research has revealed that he played a decent standard of club cricket. He was certainly good enough to play regularly for Taunton CC and hold his own in the company of many first-class cricketers. And in 1878, he was awarded a silver cup by Taunton for the best batting average that season. John was involved with Somerset from the outset and played in the inaugural match against the Gentlemen of Dorset at Lansdown in August 1876. He would appear in sixteen more non-first-class matches during the club's early years, but his only first-class appearance was in 1884 where, as a tailender, he scored 4 and got a duck in the second innings.

At long last, an image of John Winter

can be unveiled thanks to the 1881 Long Ashton photograph. And very much with a look of self-assurance as befits a man of his status, seated centre stage most likely a nod to him captaining the side. John will not be remembered for his cricket but will always have a significant place in Somerset's history because it was through his involvement as a player for Taunton CC that Somerset acquired the County Ground.

In 1880, John's club captain at Taunton, W.H. 'Herbert' Fowler **[1]** , was faced with replacing the ground they had leased from Mr Balman of Musgrove Farm since 1878. Having spent money getting the pitch into shape and building a pavilion, the club discovered that the farmer was about to renege on the deal (the field was roughly where the cemetery extension to the north of Wellington Road is situated). Herbert Fowler, speaking at his club's AGM years later, explained that he was discussing the problem of finding a ground "When Mr Winter came forward and said - Why don't you take my field? - we accepted his offer and now the field is the County Ground".

It was the perfect location, 7.5 acres of derelict scrubland, known as the Rack Field, in the centre of Taunton between the river and St James Street. A lease was all but agreed but, in the meantime, a newly formed organisation, called the Taunton Athletics Club, had been set up to act for all the major sports clubs in Taunton including the cricket club. It was agreed that Rack Field would be shared by all the sports clubs, and it was the Taunton Athletics Club that held the fourteen-year lease from John Winter, at a cost of £40 a year. The Athletics Club folded with heavy debts in 1886 long before the lease expired leading to Somerset taking over the ground and a new lease, but this may not have happened without the crucial involvement of H.E. Murray-Anderdon **[VOL.5, page 279]** in the negotiations, covered in Henry Murray-Anderdon's additional biographical notes contained on page 214.

As well as the Rack Field and the Priory grounds, John had inherited great swathes of land and property in and around Taunton which were gradually sold off to pay for living well beyond his means. He sold the area of land which surrounded the newly created cricket ground including the part that housed the Taunton Priory, dissolved by Henry VIII in 1539. This parcel of land also included two cottages in St James Street which were formerly called the Weavers Arms.

The Lambrook Farm comprising 72 acres of farmland was next to go, and eventually his principal residence, Watts House, and its contents were sold in

1891. And in the mid-1890s, John agreed to rescind the lease of the County Ground and sell Somerset the freehold. It was sold for a sum of £2,000. John, his wife Rosa, and the younger of their eight children then moved to London. The family lived firstly in Lewisham but later moved to Twickenham. It was a far cry from the splendour of Watts House and its country house cricket. John died on 15 May 1914, aged sixty-two, and left an estate of just £209 to Rosa.

JOHN BONAMY CHALLEN [41]

John was born in Ruthin, Denbighshire on 23 March 1863. John's Devon-born father, John Louis Challen, was a schoolmaster at Ruthin Grammar School at the time but Wales had little to do with his formative years. His middle name came from his mother's maiden name and her noble Guernsey family descended from John Bonamy, Dean of Guernsey from 1716 to 1739. His first taste of schooling was at Honiton Grammar School, but he then spent seven years at The Philberds, a preparatory school in Maidenhead. It was here that John learnt the rudiments of the game of cricket under the guidance of the headmaster, the Rev F.W.S. Price who had played first-class cricket for Cambridge University. He was in the school 1st XI for five years before he was sent to Marlborough in 1878.
Meanwhile his family home had moved to Wiltshire, where his father was a curate at Christ Church, Warminster and then to Somerset where John snr was the rector of Nunney near Frome.
A year after going to Marlborough College, John was in the 1st XI and played in the 1879 match at Lord's against Rugby School. A year later he was playing for Somerset. After several matches against minor opposition

John Challen, eighteen -years-old in the Long Ashton match of 1881

such as Horsington and Ashton Court, he played a county match against Hertfordshire in early August and kept his place against Leicestershire and Bedfordshire but did nothing of note in any of these matches. He finished the rest of the 1880 season playing against minor opponents such as Frome and Will 'o' the Wisps. He played no cricket for Somerset in 1881 other than the match against Long Ashton.

On leaving Marlborough, John went straight into teaching, firstly as a tutor at a private school in Thornton Heath, Croydon from 1880 to 1882 where he made three centuries for the school team and topped the batting averages for Thornton Heath CC. He was an assistant master at Wellingborough Grammar School from 1883 to 1892 and in his nine years there he recorded 6,058 runs over 150 completed innings. While teaching at the grammar school, he received a second-class degree from Trinity College Dublin, obtained by distance learning.

His teaching duties meant that he was only available for his county during the summer holidays. In the first spell of first-class cricket, he played nine matches in 1884 and 1885. He was known as a steady accumulator of runs but against Hampshire in 1884 he made runs at a rare pace scoring 93 in an hour and ten minutes. He continued to play each summer during Somerset's second-class days and was part of the victorious 1890 side responsible for a return to first-class cricket the following year. He played a further forty-three first-class matches for the county between 1891 and 1899. His one century was scored against Sussex at the County Ground on 11 August 1893. His final batting average for the fifty-two appearances was 19.71.

He moved to Devon in the Autumn of 1892 becoming the headmaster at Crediton Grammar School and remained there until 1895 when he took up the headship of the Devon County School in West Buckland. Then in 1900, he founded the North Devon School in Barnstable. John had kept in contact with his old prep school and turned out for the Old Philberdians at cricket and football. He must also have kept in touch with his old schoolmaster Frederick Price as he had married his daughter Amy in 1893.

John left Barnstable in 1909. It was assumed in VOL.1 that John handed the running of the North Devon School to his son John Bonamy Rhys Challen, but he was thirteen years old at the time. His son would later distinguish himself during the First World War winning the MC at Salonika in 1919. John had left Barnstable, probably at the behest of his wife, in a failed attempt to rescue his

father-in-law's school. The Philberds would soon close, and its buildings were used to intern German prisoners of war before it was demolished in 1919.
John moved to Eastbourne in 1910 where he became second master at the Aldro School, a position he held until 1918 when he entered a partnership with the Rev George West and Gerald Pethybridge to take over the running of St Christopher's Preparatory School in Eastbourne. The 1921 census shows that there were 84 boys between the ages of eight and fourteen being educated there though surprisingly they are described as 'inmates'. The school flourished for a while, but the partnership was dissolved in May 1931 with all the debts discharged by the partners. The school was up for sale in 1932 following the bankruptcy of the headmaster. John died in Eastbourne on 5 June 1937, aged seventy-four.

HORATIO ERNEST HALL [43]

Horatio, always known as Ernest or Ernie, was born on 25 April 1861, three years, and five months after his brother Henry (H.G.H. Hall **[10]**), always known in cricket circles as Hamlet. The two brothers were Bedminster born and bred. It has already been mentioned on page 14 that Ernest should now be reclassified as the tenth first-class cricketer to represent Somerset and that his brother Hamlet should be the forty-third.
Ernest began playing for the Bedminster 1st XI in 1881, aged twenty, when Hamlet was already an established member of the team. Hamlet had by this time played for Somerset in its pre-first-class days (he had first played for the county in August 1879 at the County Ground when the opposition was MCC). And Ernest's first senior season playing for Bedminster in 1881 also earned him a call-up for Somerset that year, also against MCC, although he was given little chance to perform. It is therefore no wonder that the identity of the brother who played in Somerset's inaugural first-class match the following year has been a matter of some doubt.
The two brothers were quite different kinds of cricketers. At club level, Hamlet was a top-order batsmen, renowned for his steady, defensive technique, and a useful change bowler when required. Ernest was played almost entirely for his bowling, described as medium paced, with very accurate line and length and good movement off the pitch. This significant difference in cricket skills

was a good reason to doubt that Hamlet played in the inaugural match against Lancashire on 8 June 1882 because the brother that played opened the bowling that day with Arnold Fothergill. The brother took 1 for 47 off 37 overs in Lancashire's only innings, and batted one place above a confirmed tailender, Harry Scott. Although Somerset did not always play to the strengths of its new recruits, it points conclusively to Ernest being the debutant. And the evidence from newspaper reports is compelling as they record the player's surname with the initials 'E.H.' which is consistent with Ernest's preferred arrangement of his forenames.

A further reason for Ernest's claim to this match can be found in the scorecards of two trial matches before the start of the 1882 season. In both trials Ernest is listed as 'Mr H.E. Hall'. The first trial in April was at Bedminster between a Gloucestershire XI and a Gloucester Colts XXII with Ernest playing for the Gloucestershire XI. Ernest did nothing to advance his future with W.G.'s county team, batting as the tailender and having little opportunity to bowl. It was followed by a second trial, this time for Somerset at the County Ground, held a week before the Lancashire match. This trial was between a Somerset XI and a Somerset Colts XV. Ernest opened the bowling for the Colts and took 5 for 55 off his 29 overs. His '5-fer' included the wickets of W.H. Fowler **[1]** and H. Fox **[8]**, both influential members of the county side who probably helped seal his debut at Old Trafford.

There is no contention about whether both brothers played for Somerset in a first-class match because it is fortunate that they were together in the XI that played Gloucestershire at Moreton-in-Marsh in August 1885. But it does mean that Hamlet only played this one first-class match and an adjustment to the brothers' first-class career statistics is needed. The figures for batting are:

Brother	Matches	Inns	NO	Runs	HS	Ave	Ct
Hamlet	1	2	0	2	2	1	0
Ernest	4	8	2	43	23	7.17	1

And the figures for bowling are:

Brother	Balls	Mdns	Runs	Wkts	BB	Ave
Hamlet	20	1	10	0	0-10	0
Ernest	466	41	192	4	2-67	48.00

Ernest was not asked to play for Somerset again until 1884 and his second call-up was because of some exceptional performances for Bedminster. By the end of the season, he would easily top the Bedminster bowling averages with 62 wickets at 5.50. And this was against some of the strongest teams in the Bristol area, including East Somerset, Thornbury, Kaleidoscopes and Lansdown. Against the latter club in July 1884, he and a professional named Pullan of Yorkshire sensationally disposed of the Lansdown batsmen for 4 runs in ten overs. Ernest bowled 5.4 overs to take 4 wickets for zero runs.

And shortly after this match he was asked to play for Somerset against Hampshire at Southampton. He was unlucky to face a team in form who rattled up 645 runs, 420 of them on day one, in the host club's innings victory. Somerset used all ten outfielders as bowlers and Ernest's figures of 2 for 67 off 38.2 overs were as good as anybody's. The ill-luck continued in his third match for the county against Gloucestershire at Moreton-in-Marsh in August of the following year. It was another resounding innings thrashing, Somerset using eight bowlers this time. He made his fourth and final appearance later that month at Southampton when Somerset disgracefully turned up with just nine men and suffered an eight-wicket loss. In the circumstances, there appears to be no reason why Ernest only bowled nine overs in the match.

At club cricket, he continued to be the mainstay of the Bedminster bowling for the remainder of the decade and well into the 1890s. VOL.1 highlighted his 8 for 24 against East Somerset CC in 1885 but did not have the space to expand further. The East Somerset team was based in Yatton and formed in the mid-1870s to further the cricketing ambitions of its benefactor T. Chamberlayne **[VOL.5, page 115]**. His clear intention was to challenge the newly created Somerset CCC for the right to represent Somerset at county level. But, as Tankerville Chamberlayne had to later admit, in a letter to the *Bristol Times and Mirror,* Yatton was in the wrong place. He wrote 'an "East Somerset" team which included Dr W.G. Grace and Mr W.R. Gilbert and other Gloucestershire cricketers suggests, to say the least, a misnomer.' The purpose of the letter, apart from having a dig at the Somerset authorities, was to inform the readers that East Somerset would be renamed Yatton CC from 1886 onwards. The match against Bedminster was therefore one of East Somerset's last serious matches played when they fielded Gloucestershire and Somerset cricketers including H.T. Hewett **[47]**, J.B. Challen **[41]**, and G.B. Nichols **[61]**, the latter playing for Gloucestershire at the time. This then was no village side and Ernest's eight wicket haul, six of them clean bowled, was an exceptional performance against quality opposition.

Ernest's brief career with Somerset would not have left him with any fond memories. He seems to have suffered the misfortune of playing in a poor-quality side which would soon have its first-class status rescinded after just four seasons. Three of his four appearances resulted in innings victories for the opponents and the fourth was lost by a margin of eight wickets which would have done nothing for the morale of an opening bowler.

The two brothers were both teachers so they would have only been available during the summer holidays. Hamlet taught at Dr Bell's National School in Bedminster where both brothers had been education. It is believed that Ernest initially taught in Bedminster but towards the end of the nineteenth century his family ties to Bedminster ended with the death of his father in 1898 and his mother's subsequent move to Stafford to live with Ernest's sister Orphelia. It prompted several life changes including a move away from Bedminster and a marriage at the age of thirty-eight.

In August 1899, he married Beatrice Maud Murdock at St Paul's Church in Bedminster. Ernest was living in Knowle at the time and Beatrice was living in Clifton. Beatrice was the sister of his Bedminster teammate E.G. Murdock **[57]** who was also living in Clifton and teaching there, at Christ Church Boys' School. And perhaps it was his wife or his closest friend who alerted Ernest to the opening of a new elementary boys' school in the Hotwells area of Clifton at the beginning of 1900. Hotwells (Primary) Council School is certainly where Ernest Hall finished his teaching career as its headmaster. And he may well have been at the school from the outset. The 1901 census shows that Ernest and Maud were living in Knowle at roughly this time. It also has Ernest as an elementary schoolteacher, but it cannot be certain that he was at Hotwells. By 1911, the couple had moved to the Hotwells area of Clifton along with their daughter Eileen, born in 1902 and baptised in St Paul's Church.

It was a matter of regret that an image of Ernest could not be found for publication in VOL.1. And it was not for the want of trying all possible sources. Perhaps if it had been known at the time that he was teaching at Hotwells the postcard image on the opposite page, would have been used. Taken in 1900, the schoolteacher could well be Ernest. He is about the right age and with more than a passing resemblance to Hamlet. Ernest died in Clifton on 1 December 1919, aged fifty-eight.

HERBERT TREMENHEERE HEWETT [47]

Herbie's unusual middle name Tremenheere came from his maternal grandfather, the Reverend John White Johns, who chose to name his sons after the village of that name. The word translates in the Cornish language to refer to the standing stone sited near the village. His mother married William Henry Hewett, a landowner and brewer from Norton Fitzwarren which is where Herbie was born on 25 May 1864. His cricket progression, via Harrow School and Trinity College, Oxford where he obtained a blue in 1886, ensured early recognition at Somerset. He played as an eighteen-year-old, left-hand batsman during the club's non-first-class days and was given the captaincy at the relatively young age of twenty-six.

The above photograph, bearing an uncanny likeness to a certain German dictator, was on the walls of the Scarborough pavilion until recently. It was presumably discarded to clear space on the walls and ditch some of the long-forgotten players. V.T. Hill **[65]** was another Somerset cricketer to suffer this indignity. Herbie was a big-match player, and he needed no encouragement to play at Scarborough. An invitation to play for the South, MCC, and Gentlemen of England among others was never refused. But memories of his festival cricket at the seaside town would have been marred by an unseemly experience during his final appearance there in 1895. He had always got on well with the Yorkshire crowds despite him having a particular appetite for Yorkshire bowlers. His double century against them in 1892, part of a then world record first-wicket partnership with L.C.H. Palairet **[68]**, was still fresh in the memory. And he was also on good terms with Yorkshire cricketers and admired their uncompromising approach to playing cricket. Herbie's brand of cricket was cut from similar cloth, the polar opposite to most of his fellow amateurs at Somerset.

In 1895 he was due to play all three matches at Scarborough Festival which was renowned as the great social event on the cricket calendar and two of these matches were against Yorkshire. The first match was for MCC against the champion county. His second was as captain of the South against the North and the third should have been as captain of an English XI against Yorkshire. Steady rain throughout the morning of the third match prevented the wicket from drying out and a section of the holiday crowd expressed their impatience by shouting and booing. Eventually, at 1.30pm in the afternoon, Herbie led out his team whereupon he was subjected to some offensive remarks. Herbie made it clear from the start that he was too upset to play and withdrew from the field as soon as Fred Spofforth, who had played for the South the previous day, could replace him. In a later interview, Herbie said that he could not be blamed for the delay in starting the match and as an amateur cricketer would not stand for the unsportsmanlike behaviour to which he was subjected.

It seems very likely that the incident influenced his decision to finish playing top-class cricket. He made only one further appearance at the first-class level, for MCC the following year. He had already abruptly ended his career with Somerset in 1893. Some commentators put that down to a fit of pique with another baying crowd when he unfairly shouldered the blame for the rain delay in Somerset's match against the Australians. He didn't help matters by pulling out of the Lancashire match two days later saying he was unfit and then scoring a century for Harrow Wanderers CC later in the week. But in truth, Herbie had publicly stated his intention to relinquish the captaincy well before the visit of the Australians and his resignation was more likely a result of disillusionment with the way the club was run. The mercurial Herbie did not suffer fools gladly and, as Sam Woods would later recall in his autobiography, there were plenty of them on the committee at the time.

The official reason for him going was that he needed to advance his career as a barrister, but this would have been no barrier to playing serious cricket. Herbie had no need to earn a living. He was the only male sibling and the main beneficiary when his father died while he was still at Harrow School. And Herbie's business in the Inner Temple did not stop him playing a dozen high-profile first-class matches in 1894 and a similar number in 1895. Losing Herbie was a blow to Somerset as he is widely regarded as being responsible for Somerset returning to first-class status in 1891. He may have been long forgotten in the Scarborough pavilion but not by the Somerset faithful who still regard him as one of the best captains in Somerset's history.

He continued to play the occasional cricket for MCC, I Zingari and Free Foresters until the early 1900s while working as a barrister and lodging in London, SW1. The profession has a reptation for its abuse of alcohol, some recent surveys have called it endemic, and Herbie was no exception. He never married but was very close to his unmarried sister Florence Ethel Hewett. She was at his side when he died from cirrhosis of the liver at a private nursing home in Hove on 4 March 1921, aged just fifty-six. His body was transferred by hearse for his funeral in Norton Fitzwarren. It ended with a solemn procession through the village with every blind closed and the flag of St George flying at half-mast on the church. Henry Murray-Anderdon and Sam Woods represented the club as president and secretary respectively. His sisters made up the family mourners and he was laid to rest in his parent's tomb. He left the modern equivalent of £1.5 million in his will to his beloved sisters, the bulk of it going to Florence.

HARRY EDMUND WINTER [48]

Harry Winter is also seen for the first time thanks to the 1881 Long Ashton photograph. He is twenty-three years old in the photograph having been born in Bampton, Devon on 7 December 1857. This match against Long Ashton

was the only time he made a non-first-class appearance for Somerset. By 1881, he was living and working in London as a solicitor, and it suggests he might have been on leave and visiting his older brother, J.A. Winter **[40]**, at the latter's home, Watts House in Bishops Lydeard.

Harry played his single first-class match for Somerset against Kent in 1884. He had a town house in Earls Court and a country house in Kent which may explain why he popped up in Tunbridge Wells to appear for Somerset. Going in ninth wicket down, he made 24 not out in a last-wicket partnership of 29 runs with G. Mirehouse **[46]**, dragging the first innings score above 200. Harry had some ability with the bat, but it clearly didn't extend to his bowling. Somerset used eight bowlers in Kent's first innings and the same number in the second before handing the ball to Harry for one over costing nine runs, including three wides. A duck in the second innings gave him a decent first-class batting average of 24.00.

Harry was a keen sportsman playing cricket for several London clubs through the 1880s. He was also a member of the Thames Rowing Club and Honorary Secretary of the London Athletic Club. With his legal background, he became involved in setting up exploration companies in the colonies, most notably Newfoundland. His brother John was sometimes enlisted as a co-director and several ventures ended in winding up and bankruptcy. At the time of his death, Harry was living in Earls Court Square, but he died in Stone, nr Dartford, Kent on 17 January 1921, aged sixty-three.

ARTHUR EDWARD NEWTON [63]

Arthur was born on 12 September 1862 at Barton Grange, Corfe, a country estate that would feature strongly in early Somerset cricket history. His father Francis Wheat Newton inherited Barton Grange in 1849 and married Arthur's mother Catherine Ainslie, the sister of A.C. Ainslie **[VOL.5, page 1]**. The Rev

Ainslie's involvement with Somerset cricket is covered in this book (page 201). Alexander and Francis were instrumental in encouraging the villagers of Corfe to start a cricket team and play matches at Barton Grange. Arthur was approaching his thirteenth birthday when Uncle Alex chaired Somerset's inaugural meeting at Sidmouth, and cricket was already in his blood, honed on the cricket fields of Barton Grange and Eton College.

Arthur played in three Eton v Harrow fixture at Lord's (1879-1881) before going to Pembroke College, Oxford, but he was unfortunate to come up against M.C. Kemp, his Harrow opposite number in the Lord's matches. Kemp, later with Kent, made four consecutive appearances in the Varsity match, his last in 1884 being the year Arthur was awarded his BA. It seems Arthur was so intent on getting his blue that he returned to play for the University in 1885. He kept tidily in the Varsity match, letting through just four byes in Cambridge's two innings. That same year he toured the United States and Canada with an E.J. Sanders' XI and played in the only two matches afforded first-class status, both against the Gentlemen of Philadelphia.

The following year Arthur played his first match for Somerset against Hampshire, and continued to play regularly for Somerset during its non-first-class days, 1886-1890. He also managed a tour of Australia with G.F. Vernon's XI during the winter of 1887/88, playing in all but one of the twenty-seven tour matches. With an impending marriage to the sister of teammate, Admiral Sir C.S. Hickley [115], Arthur needed gainful employment as his older brother, Francis Murray Newton, stood to inherit Barton Grange and the family's extensive property interests. Thanks to the research of Margaret O'Sullivan of the Mary Immaculate College, Limerick, it is now known that he served his apprenticeship as a land agent in the estate offices of William Rochfort based in Cahir, County Tipperary. William Rochfort was the land agent for several large estates in Ireland and his family were heavily involved in Irish cricket which may explain why Arthur was in Cahir at times during the early to mid-1890s. Arthur married Mina Hickley in January 1891 and the couple's absence from the April 1891 UK census suggest that they were in Ireland at the time. Mina was certainly there when her only child, Arthur Victor, was born in Dublin on 5 June 1893. Such was Arthur's dedication to Somerset cricket that two days before his son's birth, he was playing at Trent Bridge. He returned to play the final six county championship matches in August 1893, but then returned to Ireland where on 23 September 1893 he played for a Cahir X1 against Abbey School, Tipperary. Dr Pat Bracken, of the Tipperary County Council Library Service, has provided details of various matches Arthur played for Cahir CC between May 1894 and June 1896. Despite being a confirmed number eleven, he would open the innings and was the mainstay of the club's batting.

Arthur played 197 first-class matches for Somerset between 1891 and 1914 during which time he took 297 catches and made 122 stumpings. Many of his dismissals were spectacular, none more so than when he stood up to Sam Woods, bowling his first ever ball for Somerset in 1886. Arthur was expecting a loosener, but Sam bowled a fierce, fast yorker down the leg side and the unfortunate Warwickshire batsman, Claude Rock, was stumped. W.N. Roe **[26]** would later remark "It was the finest example of stumping I ever saw". There are other fine examples of his wicketkeeping. In 1901 against Middlesex, he made nine dismissals in the match which was a Somerset record equalled in 1963 by H.W. Stephenson **[367]**. This recently discovered photograph shows Arthur at work behind the stumps:

The photograph, taken at Taunton in 1910, provides an excellent view of how the river end looked during the early days with not much in the way of spectator comfort. It shows the umpire's finger raised in answer to Arthur's appeal for a catch behind against W.W. Lowe off the bowling of Ernie Robson.
Arthur's brother Francis, married Louisa Hedley, the sister of Sir W.C. Hedley **[80]**, and inherited Barton Grange on the death of his father in December 1895. Arthur was not overlooked. He received the family's freehold and leasehold interests in West Harptree and surrounding parishes, known as the West Harptree Estate. This gave Arthur the financial independence which probably brought an end to his employment in Ireland. The family first lived at Henlade Villa, in Ruishton, but Arthur soon took the opportunity of moving back to his home village of Trull when the substantial country house, known as Dipford House came on to the market in 1901. It would remain his home for the rest of his life. In later years, the house would be filled with just memories as his son died in 1915 in Flanders with the Royal Flying Corp, and Mina died in 1918. The 1921 census return, in Arthur's meticulous hand, still has him as a land agent, but, by this time, it was probably no more a demanding job than looking after the Newton family's extensive land and property interests.
Arthur, aged fifty-six when county cricket resumed after the War, was now past consideration for Somerset. An analysis of his 197 matches for the club shows that 128 of these matches were played at Bath or the County Ground. He was clearly of sufficient standing within the club to be able to pick and choose his matches, favouring the home fixtures and eschewing travel too far from home. In his last years, between 1908 and 1914, he appeared in just four fixtures outside the county and three of those were at Lord's. The committee would have tolerated his selectivity knowing it could call on a wealth of amateur wicketkeeping talent.
After the First World War, Arthur continued to play for Somerset Stragglers but here too the matches had to be at the County Ground or immediate area within cycling distance of Dipford House because this was his preferred mode of transport. On the 12 September 1932, Arthur turned up at the County Ground on an old bicycle, which was as ancient as him, to keep wicket for the Somerset Stragglers against South Devon. It was his seventieth birthday, and he must have been surprised during the luncheon interval to be presented with a new bicycle and an illuminated address by another of Somerset's great amateur wicketkeepers, Rev A.P. Wickham **[67]**.

This photograph shows Arthur receiving the bicycle:

The basket he is holding was filled with two sugar duck eggs neatly inscribed, a nod no doubt to his sweet tooth and his modest batting ability. His thank-you letter was modest too, remarking that he had done nothing to deserve the honour and had a great deal of pleasure out of cricket over the years. He ends by saying that his old bicycle was on its last legs and that he would appreciate the splendid new machine. Unlike the old bicycle, Arthur was not on his last legs and continued to play cricket for several more years. No-one is sure when he finally discarded the gloves but a report in September 1936 noted that Arthur, aged seventy-four, made five stumpings in a match at Taunton. He is also present in cricket attire in a Stragglers team photograph taken during a match against Frogs CC that same year. Arthur died at Dipford House, on 15 September 1952, shortly after his ninetieth birthday.

SAMUEL MOSES JAMES WOODS [64]

Sam was an exceptional sportsman. While he played rugby for England, football for the Corinthians, and represented Somerset at rugby, football, hockey, billiards, and skittles, it was his cricket that defined him. In a first-class cricket career spanning the years 1888 to 1910, he scored 15,345 runs and took 1,040 wickets, achieving a higher average with the bat than the ball - 23.42 and 20.82 respectively. David Foot, the late, lamented doyen of Somerset cricket writing, rated Sam as the 'greatest character in the history of Somerset cricket' and few would argue with that description. He wrote:

There is really nothing more to write about Sammy Woods. The stories tumble over each other - and most of them are true, or at least in the spirit of this immensely lovable and outsized Australian. Everything about him was bountiful: his shoulders, his smile, the thrust of his bowling arm, the playful swing of his bat, his drinking capacity, and the warmth of his heart.

To an extent, David Foot is correct about there being nothing more to write about Sam. Foot, Roberts, Roebuck, and Robertson-Glasgow among others, have covered the colourful stories and plentiful anecdotes that remain his legacy. And yet, very little has been written about his club captaincy and nothing about his three years as secretary which ended abruptly in 1922. Perhaps it was seen as unseemly to tarnish the memory of this legendary figure. Sam himself never commented on either and his rambling autobiography *My Reminiscences* gives nothing away.

Sam came to England as a sixteen-year-old with his brother H.D.L. Woods **[VOL.5, page 256]** and they completed their education at Brighton College. But whereas Harris Dunmore Lang Woods returned to Manley after making two appearances for Somerset in 1889, Sam made the West Country his home. It was Somerset's good fortune that Sam would lodge with his guardian Gilbert Burrington in Bridgwater when not in college at Brighton and later Cambridge. Burrington, who was the father of Gilbert jnr (G. Burrington **[136]**), had professional and personal links with the Somerset hierarchy and it was preordained that Sam would play for Somerset when the time was right.

His first match for the county was in 1886 and it would be another five seasons before his first-class debut for Somerset thanks to the club's spell in the wilderness during the seasons 1886 to 1890. By then, he had been called up to play for Australia during the 1888 tour of England, appearing in three Tests, had played regularly for the Gentlemen against the Players, and appeared in three Varsity matches. It was enough for *Wisden* to name him as one of the 'Six Great Bowlers of the Year' in 1889. He had also managed to play rugby for England. No wonder then that his championship debut against Middlesex at Taunton on 18 May 1891 was eagerly anticipated. In a drawn, rain-affected, match he took 2 wickets for 28 runs in Middlesex's only innings.

Sam inherited the captaincy in 1894 after the resignation of H.T. Hewett **[47]**. He was the natural choice, the outstanding player in the team with the possible exception of L.C.H. Palairet **[68]**. Herbie Hewett, arguably one of the best captains in Somerset history, was a hard act to follow. Herbie was an exceptional cricketer, but his gruff, direct, and temperamental demeanour made few friends, especially at committee level. In contrast, the extrovert Sam was loved by everyone, and his teammates would have followed him to the ends of the earth. But whereas Herbie was tactically astute, the happy-go-lucky Sam never worried his head about such things. For him, the game was there to be played with generosity of spirit where the social side of playing was valued as much as the result. Sam would go all out to win the match but lost no sleep over a defeat. As he famously remarked "Draws? They are only for bathing in". And lose they frequently did, to the point that, by the end of his captaincy, rumours had to be scotched that Somerset's first-class status was in jeopardy. During Sam's thirteen-year tenure as captain, Somerset lost 46% of the championship matches played and won just 23% of them (Herbie had won 39% of his championship matches in his three years as captain).

Sam's captaincy dragged on far too long. By 1904, he was not in great shape. His bachelor lifestyle and excessive consumption had taken its physical toll and he was only capable of bowling in short spells. He took just four wickets that season at a high cost and the team lost eleven of the eighteen championship matches. The 1905 championship season was even more of a disaster with one win out of eighteen and ten defeats. Such was the paucity of bowling, the club used twenty-three bowlers during the season in which Sam managed just two championship wickets. And yet there was no clamour for his resignation because he was so well liked, and there was no obvious replacement. Sam soldiered on throughout the 1906 season missing just the last match of the season after his leg gave way attempting a quick single and failing to make his ground. He took no further part in the match and officially announced his resignation, although he had already mentioned his intention to resign to Albert Trott when Somerset had played Middlesex earlier in the month. It was an ignominious end to his captaincy. He had bowled just fourteen overs during the season and had not taken a wicket. Lionel Palairet captained the club in the last match against Yorkshire, his first appearance that year, and showed how much he had been missed, top scoring in both Somerset innings. And to the committee's great relief Lionel agreed to captain the side in 1907 after obtaining permission from his employer to take the summer off.

Sam was given a presentation to mark his retirement as captain during the opening championship match of 1907, against Yorkshire. He was given a framed illuminated address, a gold watch, and a cheque for £1,620 (equivalent to a quarter of a million pounds in today's money) which had been collected by private subscription. This photograph of the presentation has surfaced and offers a fine reminder of the upper tier of the Old Pavilion:

On resigning the captaincy, he had said he would continue to play "as a private member of the team but not in the cold, wet weather", a consequence of the rheumatism that plagued him. 1907 turned out to be the coldest and wettest summer of the 20th century, yet typical of the man and his good nature, Sam played in the Yorkshire match and appeared as a batsman in most of the championship matches that season. He played a handful of matches thereafter and the last of his 299 appearances for Somerset was against Middlesex at Lord's in June 1910, when he was caught in the slips off the rapid bowling of Edward Mignon for a duck in Somerset's first inning and scored 10 runs in the second. Sam never really left Somerset after 1910. He would attend matches, holding court and dispensing sound advice to the younger members of the team who held him in awe. J.C.W. MacBryan **[208]** who first played for Somerset in 1911 was one of his most ardent disciples. And he was a major influence within the Somerset hierarchy, attending and speaking at public meetings and becoming a vice president in 1913. If he were not at a cricket match, he would be found at Burnham Golf Club where he played off a handicap of two.

He was forty-seven years old when War was declared and made several attempts to join up. Eventually the Somerset Light Infantry was persuaded to grant him a commission as a lieutenant, despite being considerably overweight and suffering from an arthritic hip. He did serve with the 9th Somersets for a year or so in Khartoum before contracting malaria and having to return to England. His active service had included breaking a leg jumping off a runaway camel during a spot of leave in Cairo. This once great athlete presented a sad sight after the First World War, limping badly from the cumulative effects of his sporting injuries, war escapades and the increasingly troublesome hip.

Back at the County Ground, Reginald Brooks-King, who had been honorary secretary at the club since 1913, handed in his resignation at the AGM in January 1920. As a parting shot, he said the time had come to have a paid secretary as was the case in every other first-class county. This course of action had been recommended in 1912 before Brooks-King came to Somerset's rescue and did the job for nothing but expenses. The committee could ill afford to pay for a secretary but were forced to agree that one was necessary. Six weeks later Sam was appointed the first paid secretary, on a salary of £250 per annum, after four candidates were interviewed from over two hundred applicants. Nothing is known about the other interviewees, but they could hardly have been less qualified for the administrative role. Sam's employment CV outside of cricket would have stretched to seven months as a bank clerk and some part-time working in a brewery. There was probably no other candidate as ill-suited for the job but perhaps there was method in the committee's madness. His immediate job was to launch an appeal for funds to repair the ground after its use by the military throughout the war and there was no better figurehead to front such an appeal. In newspapers and the 1920 yearbook, Sam wrote:

FUND FOR THE RESTORATION OF THE COUNTY GROUND: The occupation of the ground by so many soldiers during so long a period led to much damage being done to the seating accommodation around the ground and to the pavilion and stands generally. It is found impossible to pay for the necessary renovations out of ordinary income of the club and I am therefore making an appeal for subscriptions for this special purpose. It is hoped that many will give, no matter how small an amount, in order that our historic County Ground may be restored to its pre-war state. It is estimated that at least £500 is required.

Sam was correct in saying there was no money for the restoration. The 1920 annual accounts make an interesting read. Total receipts of £2590.15s.11d were spent mainly on professional wages of £460.12s, amateur expenses of £682.19s.8d, umpires and scorers' expenses of £270 and the secretary's salary and expenses of £246. 5s.5d. A surplus of just over £100 was made after other expenses were taken into account. The Restoration Appeal Fund did not catch on and it does not seem to have been pursued with much vigour, as there is hardly any reference to it in contemporaneous newspapers. The failure to achieve any success with the appeal was confirmed in the 1921 yearbook by a footnote hidden away amongst the results of the previous season. It noted that 'Mr Woods informs us that the subscriptions hitherto received and promised fall far short of the amount required, while there is still much work necessary to be done on the ground'. This second brief mention failed to raise any new funding, and it would be left to Sam's successor as secretary, A.F. Davey, to re-invent the appeal in 1923. Under the guise of 'The Shilling Fund', it proved to be a great success.

Sam continued as secretary throughout the year and was still receiving accolades in that office as late as November 1922 when he attended the Taunton CC AGM. But he was having trouble with the area committees. There

John Daniell (left) with Sam. Captain and Secretary together during the match against Hampshire at Weston-super-Mare in 1921

were grumblings from the Weston-super-Mare area committee, arguing that annual subscriptions should reflect the fact that Taunton had more than twice the number of home fixtures than Weston. And he had to attend a special meeting of the Bath committee in the Guild Hall to defend the decision to give Bath a fixture against Surrey in early May. The Bath committee had protested vigorously because it left them just a few days after the last rugby match was to be played and counter-argued for the fixture against Middlesex in June. The Bath area secretary said that his protest had not been treated with fairness or courtesy and suggested Taunton should take the Surrey match. Sam, clearly exasperated, replied "if that happens, Bath will only get two games. Taunton had all the worst fixtures in 1922 and there was enough grousing there about the matches they got".

And the 'grousing' from the area committees continued at a heated AGM in March presided over by A.E. Newton **[63]**. It was not helped by Sam's report on the annual accounts, which showed a deficit of £447, and he was clearly troubled by the minutia of questioning that followed. His recommendation that his very good friend Ernie Robson be given a benefit in 1923 was also turned down and this may well have been the last straw for him. When it came to voting in the officers for the next year, he dramatically announced his resignation, much to the surprise of everyone present. In what must have been an emotional outburst he said "When I was appointed two years ago there were many doubts about my business capabilities, and I feel that those doubts have proved to be well-founded. The sooner the committee get a secretary with a much more business-like head than mine the sooner things will be rectified in Somerset".

Arthur Newton accepted his resignation and said Somerset owed him a great debt of gratitude, although it was referenced to his cricket rather than his time as secretary. He agreed with Sam's remarks that the club needed someone from business to run it properly (A.F. Davey, Sam's successor, was an experienced administrator and secretary of the Somerset County Agricultural Association). It was tantamount to an acknowledgement that Sam's appointment had been a mistake. Sam's resignation did not go down well with the members. At a special meeting of the club in April, called specifically to discuss subscriptions, the mood turned ugly with such loyal supporters as W.G. Penny from Watchet condemning Sam's departure, calling him a "beacon light" to Somerset cricket, and claiming that Sam had been forced out. Arthur Newton, who was also chairing this meeting, replied that he had been connected with Sam longer than anyone in the room and was as sorry to see him go. He added that Sam had been offered a place on the committee, but he had written to say that he could not see his way to serve.

As a postscript, the 1922 yearbook was published soon afterwards. It contains a glowing tribute to Henry Murray-Anderdon who died the previous December but not a word of thanks for Sam's work as secretary. He is still recorded as being in post, but there is a bizarre, unattributed, page headed 'DROPPING THE PILOT Mr S.M.J. Woods (a slight appreciation by one who knows him)'. It refers to Sam's resignation claiming that 'the cause of his regrettable decision is apparently to remain obscure, but one fact stands clear, and it is that Mr Woods went to the annual meeting of the club with his friends, totally unprepared for what eventually took place. *Verb sap* [the Latin abbreviation meaning a word is enough to the wise]'. A not too subtle hint of skulduggery to 'wise' members. And a very odd insertion in an official yearbook.

In was a sad departure from Somerset cricket after everything he had given to the club, but Sam was not one to hold grudges. It gave him more time to spend on the links at Burnham, and he was still a common sight at the County Ground and the outgrounds of Weston and Bath. Sam had never bothered with a home of his own and just relied on friends, supporters and publicans for bed and board. He had been based in Burnham since before the war and the 1921 census confirms that he was almost a permanent resident at The Hall, Berrow Road, Burnham, which was the family home of Thomas Holt, a director of the Holt Brothers Brewery. Thomas Holt was a keen cricketer, a Somerset member, and the father of E.G. Holt **[306]**.

In time, he drifted back to Taunton where he would hang his hat in the gentlemen's club at 39 Fore Street, known in the 1920s as the *Somerset County Club*. He could be found here most days or at *The George Hotel* in the company of his host and good friend E.J. Lock **[70]**. The *County Club* was the address given in probate documents which disclosed that he left his very modest estate to his sister Florence. He died of oesophageal cancer on 30 April 1931, aged sixty-four. Flags were lowered at half-mast throughout the town, and some said as far away as The Oval. Crowds lined the streets to pay their respects to his funeral cortege as it travelled the short distance, along the Wellington Road, from a packed St John's Church, in Park Street, to St Mary's Old Cemetery where he was laid to rest.

VERNON TICKELL HILL [65]

Vernon was born in Llandaff, Cardiff on 30 January 1871 and grew up with a sense of entitlement and self-assurance which did not always endear him to others. He shared a close family upbringing with his parents, three brothers and three sisters in Rockwood, a grand house built on Fairwater Road, Cardiff, now the Rockwood Hospital. The family scrapbooks, held by Glamorgan Archives, depict concerts and social gatherings as well as less formal occasions showing the family involved in games of cricket, including his sisters, Gladys, and Constance. Constance was particularly adept at the sport. In a match for Glamorganshire Ladies, she captained her team, opened the innings scoring 56 of her side's 100 runs, and then took four early wickets.

And their father, Colonel Sir Edward Stock Hill, was still turning out for the South Wales Cricket Club before his duties as MP for Bristol South required a move to Walton-in-Gordano in 1886. All four brothers (Vernon, Eustace,

Roderick, and Percy) were educated at Winchester College where both Eustace (E.T. Hill **[113]**) and Vernon made the cricket 1st XI. Vernon was an ever-present member of the 1st XI team during the last three years of his time there. After Winchester, he went up to Oriel College, Oxford in 1889.

This recently acquired photograph, is of the Oriel football XI from the 1890/91 season. Vernon is seated centre on the sofa and has already perfected the haughty, aloof look that would later define him. The photograph has added interest because L.C.H. Palairet **[68]** is seated second left, and R.C.N. Palairet **[69]** is seated on the chair far right. The presence of Rags the terrier and Bill the bulldog enhances this evocative image. Richard 'Dick' Palairet was the only one of the three to earn an association football blue but both Palairet brothers were very decent footballers, playing football for Bath AFC and good enough to represent Somerset at the sport in 1889.

Vernon made his debut for Somerset in 1890 against Hampshire, aged nineteen, and his first-class debut the following year against Middlesex at Lord's. Six weeks later the Palairet brothers also made their first-class debuts. The three young Oriel College graduates would go on to play a combined total of 455 first-class matches for the county. Lionel was the most gifted cricketer of the three, and quickly earned a place in the University XI obtaining his blue in 1890 and 1891.

Vernon was not picked for the Varsity matches in either of these years and was no doubt determined to prove the selectors wrong when he was finally chosen in 1892. George Chesterton, writing in *Oxford and Cambridge Cricket* published in 1989, reported that 'Oxford made a disastrous start [both openers out for a duck] but recovered decisively when the left-handed Vernon Hill joined Jardine [M.R., father of Douglas] and from the very start he hit with whole-hearted vigour and a fine contempt for consequences – and they put on 180 in an hour and forty minutes'. Jardine scored 140 and Vernon achieved his maiden first-class century with a score of 114.

His only other first-class century was scored on the County Ground against Kent in 1898 when, with Sam Woods, the pair proceeded to 'hit out with tremendous power' according to the *Taunton Courier*. In the space of two and a half hours they had raised the Somerset score from 262 for 6 to 502 for 7. Vernon's career best innings of 116 runs included a six and sixteen fours.

There were other examples of his powerful hitting and none better than his innings at Lord's against Middlesex in 1900. Somerset's first innings got off to a poor start and the team were in some trouble at 55 for 4 when Vernon came to the wicket. According to *Cricket: A Weekly Record of the Game* it had been 'lifeless cricket' up to this point when 'the amateur woke up players and spectators alike with some brilliant cricket'. With complete distain for Jack Hearne and Albert Trott who had already taken four cheap wickets, Vernon hit 72 runs in 35 minutes, an innings that included 64 runs in fours and this at a time when a six only counted if hit out of the ground. One stroke hit the top of the pavilion, another into the first tier, but they still counted as fours. The remarkable thing about Vernon's innings was that while the pyrotechnics were happening, his partner Len Braund scored just three singles in their fifth-wicket stand of 75 runs. These explosive innings were the exception rather than the rule. He played 121 first-class matches for Somerset during the period 1891 to 1912 and finished with a modest batting average of 19.21.

He returned to South Wales during the early 1900s and took on the captaincy of Cardiff CC. He raised funds for Glamorgan and was heavily involved with Glamorgan's campaign for first-class status. He is recorded as playing for Glamorgan from 1903 onwards and he also made three appearances for

Glamorgan in the Minor County Championship of 1905. Vernon returned to English county championship cricket in 1908 after he moved back to the West Country and played a dozen championship matches for Somerset during the 1908 and 1909 seasons. His final appearance for Somerset was against Hampshire in May 1912.

Cricket appears to have consumed his early adult life. Apart from the English and Welsh county-level cricket, he played regularly for the MCC and the Somerset Stragglers and went on two overseas tours to America (in 1895 with F. Mitchell's XI and in 1898 with P.F. Warner's XI). The wonder is that he managed to qualify as a barrister during this period of his life. The London City directory of 1900 confirms that his official chambers were at 8 Figtree Court, Temple EC.

Vernon married Gwynidd Blanche née Llewelyn in 1901. Her father was Evan Henry Llewellyn **[VOL.5, page 30]**, MP for North Somerset, who had made his debut for Somerset against Incogniti in 1876. They purchased the ancient Woodsprings Priory, near the Sand Bay promontory at Kewstoke, Weston-super-Mare, probably because of Vernon's keen interest in archaeology. Over the years, Vernon and Gwynidd made a huge contribution to the understanding of the original layout of the 13th century priory. Vernon took to farming and in time became regarded as one of the most modern-minded agriculturalists in the West Country. He also became a member and steward of the Bath and West Society. He even found time in 1911 to patent a contraption for the humane killing of slugs.

Vernon Hill, called to the bar but preferring a call to the fields and cricket grounds of the West Country

Throughout this time, he did not neglect his civic duty. He was a JP for Somerset and a councillor on the Axbridge Rural

District Council. He was also a churchwarden at his local Kewstoke Church. And on the outbreak of the First World War, he lost no time persuading the War Office to grant him a commission despite being in his early forties and well over military age. He served in France for a year with the King's Royal Rifle Corps and reached the rank of major.

Cricket was still a great interest, playing for the Somerset Stragglers and the Free Foresters until into his mid-fifties and he maintained his links with the county serving as an elected vice-president on the committee and holding the office of president in 1930. He even managed an MCC tour of Denmark in 1922. Towards the end of his life, Vernon suffered badly with rheumatism and the running of the farm became too much for him. He first offered the priory to the council in 1926 and when that fell through, he sold it to the Agricultural Land Company which rented it out to local farmers. It was purchased in 1968 by the National Trust.

He died at Sand Bay, on 29 September 1932, aged sixty-one. His funeral was so well attended that it filled the parish church at Kewstoke to overflowing. He was buried there alongside his beloved wife who had been interred two years previously. He lived long enough to see his two sons, M.L. Hill **[261]** and E.V.L. Hill **[280]** play for Somerset.

ARCHDALE PALMER WICKHAM [67]

VOL.1 mentioned Archie's unique claim to have kept wicket for both teams in a first-class match, against the Oxford University on 6 and 7 June 1901, but there has always been some doubt over whether this was fact or myth. He certainly kept for the University when Bill Findlay had to retire towards the end of Day One after receiving a blow to the face. The *Field* reported that Archie's offer to keep for the University [while the Oxford replacement, B.A. Collins, was summoned], was a 'somewhat unusual but very generous proceeding'.

The doubt rests on whether Archie kept wicket for Somerset at all during the match. H. Martyn **[131]**, who was on debut for Somerset, kept wicket during the University's first innings on Day One, taking two catches. Sam Woods was aware of the young Oxford man's ability having seen him keep wicket for the University against Somerset and having played with him for the

Gentlemen against the Players at Lord's the previous year. It suggests that Sam may have wanted to have another look at him behind the stumps. Archie would have expected to play as wicketkeeper and must have agreed to his captain's decision with some reluctance. Whoever kept wicket during Oxford's second innings had no hand in a dismissal and contemporaneous newspaper reports and the original scorebook shine no light on the wicketkeeper's identity.

A rare photograph of Archie in trademark stance, taken by George Beldam c1904

Would Sam Woods have had the temerity to ask Archie to stand down for a second time? Probably not. Archie, the senior amateur twice Henry Martyn's age, would not have been so agreeable and may have pulled rank when faced with another day in the field. And if Archie didn't keep wicket in the University's second innings, why would such an unusual event have ever gained credence? On the balance of probability, the record should stand.

EDWARD JOHN LOCK [70]

Ted Lock was born on 21 November 1868 while his father was butler at Cothelstone House, near Taunton, owned by Edward Jeffries Esdaile, the son-in-law of the poet Percy Shelley. The Esdaile family had restored Cothelstone House and Manor in the 1850s after purchasing the dilapidated estate which had never recovered from civil war damage. John Lock remained with the Esdaile family until he moved into Taunton during the early 1870s, first taking on the *Old Angel Hotel*, then the *Fleur de Lis Hotel* in North Street. His final move was to take over the running of *The George Hotel* on the High Street in 1875. John would be the proprietor of the hotel for the next thirty-three years until his death in 1909.

Ted was educated at Huish's Grammar School where he received a prize for punctuality, not difficult when you live a couple of hundred yards from the school. He was a good enough cricketer at Huish's to be in the 1st XI at fourteen and he first joined Taunton CC as an eighteen-year-old. By the summer of 1887, he was playing regularly for the 1st XI in the company of many first-class cricketers such as T. Wood **[92]**, the Rev E.P. Spurway **[58]**, and E.J. Tyler **[62]**. Ted Lock and Teddy Tyler, who was serving his residential qualification until he could turn out as a professional for Somerset, would become great friends over many years in Taunton.

Ted was fortunate to have gained two championship appearances for Somerset in 1891 and 1893. Neither occasion was auspicious, and he ended his first-class career with a top score of ten and a batting average of 5.33. His elevation from useful club cricketer to first-class cricketer was most likely due to his links with other Somerset cricketers, especially with the influential Sam Woods who was probably responsible for his selection. *The George Hotel* was a popular meeting place for Taunton athletes and cricketers, and Sam was a frequent guest, availing himself of its free hospitality. Sam and Ted were of similar age, and it was natural for them to form a strong bond over the years. Later, after the death of John Lock, Ted would become 'mine host' at the hotel, though the duties appear not to have affected his cricket availability as he seems to have played at every opportunity.

Apart from his cricket for Taunton CC which appears to have lasted as a 1st XI player until at least the early 1900s, (thereafter serving as the club's honorary secretary), he turned out regularly for Somerset during the pre-first-class days of the late 1880s, Somerset Club & Ground, the Taunton and District Licensed Victuallers, Wilton CC, Quantock Lodge CC throughout the 1890s, Somerset Stragglers, and Taunton Thursday CC from its formation in 1899 up to the First World War. And he was a committed tourist, at first during the 1890s with the Moonlighters, a wandering club formed and organised by G.B. Nichols **[61]**, and then, for some thirty years, with the Devon and Somerset Wanderers. As Ted remarked at a presentation from members of Taunton CC on his marriage to Agnes Couper née Symington in 1902, "It is quite true that I take a keen interest in the game of cricket, and I have always endeavoured to play my hardest in a sportsmanlike way".

He was so proud of his cricket career that he kept an album to house the photographs taken of matches and tours in which he played. The album was sold at a Taunton auction house in March 2000 after the death of his eldest son Arthur in 1999, and more recently the album came back onto the market again. The album was the prime photographic source for the book *H.T. Stanley: Too Fond of Winning* published in 2018 and apart from the superb Quantock Lodge CC team photographs, there are photographs of him in the Devon and Somerset Wanderers touring teams, starting with the eleventh tour of the Channel Islands in 1904 and ending with the thirty-fifth tour of Hampshire in 1934. Other photographs include several of Wilton CC and the Taunton Thursday Club CC which Ted helped to form.

This previously unpublished photograph is of the Taunton Thursday Club XI in its first year of formation. It includes five cricketers who played for the county:

Standing L-R: C.J. Bale (umpire), B. Edwards (scorer), A.E. Lewis ***[119]****, J.F. Ebdon* ***[116]****, J. Robins, C.R. Lyall* ***[204]****, H.T. Gamlin* ***[99]****, N/k (umpire);*
seated L-R: E.J. Pope, A. Davey, **E.J. Lock [70]***, R.F.A. Farnham, E.E. Luke, E.B. Thornhill*

Taunton CC formed the Thursday XI in 1899 and this photograph was taken at the County Ground during the inaugural home match against Bridgwater in May 1899. Sixteen fixtures were arranged against local club sides in Taunton Thursday's first season with Ted Lock appointed as captain. The fixtures included matches against Wilton, Wiveliscombe, Corfe, Ilminster, and Bishops Lydeard as well as matches against the 2nd XIs of Wellington and Bridgwater. The Somerset cricketers J.D. Harcombe **[167]** and E. Shorrocks **[166]** would also play regularly for Taunton Thursday at this time.
The significance of Thursday? It was half-day closing in Taunton. The half-holiday as it was generally called was gradually adopted throughout the county during the early 1890s although not all shops closed and, where they did, it was on different days of the week. In Taunton, shops closed on a Thursday at 2pm, the popular choice, but for example it was Wednesday at 2pm in Exeter and Friday at 1pm in Wellington. At the time, there were no matches on the Sabbath, so the half-day gave tradespeople and shopworkers who worked on a Saturday a chance to play organised cricket. Later, the club would play around twenty fixtures a year against club sides such as Taunton Deane and continued to do so until the 1930s when its original purpose had all but passed into social history.
VOL.1 mentioned that Ted took his singing seriously which is something of an understatement. He was a member of the Taunton Operatic Society and the Taunton Madrigal Society taking part in productions during his younger days. And he needed no encouragement to sing as the after-dinner entertainment. The Lock family were committed Christians and, like his father before him, Ted attended St Mary's Church. His obituary confirms that he was in the St. Mary's Church choir for over seventy years from boyhood to just before he died. Ted's album contains photographs of the choir, against the backdrop of the church, dating back to the 1890s and there are others of the Madrigal Society. They can be viewed by contacting the writer should anybody be interested in seeing them. Ted died at his home in Elm Grove, Taunton on 3 May 1949, aged eighty.

WALTER HENRY HALE [76]

Wally's first-class career statistics were initially credited to someone with the same name and born in Bristol at the same time. It was an understandable mistake because Wally's birth registration was hidden away under the surname HEAL. His mother Pauline née Hinton registered the birth and perhaps her Bristolian accent was the cause of the registrar's error. There was additional confusion about his date of birth. It is *not* 10 April 1870 as stated in VOL.1. This is his date of baptism; he was born on 6 March 1870.

Wally's father John worked as a labourer in a corn warehouse in the centre of Bristol and Wally was born close by in one of the tightly packed and very basic communal houses provided by the employer. Much later, John worked as a haulier which at least allowed the family to enjoy the more comfortable surroundings of Arno's Street in Totterdown.

Playing and coaching cricket was in Wally's blood from an early age. He was the professional for Minehead CC as a nineteen-year-old and a year later became the coach at Ilchester CC. He was Shropshire CC's professional during the 1891 season, and then began the 1892 season as the professional for Bedminster CC.

It was a trial match at the County Ground on 9 May 1892 that kick-started a brief career with the county. Wally was asked to captain the colts against a full Somerset team which included the twin strike bowlers of Tyler and Nichols. He scored 49 in the first innings 'without the vestige of a chance' and 135 in the second. He so impressed the authorities, that three weeks later he was playing in a championship match at the Oval. There was clearly some subterfuge over his residential qualification as according to the local newspapers he is reported as 'having first seen the light at Wells' rather than Bristol city centre. Runs against the Surrey XI were harder to get and worse was to come in the coming weeks, two run outs and a stumping not helping his cause. In all, he played eight times for the county in the early part of the 1892 season as well as playing in a first-class match for an H.T. Hewett XII against Cambridge University. He was never able to repeat his trial success and it was back to Bristol, leaving with a batting average of just under ten and a top score of 37 (caught & bowled W.G. Grace).

Wally married in 1893 and seeking security as a cricket professional he moved to Burnley CC in the Lancashire League, playing three full seasons for them between 1893 and 1895. Wally had played for Gloucestershire colts as a teenager and the county of his birth were belatedly showing an interest, prompting a return to Bristol. During the thirteen seasons between 1895 and 1909 he played sixty times for Gloucestershire with much more success than

he achieved with Somerset.

During his time with Gloucestershire, he scored two centuries, eight fifties and finished with a batting average of 20.47. In one season, 1901, he headed the Gloucestershire averages above Gilbert Jessop. His last first-class match was fittingly against Somerset in his thirty-ninth year. When not required by Gloucestershire he enjoyed great success as an allrounder for Knowle CC and received a benefit from the club in 1904. And as late as 1911 he was still setting records for his local club – the first, and perhaps, only player to score 1,000 runs in a season (1,016) in addition to the 80 wickets he took that year.

The Cricket Museum has recently been gifted a photograph which was in Wally's possession. The photograph is of a Gloucestershire XI taken during the 1899 season and offers this excellent close-up image of Wally, which was not available previously.

His VOL.1 biography mentioned his rare achievement of playing cricket and rugby for Somerset and Gloucestershire. His club rugby career for Bristol, and later Knowle was also mentioned. He is well-known for his coaching of promising young cricketers but not much has been written about his contribution to coaching youngsters at rugby. One of his protégées went on to captain England. J.S. Tucker, the famous Bristol hooker, revealed that Wally taught him to play rugby on Durdham Downs. Wally's son William H. Hale also played his rugby for Bristol. Wally died in Bristol on 12 August 1956, aged eighty-six.

CHARLES EDWARD DUNLOP [79]

Charles came from a distinguished Scottish family. His grandfather Edward

Dunlop had been President of Glasgow Chamber of Commerce in the mid-1850s and Lord Provost of Glasgow. His father, Charles snr, chose to work as a merchant overseas and spent his entire working life in Singapore. He married Amy née Sinclair at St Andrews Church, Singapore in 1867. The family's UK home was in Edinburgh, and it was here that Charles jnr was born on 23 June 1870. The younger Charles was known within the family as Karl, perhaps to distinguish himself from his father.

Charles Dunlop as he appears in the Gentlemen of Somerset team photograph that played Dorset in 1900. The team photograph is on page 223

He was educated at Merchiston School in Edinburgh where he was in the cricket 1st XI between 1886 and 1888. From there he went to Wadham College, Oxford and during his time there played in several trial matches without ever making the University XI. Charles qualified by residence for Somerset despite being a Scotsman based in Edinburgh. It was thanks to a holiday home in Chew Magna called Sunnycote where his mother spent the summers of 1890 and 1891. It was chosen perhaps for being close to Bath and to Bristol where there were relatives. Charles would join her when down from college and play cricket locally, mainly for the nearby village of Felton. This resulted in an invitation to play for the Gentlemen of Somerset in the last match of the 1890 season at the County Ground against the Ishmaelites.

Charles returned to Chew Magna in the late summer of 1891 but did not appear for Somerset that year. He made 43 appearances for the county between 1892 and 1905. It was said that he was only picked for his enthusiastic fielding, but he ended with a first-class batting average of 16.50 and his highest first-class score of 65 was made in a winning run-chase against Kent in 1895. The Rev R.S. Holmes writing in *Cricket: A Weekly Record of the Game*, described this innings as 'of infinitely greater value than a hatful of hundreds'. This was the same year that he made his single appearance for Scotland in a two-day, non-first-class match against Lancashire.

He would probably have played more often for Somerset, but his appearances were limited when he turned to teaching after obtaining his BA in 1893. He also spent parts of his summers in Scotland where he would appear for one of Scotland's leading cricket clubs, the Grange CC.

His chosen career as a schoolmaster did not always run smoothly. In 1901, he went into partnership with a Mr Balshaw, for the purpose of running a boy's school called Hermitage School in Lansdown and for which Charles acted as proprietor and headmaster. It was an ill-judged arrangement, with Balshaw much to blame, and it resulted in Charles being declared bankrupt. To make matters worse, it also resulted in the loss of his wife's legacy which had been ploughed into the school. VOL.1 mentioned that he gave assurances that he would endeavour to pay off his creditors and it was achieved in sufficient measure for the bankruptcy court to give him an unconditional discharge in March 1903. The newspaper reports of the hearing suggest that the judge had great sympathy for the situation in which Charles had found himself.

By this time, he had briefly taught 12 to 13-year-old boys from his home in Edinburgh before returning to his alma mater in Edinburgh to teach classics and mathematics. He remained at Merchiston for several years during which time he and his wife Isobel had two daughters. By 1910, His reputation and integrity were sufficiently restored for Charles to be appointed headmaster of Larchfield School in Helensburgh, a coastal town in Argyll and Bute. This must have been some achievement as Larchfield, founded in 1858, was a highly regarded school which would later count John Logie Baird as an alumnus and Cecil Day-Lewis and W.H. Auden as teachers. Unfortunately, Charles would not have much time to leave his mark on the school.

Charles died from heart failure the following year in Kensington on 21 August 1911. It is assumed that he was paying a last visit to his father, a Kensington resident, who died the following month. He would have been due to return to Helensburgh for the start of the Autumn term and it must have been a great shock for his young family as he was just forty-one years old. Isobel lived another fifty years but never remarried, dying in Bristol in 1961.

HENRY THOMAS STANLEY [86]

Henry led a privileged but tragically short life growing up at the large county estate called Quantock Lodge, near Over Stowey. Although born in Hanover Square, London on 20 August 1873, he spent most of his childhood on the estate when not being educated at Eton College and Christ Church, Oxford. Henry was a slight and sickly child, and left no impression at Eton College, academically or sportingly. He was not good enough to get into the Eton XI, so he formed his own team at the tender age of sixteen having persuaded his father, Edward Stanley, MP for Bridgwater, to create a cricket pitch in the grounds of the estate. This photograph from 1899 is of a Quantock Lodge team packed with Somerset cricketers:

*Standing L-R: (Umpire, possibly H. Amory), A.H. Westcott **[85]**, E. Palmer, R.B. Porch **[97]**, Rev G. Cuming, R. Humphrey (Umpire); seated, chairs L-R: A.P. Wickham **[67]**, J. Daniell **[114]**, **H.T. Stanley [86]**, C.E. Winter **[21]**, E. Robson **[95]**; seated on ground L-R: G.C. Gill **[108]**, T. Wood **[92]***

Henry (in traditional captain's position) is sporting a Harlequins cap.

The family's social influence was so great that Henry was able to command or invite the best cricketers from the South West to play for his team, which he would naturally captain. In this case, the team contains nine Somerset players; Edmund Palmer and Gordon Cuming being the exceptions. Edmund was one of the Lodge's estate workers. He was a fine fast bowler who played more often for Henry's team than any other player, but then Henry's father did pay his wages. Edmund was born in 1873, the same year as Henry, though there the similarity ended as they were at opposite ends of the social scale. Gordon Cuming was the vicar of nearby Over Stowey and he was a good enough cricketer to be in this company (he averaged 25.8 with the bat for the club). He had been a stalwart of local club cricket in the Quantocks for many years and must have been close to Somerset selection at times.

This photograph was taken at the match between Quantock Lodge CC and Kaleidoscopes CC on 4 September 1899. The opposition was a touring side from Bristol whose honorary secretary was the Somerset scorer, Tom Knight. This annual fixture was an incredibly competitive affair with both sides engaging first-class cricketers from their respective county teams. On this occasion, Henry's team made light work of the opposition. Henry made 63 not out in the Lodge's innings of 150 and the visitors were unable to cope with the bowling of Somerset's regular openers, Gill, and Robson, who took five and four wickets respectively. Quantock Lodge played 135 matches between 1889 and 1903 and during the club's short existence, eighty-two cricketers with first-class or minor county experience played for the club, including Test cricketers such as Gilbert Jessop of Gloucestershire and Walter Lees of Surrey.

There were inevitably a great number of one-sided contests at Quantock Lodge, leading to the comment of Sam Woods in *My Reminiscences* that young Master Stanley was 'too fond of winning', the title of Henry's biography published in 2018. The visit to Quantock Lodge was never about winning however which is why few cricketers and few teams turned down an invitation to play. The Estate's butler was always on hand to dispense the Stanley family's legendary hospitality, both during the match and later at the post-match dinner, ensuring that visiting teams, even in defeat, would return home in high spirits.

Henry Stanley played fifty first-class matches for Somerset between 1894 and 1899 and, just two months before this Kaleidoscopes match, had scored his maiden first-class century for Somerset against Gloucestershire at the Spa Ground in Gloucester. He had been in and out of the Somerset side during the

1899 season, but he was beginning to establish himself as a steady, reliable opening bat during the latter part of the season. Henry would have been looking forward to many more seasons playing cricket for his county, and he was not to know that it was to be his last.

The season was played out against a backdrop of simmering tension between the British, in control of the Natal and Cape colony regions of South Africa, and the Boer community in the Transvaal and Orange Free State. And within three months of the Kaleidoscopes match, the two sides were at war. The British, used to conventional, cavalry-led warfare, were critically unprepared for the Boer hit and run tactics practiced by their inspirational leader Christiaan de Wet. During the week before Christmas 1899, the British sustained heavy losses, with thousands of regular soldiers killed at Colensa, Magersfontein and Stormberg. The newspapers dubbed it 'Black Week.' But worse was to come for the British Army, it lost approximately 1,250 men during the battle of Spion Kop. Volunteers were desperately required, and the Government turned to the Yeomanry Regiments. For more than a century, Yeomanry membership had been *de rigueur* for high-born gentlemen, a chance to don fancy uniforms and pretend to be real soldiers. Henry, who was a Lieutenant in the West Somerset Yeomanry Cavalry, could never have imagined he would be called upon to fight a real war when he joined the Yeomanry, but he answered the call for volunteers without hesitation.

Henry landed in South Africa on the 29 March 1900 with the advanced party of the 7th Battalion of the Imperial Yeomanry and showed himself to be a brave and popular officer during various skirmishes with the Boers. A trooper would later comment that his bravery bordered on the reckless. Within three months of his arrival, the fortunes of war had turned. Pretoria, the Boer capital, was taken in June and the whole of the Transvaal annexed by 1 September 1900. It was typical of the British that thoughts immediately turned to cricket.

The *Black & White* magazine dated 15 September 1900, reporting on the sporting proclivities of the British soldier at war, remarked 'Scarcely had the British flag been hoisted at Pretoria than Major Poore, of the 7th Hussars, the well-known Hampshire cricketer, had organised a cricket XI. Matches were arranged and played with the utmost keenness before large crowds of spectators'.

This was the same Major Poore whom Somerset had helped achieve a first-class average of 91.23 in the 1899 season (he had taken 304 runs off the

Henry in Boer War battledress, from a memorial supplement published by the Somerset County Express

Somerset bowling in one innings at Taunton that year). He was in a good position to organise the matches as he was Provost Marshall of Pretoria.

It is frustrating when a significant discovery occurs after publication, and this is the case with Henry's biography *Too Fond of Winning*. There was just a brief reference to Henry playing for Major Poore in *Cricket: A Weekly Record of the Game*, but nothing was available about the matches from traditional sources. More recently, original copies of an obscure illustrated magazine, titled the *Black & White*, have been found at the British Library. And they have proved to be an invaluable source for these Boer War matches. This panoramic photograph of a Major Poore's XI match in progress is a great example:

Major Poore's team v. Pretoria. Scores:- Poore's team, 180: Pretoria, 176

The report in *Cricket: A Weekly Record of the Game* mentions a match involving Major Poore and Henry Stanley that was played on 8 August 1900, but the *Black & White* magazine report and the photograph opposite concerns a later match confirming that there was more than one match played between the two teams.

The *Black & White* magazine also includes a photograph of Major Poore's XI, shown below, with Poore seated middle holding a bat, and Henry seated on the ground, left with a pipe in his mouth:

The magazine was published on 15 September 1900, one day before Henry Stanley's tragic death. By this time, he had left Pretoria in pursuit of the illusive General de Wet. On the morning of the 16th, he was leading a scouting patrol at Hekpoort, about 50 miles from Pretoria, when his company fell into a trap set by the Boers. In the battle that ensued, Henry took a bullet to his head which left him mortally wounded. He died a few hours later; he was just twenty-seven years old.

He was buried the following day, close by to where he fell, but two years later, on the ending of hostilities, he was re-interred in the Bergershoop Cemetery in Krugersdoorp, about thirty kilometres from his original resting place. Visitors to the cemetery will find a large stone memorial in the section given over to the British soldiers interred there, but Henry is not amongst the names on the memorial. As in life, as in death, all men are not equal. He has a separate marble memorial paid for by the family. There are also memorials to be found in and outside the church of St Peter and St Paul, Over Stowey.

More recently, a Boer War photograph was sold at Knight's Sporting Auction. Although lacking in any detail, it clearly contains Major Poore seated third from right, the captain of Pretoria CC stood fourth from left at the back wearing a cravat and Henry who is stood at the back fourth from right:

The rudimentary pavilion and the rural background indicate that this is a different match from the one portrayed in the Black & White magazine and this photograph may well relate to the match mentioned previously that is featured in *Cricket: A Weekly Record of the Game* and dated the 8 August 1899.

Henry would have inherited the Quantock Lodge estate and this man of sober character would have managed the family's wealth responsibly. But the estate passed to his younger brother, Edward, on the death of their father in 1907. Edward was a bon viveur and 'Champagne Charlie' whose profligacy and fondness for wine, women (especially actresses), hunting, horses, and greyhounds would soon lead to the decline and eventual break-up of the estate.

ERNEST ROBSON [95]

Ernie was not a native of Somerset. He was born in Chapeltown, Leeds on 10 May 1870 and arrived at Somerset as a seasoned Cheshire and Lancashire league professional who had to qualify by residence. In March 1895, the *Pulman's News and Weekly Advertiser* carried an interview with Sam Woods on Somerset's chances for the coming season. When asked 'you have some young professionals coming on, don't you?' he replied 'Yes, the two Smiths, Farmer and Robson, their qualification terminates in July' (a reference to D.J. Smith **[101]** & W.R.R. Smith **[100]**, Farmer, on Somerset's books since 1893, never made a 1st XI appearance).

When asked whether they were batsmen or bowlers, Sam said they were mainly batsmen. It is odd that Sam had yet to discover he had a major bowling asset at his disposal. It did not escape Raymond Robertson-Glasgow who would describe Ernie as 'the most accurate of right-hand bowlers of medium pace I ever saw'. Ernie played in both first-class University matches that year but had to wait until the next year before making his championship debut at Ashley Down against Gloucestershire. He went in second wicket down making scores of 20 and 41, and perhaps of most surprise to Sam Woods, he took 3 wickets for 28 runs in 25 overs during the match as a third change bowler. In 424 first-class matches for Somerset, he scored 12,427 runs at an average of 17.65 and took 1,122 wickets at 26.56 apiece. This makes him fourth on the all-time list of Somerset wicket-takers. Only J.C. White **[194]**, A.W. Wellard **[288]** and B.A. Langford **[392]** have taken more.

Few Somerset cricketers have deserved a benefit more than Ernie Robson who gave the club twenty-nine years' loyal service from 1895 to 1923. His official benefit match against Kent in 1905 raised £400 (equivalent to £34,000 today), but fifteen years later, Tom Kelway organised a one-off benefit for him at Bridgwater. Tom, a decent player for Sherborne CC before he moved to Bridgwater as headmaster of Eastover Council Boys' School, had played with and against Ernie on numerous occasions and counted him as a good friend. Tom organised the match because of Somerset's lack of compassion in granting a second and overdue benefit. The proceeds of the benefit came to £173 which was presented to Ernie at a dinner held on his behalf at the *White Hart Hotel* under the presidency of Sam Woods. In making the presentation of the cheque, Sam referred to Ernie as 'Robbie' the nickname universally used

Starding L-R: J. Bridges [203], ?, E.H. Staddon (Gloucs), H.A. Reed (Gloucs), W.S.A. Brown (Gloucs), T. Kelway (Bridgwater), ?, ?, J. Tunnicliffe (Yorks), P.F.C. Williams (Gloucs), ?, ?;
middle row L-R: V.T. Hill [65], P.G. Robinson (Gloucs), S.M.J. Woods [64], **E. Robson [95]**, A.F.A. Lilley (Warks), J. Daniell [114], F.G. Robinson (Gloucs), J.C. White [194];
front row L-R: C. Parker (Gloucs), M.L. Hill [261], J.D. Harcombe [168], P.C. Ewens [267], H. Chidgey [129], H. Smith (Gloucs), W.M. Milton (Bridgwater), H. Gibbs [232], H.W. Saunders [205]

in cricket circles. Sam now described him as the best allrounder that Somerset had ever had. The rare photograph of the match shown opposite is believed to have been Ernie's presentation copy.

Ernie was a shy man, not much of a conversationalist, and it would have taken some effort to respond to Sam's glowing tribute. He thanked Sam and Tom Kelway and reserved a special thanks for Dick Lilley as he recalled first playing against him some thirty years previous when Ernie was playing for Cheshire. He finished his short and emotional reply by saying "I was never sorry that I came to Somerset, and I hope I will be spared for many years to achieve some more good performances for the county".

It was some hope considering he would be celebrating his fiftieth birthday before the start of the coming season. And Ernie would sadly not be spared for many years to come, for cricket or life itself. His application for a second official benefit in 1922 was discussed at the AGM but the meeting decided it was out of the question given the club's parlous financial state.

Ernie turned fifty-two during the 1922 season but was remarkably fit for his age. He played in all twenty-four championship matches that season taking 54 wickets at 26.61 apiece. And the Somerset supporters who were at Weston-super-Mare to watch the match against Middlesex that July would never forget Ernie's part in the run-chase that resulted in a thrilling two-wicket victory for Somerset. They were privileged to witness Ernie hitting a six off the England leg-break bowler John Hearne to win the match in the last over, on the stroke of 7pm. M.D. Lyon **[237]** was playing in the match and his father was so impressed that he wrote out a cheque for £50 there and then presenting it to Ernie as he came in.

Ernie would have been quietly confident that his application for a benefit in 1923 would be successful especially as he had the support of the club secretary Sam Woods who spoke in favour of his application at the AGM. A.E. Newton **[63]**, presiding at the meeting, took a contrary view as would be expected of an amateur who had never needed to worry about money. He remarked that Robson had had one benefit and thought the Club had been as generous as possible. The matter was once more deferred for a year, but before that year was out Ernie was diagnosed with terminal cancer. He played his last first-class match at Edgbaston against Warwickshire in May 1923. He became ill during the match and went home to rest. Injury was the explanation for his absence during the remainder of the season though it was obvious that he was not well.

But 'injury' did not stop him from turning out for Taunton CC during the rest of the season. And, having put his name forward for the umpires list, he also made his one and only first-class umpire's appearance in August for the match against the West Indian tourists at Clarence Park. He even fielded as a substitute in the final championship match of the season against Yorkshire when Jim Bridges met with a 'motoring mishap' on the third day of the match (this was not the only motoring mishap to befall Jim Bridges as will be recounted on page 153).

Ernie Robson at the Oval in 1922. The weary look of a man who would bowl 64,133 balls in his first-class career

This was therefore the last day on which he graced the County Ground as a player. When it came to the Somerset AGM in March 1924 the committee relented and awarded Ernie a second benefit match which was to be against Worcestershire at Taunton, the last game of the season. But this second official benefit match came too late for him.

Ernie died at the Bristol Royal Infirmary on 23 May 1924. However, the benefit still went ahead, and the gate receipts helped swell the 'Ernest Robson Fund' which was set up after Ernie's death for the benefit of Mary, his widow. Somerset reported later in the year that the money raised amounted to £930 (equivalent to about £60,000 today) but neglected to mention that the bulk of the funds had come from the various sporting and social events organised by his many friends and supporters throughout the summer.

£14 of the Fund came from the auctioning of a bat which Phil Mead of Hampshire had donated. Phil had taken it with him around the county circuit and it was autographed by over one hundred and sixty county cricketers and tourists. The high esteem in which Ernie was held was amply demonstrated when a Somerset member by the name of A.C. John became the successful bidder paying £3.15s for the bat. He then handed it back to be re-auctioned and second time around he won the bat for £10.5s!

JOHN BUCKNELL [96]

John, known as Jack, was born in Bedminster on 7 June 1872, the second son of John Bucknell and Mary Kezia née Mitchell. John snr and Mary had married in 1870 and had William as their firstborn, followed by Jack, then Mary and finally Arthur (A. Bucknell **[120]**) born on 31 January 1877. Tragically, John snr was left to raise the four children when Mary died two years later from complication when giving birth to a fourth son, Edward, who also died the same time as his mother.
John's sister Elizabeth was tasked with looking after the children while John went to work in Bristol as a solicitor's managing clerk.
During the weekends, John snr played his cricket for Bedminster CC. He had played for his local club since the mid-1860s when it could boast W.G and E.M. Grace as players. John snr would continue to play for the Bedminster 1st XI until well into his forties and was a good enough player to be selected for a Bristol and District team to play a W.G. Grace XI in August 1881.
His selection for this exhibition match held as the last match of the season at Bedminster was not quite as much an honour as it seems because his side consisted of twenty-eight players, and they still lost to W.G.'s eleven.
By the mid-1880s, John snr had dropped to the Bedminster 2nd XI and was also playing for Southville CC at Bedminster Park. He was joined by his eldest son William who in one match for Southville against Hebron CC in 1885 returned

the remarkable bowling figures of 4 overs, 7 wickets for 1 run. Hebron scored just 3 runs.

With John playing so much cricket during the children's upbringing, it was inevitable that his three sons would all play to a high standard. William joined the Scots Guards at eighteen but later played for Bloxwich CC as a talented allrounder. Jack and Arthur would in due course play for the Bedminster 1st XI before having brief spells as non-contracted professionals with Somerset. The rare image of Jack shown on the previous page was discovered too late for inclusion in VOL.1.

Readers of VOL.1, specifically of pages 200 and 201,will be aware that research into the Bucknell brothers proved that six of Jack's recorded ten appearances for Somerset should have been credited to his brother Arthur. The confusion, arising from the practice of only including the surnames of professionals in match reports and scorebooks, meant that Arthur had been missed as a first-class cricketer for Somerset for some one hundred years. The CricketArchive database has since been corrected.

Jack played three of his four matches for Somerset in 1895 before moving to the North East to pursue life as a professional cricketer for Darlington CC. Four years later in 1899, he was asked to appear in his fourth match for the county when in all probability he played because of his proximity to the match venue, Hull. His averages for all four matches amounted to 18.60 with the bat and 48.29 with the ball.

Jack was first appointed as the Darlington CC professional in December 1895, and remained as the club professional for three years, succeeded by the young Durham cricketer George Turnbull in 1899. He tried his luck in various Lancashire leagues, playing for teams such as Burnley St Andrews and Royton, before returning to play for Darlington as an amateur. He was still playing for the club up to 1913 and played for Durham as late as 1909.

In 1905, he had married Maria née Thompson whose father ran the *Black Swan Hotel* in Darlington up to the time of his death in 1903. Harry Thompson had been a well-known cricketer in the town playing for Darlington and Durham. And it was probably the family connections in the hotel trade that led to Maria and Jack taking on the running of the *Waterloo Hotel* in Darlington soon after their marriage. It became a popular meeting place for the cricket club and the Darlington Harriers Cycling and Athletics Club. Cycling had been Jack's other passion and he was a prominent member of the Darlington Harriers. The

cycling and cricket participation came to end after a serious knee injury led to a leg amputation in 1914.
It was hard to establish what became of Jack in the following years, but the recent release of the 1921 UK census confirms that he was still running the *Waterloo Hotel* with Maria that year. The couple had no children. Four years later, on 5 March 1925, Jack would die of tuberculosis, aged fifty-two. He had been suffering from tuberculosis for many years.
Jack's brother Arthur had died of the same disease at an even younger age. Arthur who had considerable success for Staffordshire while a professional for Walsall CC died in that town on 28 October 1922, aged just forty-five.

DOUGLAS JAMES SMITH [101]

It was Douglas Smith's destiny to become a professional cricketer and his biography in VOL.1 did not capture the sense of how inevitable this was for both him and his brother William (W.R.R. Smith **[100]**). Their father John plied his trade as a professional cricketer in Scotland. Among numerous engagements from 1855 to 1862, he played for Hawick, Melrose, Kelso, Langham, Dunce Academy, and Glasgow Caledonia. John then returned to England with his Scottish wife Agnes née Rutherford where he played for a succession of clubs in the Lancashire and Yorkshire leagues, briefly playing for both counties in the mid-to-late-1860s.
When Douglas was born on 29 May 1873, John had been with Batley CC for three years and continued to play for them until 1878. To support his family, which included six sons and a daughter, John worked as a woollen weaver out of season before becoming 'mine host' at the *Commercial Arms Inn* and later the *Old Mill Inn*, both in Batley. The family moved to Worcester in the mid-1880s where John became Worcestershire's coach and groundsman at the old County Ground, Boughton Park. He would also play when needed and his last recorded match was against Staffordshire in 1887 when the fifty-four-year-old was in the same team as his eldest son Alex. Alex played for Worcestershire between 1885 and 1895 but he is *not* recorded in CricketArchive as John's son nor as a sibling of Douglas and William.
Douglas was first engaged as a professional for the National Federation Bank of England at the Alexander Park ground, when in his late teens. That was

followed by a season with Meigle CC in 1892, almost certainly organised through his parents' family and cricket contacts in Scotland. Douglas was Worcestershire's professional in 1892 and 1893, often playing with at least one or other of the Smith cricketing family, and then moved to Somerset in 1894. He would have had to serve a residency qualification and an interview with Sam Woods in March 1895 (referred to on page 79) reveals that both Douglas and his brother William would be meeting that requirement by July 1895. In the meantime, there were club and ground matches to be played for the county and in Douglas's case club cricket for Yeovil CC. During one remarkable spell of batting for Yeovil in 1897 he scored 155 not out against Dorchester, 122 not out against Weymouth and 122 not out against Stoke in successive matches. He finished at Yeovil with a batting average of 63 and 100 wickets at 5 apiece. He played twenty-one first-class matches for Somerset between 1896 and 1898 but was never able to repeat his Yeovil exploits at the higher level. He left Somerset with a batting average of 13.45 (his nine first-class appearances for Worcestershire yielded an even lower average of 7.60). His highest first-class score was for Somerset against Middlesex in 1896 when, opening the innings, he made a dogged 62 while all around him gave their wicket away. Thereafter, Douglas remained in the Worcester area but spent his summers in Scotland playing for Perthshire CCC where he was following in the footsteps of his brother Alex.

The photograph, on the opposite page, courtesy of Richard Miller, is of the Perthshire XI from 1901. Douglas is seated far left.

Douglas appeared for Glamorgan, between 1898 and 1907 when it was a minor county. He also played for other Welsh teams, and the highlight must have been his inclusion in the Glamorgan and Wiltshire XI that played the Australians at Cardiff Arms Park in 1902. Somewhere amongst all this cricket it is recorded that Surrey wanted to engage him, but Worcestershire who held his registration at the time would not allow him to get away.

Throughout the early 20th century, he spent his winters in the sunnier climes of South Africa where he eventually settled as the cricket coach at St Andrews School, in Grahamstown. He made his last visit to the UK in 1939 and attended the Forfarshire versus Perthshire derby match at Forthill where he renewed old acquaintances. He was never married, and he died in Grahamstown on 16 August 1949, aged seventy-six.

He had not forgotten Perthshire CCC in the fifty years that had passed. He

bequeathed £50 to the club in his will.

ALEXANDER GOULD BARRETT [104]

VOL.1 described Alexander's life as one of unabashed privilege. He was born on 17 November 1866 on his family's estate at Moredon, near Curry Rivel. After Eton and Lincoln College, Oxford he devoted himself to his three passions: the military, hunting, and cricket. He was an enthusiastic, if not the most skilful cricketer, and he had the advantage of owning his own ground at Moredon, used by the local cricket club and his own team. He organised and captained the A.G. Barrett XI, playing country house cricket as well as an annual fixture against the Somerset Light Infantry. His interest in the military stemmed from being in the West Somerset Yeomanry serving until 1911 leaving it with the rank of Major.

Alexander played his only match for Somerset against Cambridge University at Fenners on 11-12 June 1896. He scored six runs in his two innings and did not bowl. Sam Woods had struggled to form a side against his old University, and Alexander was almost certainly making up the numbers. So were H.L.S. MacDonald **[105]**, at thirty-five well past his best days, and the Cambridge rowing sensation D.H. McLean **[106]**. It would be the first and last appearance in a first-class match for all three, and it is hardly surprising that Cambridge, led by F. Mitchell of Yorkshire and England and supported by W.G. Grace at the top of the order, won the match by a margin of ten wickets. Alexander also played for and against the Somerset Stragglers for many years. The photograph included below is a rare example from 1906 in which Alexander features as captain of the team:

There is lots of Somerset interest in this photograph. A.E. Lewis **[119]** is the umpire, the Rev A.P. Wickham **[67]** is seated on Alexander's left. R.E. Hancock **[183]** and J.A. Hellard **[180]** were both killed in action during World War One. Records show that he was still playing for the Stragglers during the early 1930s as indeed he was for his own XI against the Somerset Light Infantry, his last appearance being in 1939, aged seventy-two.

One hugely significant event in Alexander's life was overlooked in VOL.1 and the details, concealed as best the authorities and family could manage, are quite extraordinary. Alexander's engagement to Edith Alice Miles, a staff college colonel's daughter, was announced at the beginning of January 1899. And two weeks later, on Saturday 15 January at two in the afternoon, he walked onto the platform at Basingstoke railway station, jumped on to the track and laid his head on the rail in front of a goods train entering the station. The protective guard at the front of the engine caught his head and knocked him into the foot way between the rails whereupon some fifteen waggons passed over him. Apart from shock and a slight head wound he was uninjured. He remarked to the constable who took him into custody "I cannot think what on earth made me do it".

The following Monday he was before the magistrates on a charge of attempted suicide and his brother pleaded for him to be discharged arguing that he had temporarily lost his mind. The magistrates were swayed by the plea after his brother explained that he had been depressed for some time. Alexander was discharged on the assurance that he would be properly looked after. The court's lack of empathy for his plight is quite shocking. Alexander may have been concerned about the escalating tension in South Africa or perhaps there was a more personal reason for his anxiety as he faced the uncertainties of an impending marriage. In the event, the marriage did not go ahead, but Alexander did eventually marry ten years later in 1909. His wife was Dorothy Cartwright, thirteen years his junior, whose father was the rector of the parish church in Hornblotton, nr Castle Cary before his death in 1906. The couple were married at North Curry Parish Church and lived at Eastbrook House, Trull.

He remained a committed supporter of Somerset, serving as its president in 1931 and 1932. Alexander inherited some of the family fortune and had no need of work. There was no repeat of the mental health episode which almost cost him his life in 1899 and perhaps his brother was right when he referred to it as nothing more than a fleeting moment of madness.

There was one last twist to his life or rather to his death on 12 March 1954. At eighty-seven he would have expected a more dignified ending, but he died from injuries sustained the previous day when his car hit a wall near his home. His sister-in-law, Miss Monica Cartwright, who had lived at Eastbrook House since his wife's death, was at the wheel of the car and escaped serious injury.

EUSTACE TICKELL HILL [113]

The image used for Eustace in VOL.1 was of O.M. Samson **[125]** and this was corrected in the addenda to VOL.4 with a photograph of him, in Hussars uniform. No image of him in cricket attire could be found at the time but one has since been found in the collection of the Cricket Museum.

Standing L-R: W.S.A. Brown (Gloucs), ***Capt. E. Hill [113]****, H. Wrathall (Gloucs), W. Mead (Essex & England), G.G. Hearne (Kent & England);*
seated chairs L-R: Major A.C.G. Banning, S.M.J. Woods ***[64]****, F.T. Welman* ***[4]****, W. Morgan (Glamorgan), F.A. Tarrant (Middx & Victoria);*
seated floor L-R: F.M. Lee ***[141]****, V.T. Hill* ***[65]***

This photograph had been overlooked because it held no notation, and most of the players were not recognised as Somerset cricketers. As the caption reveals, Eustace is standing second from the left.

Further research confirmed that this team was the MCC side which played Monmouthshire CC on the 6 and 7 July 1904 at Rodney Parade, Newport. Eustace's identity as the 'Captain E. Hill' in this photograph can easily be confirmed by comparison with the one in Hussars uniform and others held by Glamorgan Archives. The presence of William Morgan in this team explains why twelve players are in the photograph. Harry Wrathall was late getting to Newport and William Morgan stepped in. William, who was responsible for assembling the MCC team, also had Somerset connections. After moving to Bath in 1898, he served on Somerset's Bath area committee and helped to oversee the county's matches at the Recreation Ground until his death in 1914.

Arthur Charles Greaves Banning also had Somerset connections. A member of Somerset cricket club living in Pitminster, he met the ultimate cricketer's end by collapsing dead in the Lord's pavilion at the start of the day's play during the New Zealand Test match on 29 June 1931.

CricketArchive has incorrectly credited Edward Roden Hill with this match. It was an easy mistake to make as he and Eustace were both Army captains in 1904. E.R. Hill was a career officer in the Highland Light Infantry and his regiment was stationed overseas at the time of the match. The MCC matches against Wiltshire and Glamorgan in 1903 have also been awarded to E.R. Hill when they should have been credited to Eustace.

Poor Eustace must have become resigned to not receiving credit for matches in which he played. For over seventy years, the identity of the 'E. Hill' who made two appearances for Somerset in 1898 and 1901 was unknown. A quick inspection of the original scorebooks would have revealed that Captain E.T. Hill was playing in both matches. But the newspaper compositors left out his middle Tickell initial (derived from his mother's maiden name) and it was the newspapers which were used as the source for the players' records in *Somerset County Cricket: Facts & Figures from 1891 to 1924* and *Facts & Figures of Somerset County Cricket Club (including all players) 1891-1946*. Eustace's identity was not corrected until 1975 when the Association of Cricket Statisticians and Historians (ACS) produced *Somersetshire Cricketers 1875-1974* to coincide with Somerset's centenary. It would be nice to think that when the ACS researcher quizzed the Hill descendants about the biographical details of brother Vernon and nephews M.L. Hill **[261]** and E.V.L. Hill **[280]** one of the family interjected with "Don't forget great-uncle Eustace"!

And it would have been easy to forget his modest contribution to Somerset cricket history. After Winchester College, where he and younger brother Vernon (V.T. Hill **[65]**) were both in the Winchester College 1st XI that played Eton in 1887, he attended the Royal Military Academy before joining the 19th Hussars. Much of his early Army career was spent in India where there were plenty of opportunities to play cricket. Some noteworthy matches included appearing in two matches, for the Madras Presidency and Bengaluru (Bangalore) & District XI, against Lord Hawke's visiting tourists of 1892/93. He was also in the Madras Presidency team that played the Parsees in December 1893.

Eustace made his belated Somerset debut against Oxford University in 1898 while on leave from the Army. His younger brother was also playing and by this time Vernon was an ever-present member of the Somerset side, it being his sixty-ninth match for the club. It is safe to assume that Eustace's appearance owed much to his brother's influence. Eustace acquitted himself well, with scores of 31 (the second highest) and 17, outscoring his brother. Three years would pass before he played his second and final match for Somerset in 1901. The match was against the same opposition at The Parks in Oxford and both brothers played. Scores of 0 and 22 left Eustace with a first-class average of 17.50. Much of the time gap between Eustace's first and last appearance was spent overseas, and he was mentioned in despatches while serving in South Africa during the Boer War with the Gloucestershire Imperial Yeomanry.

He married Florence Bowen, daughter of Sir George Bevan Bowen, in 1904 and they had five children. After resigning his commission, he joined his cousin Charles Gathon Hill in the running of a shipbuilding and ship repair business in the Bristol dry dock. By this time Eustace, as the eldest son, had received a large inheritance on the death of his father in 1903 (Sir Edward Stock Hill left the modern-day equivalent of £30 million). Eustace retired with his family to the country of his birth and lived at Llansantffraed Court, near Abergavenny. He died on the 11 January 1933, aged sixty-three, in Ruthin Castle, a private hospital for 'obscure internal diseases' which in Eustace's case involved sclerosis of the liver, colon disease and bronchial pneumonia.

N.B. the MCC matches played by Eustace have necessitated corrections to the CricketArchive database as well as an additional correction to the Somerset match against Hampshire in 1890 which should not have featured Eustace. See page 212 for an explanation.

JOHN DANIELL [114]

John's father, Andrew Frederick Daniell, was the son of a commander in the Indian Navy and the grandson of a major general in the East India Company. His mother Joanna née Mickleham was the daughter of the Inspector General of Army Hospitals. The family business in India was growing and manufacturing tea in Panighatta, a Darjeeling tea estate village situated on the foothills of the Himalayan Mountains. Andrew and Joanna had a daughter there the following year, but the infant Katherine only survived the subtropical, high-altitude climate for eighteen months. John was their second and last child born in Bath, while his parents were on leave, on 12 December 1878. John's father died in 1890, en route from India, and John was sent to England to be educated at Clifton College, chosen for its proximity to his maternal grandparents. He was in the 1st XI at Clifton from 1894 to 1897 and played his first cricket match for Somerset in June 1898 when he was in his first year at Emmanuel College, Cambridge. He played no university cricket that year, but he did feature in the Seniors' match of 1899 as shown in the photograph below. This was the traditional early season trial for the University XI and John appears second from left in the second row up.

He made no impression in the match, and it was his timely century for Somerset against Lancashire a few days before the Varsity team was due to be announced that earned him his blue. He kept his place in the team for the Varsity matches of 1900 and 1901 and he was also a triple blue for the University XV. John appeared regularly for the county up to 1904 before his move to India. His father had left the tea factory, estate, and extensive Indian property interests in trust to be accessed when John was twenty-five years old, so it was now time to sort out his father's affairs. He delayed the move until the cricket season was over and probably never thought it would take three years to settle.

He returned to captain Somerset in 1908 and held the position until the end of the 1912 season. No reason was given for his decision to end his five-year reign, but 1912 was a particularly poor season when Somerset managed just two championship match wins out of sixteen played. John continued to play the following season under the captaincy of E.S.M. Poyntz **[163]**, but in May 1914, at the end of the match against Surrey at the Oval, he announced that he was giving up county cricket. The events on the pitch had probably made up his mind. Some indifferent bowling had allowed Surrey to make 397 by the end of day one and Somerset eventually lost by 241 runs, despite John scoring a dogged 84 in Somerset's first innings which was reported as one of 'sound defence'. Perhaps he was making a point to his teammates because sound defence is not normally associated with a Daniell innings. This photograph is more in keeping with John's style of batting:

This posed photograph was taken during the match against Surrey at Bath in 1920 and would do justice to those more famous studies by George Beldam. It has been copied from an article in *Land & Water*, dated 10 June 1920, and entitled *'Cricketers in Action: IV. Somerset'*. The article was written and photographed by E.H.D. Sewell and came with the caption 'JUMPING IN TO DRIVE A STRAIGHT BALL: A good example of J. Daniell's fine free style, though with a rather pronounced uplift of the foot'. Many of the photographs used in the article have been used elsewhere in this book.

During the First World War, John served as a captain in the Territorial Force of the Royal Army Service Corp, serving in France until the Armistice. When the hostilities ended, it must have been a surprise to see him back in the side by the mid-season of 1919 and taking over the captaincy from Jack White. He vowed to run Somerset in his own way and on his own terms, a coded message which meant it would be run autocratically according to his will.

It is a measure of his durability and stamina that he would play over half his first-class matches for Somerset after the War (153 out of 287) while in his forties. And make his highest first-class score as late as 1925 in a match against Essex at the County Ground. He scored 174 not out in the first innings and followed up with 108 in the second. At the end of the 1925 season, the president, Sir Dennis Boles, presented John with a scorecard of the match, printed on silk, and framed in gold, which had been subscribed by past and present members of the Somerset XI.

There would be speculation every year about whether John would carry on as captain. And finally, at the AGM in January 1927, he announced his resignation saying that the pressures of the job had become too much for him. He played his last match for Somerset at Edgbaston against Warwickshire on 9 July 1927. He was forty-eight years old, and it was not the auspicious ending that he deserved. There were just four hours play in the match due to heavy rain, thunderstorms, and flooding to a depth of three feet. And John did not even last that long after receiving a severe blow to the right knee stopping a drive from Kilner. He could be forgiven there and then for thinking it was time to pack it in.

He continued playing for the Somerset Stragglers for several more years and made useful contributions with the bat. The highlight was a century in 1928 at the County Ground against a Captain Amory's XI (R. Heathcote Amory was the captain of Devon CC at the time). At the end of 1931, A.F. Davey

resigned as Somerset secretary, a position he had held since taking over from Sam Woods in 1923. He was taking on the coveted role of Surrey secretary which had been vacated by R.C.N. Palairet **[69]**. Somerset received over one hundred applications for its secretarial vacancy, but most applicants needed to be paid and Somerset could ill afford to pay them. John stepped into the breach and volunteered to take on the role for a twelve-month period *pro bono* which was welcomed by the club, noting that it would save £250-£300.

The temporary arrangement lasted five years and by the end of his tenure it was agreed that he was leaving Somerset in a better position than when he took office. At the AGM in January 1936, he was able to report a surplus of £789 compared with a deficit of £2,437 when he took over in 1932. In responding to the vote of thanks for his 'valuable' service, he remarked in his usual direct manner "The best thanks you can give me is for each member of the club to get another member. If they did, we could afford to get a paid secretary, start a nursery, and put Somerset cricket in a better position than it has ever been before". John remained a huge influence at Somerset and after the Second World War became president of the club, a position he held for three years.

His other lifelong sporting interest was rugby. He was in the Clifton College XV by the age of fourteen and he was the Cambridge hooker in three successive Varsity matches. His club rugby was for Richmond RFC, and he was first called up to play for England while still an undergraduate. He played seven times for England between 1899 and 1904, captaining the side on each occasion. He served on the Rugby Football Selection Committee from 1913 to 1939 and was its chairman from 1932 to 1939. He was a vice-president of the R.F.U. from 1938, acting president from 1940 to 1945 and president from 1945 to 1947.

Among the hundreds of tributes to John's life there is no better story than the one recounted by N.S. 'Mandy' Mitchell-Inness **[312]** in the Guardian obituary which sums him up completely. Sitting alongside John at Taunton, Mandy remarked that Jack Lee had been hit in the box. "The box?" thundered John, "What namby-pamby nonsense is that?" A while later it happened again. John exploded "What does he need a box for? In my day, we hit fours with our private parts!"

This collotype is by Ernest Clarence Elliott, published in 1904

He had not been well for about five years before his death at his farmhouse in Holway, Taunton, but during that time he had celebrated over fifty years of marriage to his devoted wife Manora. They had a son Nigel and daughter Joan. Nigel played rugby and cricket for Taunton and was Somerset's secretary in 1950. Joan married W.F. Baldock **[243]**. John died at the farmhouse on 24 January 1963, aged eighty-four.

OLIVER JAMES GRIFFIN [117]

The observant reader will have noted that the 117th Somerset cricketer in VOL.1 was named Harry Griffin, but it is now clear that Harry was not the professional named Griffin who appeared in four matches for Somerset in 1898 and 1899. Harry Griffin was a talented all-rounder who played his club cricket for Street. In May 1898, he played for Lionel Palairet's XI in an early-season trial match, and bowled well, taking 4 for 21 off his ten overs. Harry was clearly well-known to Sam Woods and the club (he had bowled Sam in the trial). He also had a good match for Street against Sam's local club in early July 1898 taking the wickets of the first six Bridgwater batsmen. It was therefore reasonable to assume that the professional 'Griffin' who made his debut against Lancashire at Liverpool beginning 25 July 1898 was Harry. *Wisden* credited this match and three others to Harry, and this was enshrined in Somerset's early facts and figures 'bible' produced by F.J.C. Gustard in 1925 which used *Wisden* as its source.

However, Gustard's attribution should have been challenged in VOL.1. For a start, Harry was not a professional cricketer, and his scorebook entry would have read 'H. Griffin' if he had played. And it would also have been challenged if sense had been made of a brief reference in the summary of Somerset's season by the *Taunton Courier* which noted that the county had used 'Griffin of Todmorden, formerly of Taunton Cricket Club'. This should have ruled out Harry because he had never played for Taunton. Indeed, he never strayed too far from his native Street so was highly unlikely to have been playing Lancashire League cricket as a professional. Taunton did have a professional named Griffin who had played for them a few years previously, and although generally appearing under his surname, he is crucially referred to as 'J. Griffin' in a match for Taunton against Minehead CC in 1892. And J. Griffin also appears for the Moonlighters CC, a Taunton-based touring team, organised by George Nichols and Teddy Tyler, that travelled the West Country during the 1890s after the close of the county season. The tour traditionally ended in a match against Quantock Lodge CC recorded in the photographs that appear in Ted Lock's album.

VOL.1 used two close-ups from these photographs to illustrate Harry's biography, but it is now clear that these were not images of Harry but were images of the Taunton cricketer James Griffin and it is the latter player who should be credited with the four first-class appearances for Somerset. This is another fine photograph taken from the E.J. Lock album, shown opposite. It features thirteen first-class cricketers from Somerset plus J.H. Board of Gloucestershire. James Griffin is the player seated far right in the wicker chair:.

Quantock Lodge v Moonlighters 18 September 1896.
Standing L-R: W.T. Webb, N/K (umpire), T.A. Cousins, E.J. Lock ***[70]****, P.T. Mitchell, C.M. Lewis, A.E. Clapp* ***[51]****, A.H. Westcott* ***[85]****, R. Humphrey (umpire), J.H. Board, G.C. Gill* ***[108]****, C.E. Brown* ***[139]****;*
seated in chairs L-R: W.H. Randolph, A.E. Newton ***[63]****, W.B. Sloman* ***[93]****, G.B. Nichols* ***[61]****, H.T. Stanley* ***[86]****, T. Kelway, S.M.J. Woods* ***[64]****,* ***J. Griffin [117]****;*
seated ground L-R: E.H. Gill, F.C. Goodman, E.W. Bartlett ***[88]****, E. Robson* ***[95]****, H. Samson.*

Harry's biography needs to be replaced with one for James Griffin and this has been achieved with the help of Chris Gore, whose research for the Cumbria Cricket League has helpfully established that when James was playing for Todmorden, his initials 'O.J.' were provided.

Oliver James Griffin was the son of James Griffin and Susan Emma née Davey. James snr was from Luppett, Honiton, and Susan was from a 40-acre farm at Cowley, Honiton. They were married in Axminster in 1866 and had a daughter while living in Brixton, London where James was working as a provisions dealer. They returned to Honiton in 1871, where James found work as a farm bailiff, and where Oliver James was born on 1 June 1872. A second daughter was also born there on 22 May 1874 and her birth certificate reveals that James snr was deceased. The 1881 census has Susan and her three young children back at her parent's farm in Cowley. Oliver's first name had been dropped in favour of his second name, perhaps as a tribute to his late father.

As far as can be ascertained, Susan and her family remained in Devon for the rest of the decade, and it was not until the winter of 1890 that James found himself in Taunton. Susan had become the licensee of *The Devonshire Inn*, 36, Paul Street, Taunton which she politely called an 'eating house'. The inn was otherwise known as 'Evans's Refreshment Rooms'. She didn't remain long at the inn after marrying a widower named Richard Foster from London in August 1893 and eventually moving to Sussex where she died in 1905.

James first played for the Taunton 1st XI in 1891. He was nineteen and it seems inconceivable that he had not played a high standard of cricket in Devon before moving to Taunton, but an exhaustive search has failed to find any evidence. Tellingly the census of April 1891 makes no mention of his employment as a professional cricketer. His first proper engagement as a professional cricketer was in 1894 for Lancaster CC of the North Lancashire and District league. A piece from the *Lancaster Guardian* states that he was an assistant to Bulmer, the senior pro, and describes him as 'a Somerset man with a good reputation'. It added that 'as he is an effective medium pace bowler, he will supply a want in the team which has long been felt'. James remained with the club for three seasons and did well with both bat and ball in 1897, helping Lancaster to end the season top of the league. In one match against Barrow CC, he achieved the rare bowling feat of taking five wickets in successive balls, four bowled and one lbw, to finish with figures of 8 for 15.

Perhaps this was the reason for Todmorden CC offering James a contract to play for them in 1898. It was a step up for James who played in twenty-two of the twenty-six Lancashire league fixtures that year. He finished the season with a batting average of 20.42, including a top score of 75 against Haslingden CC, and took 47 wickets at an average of 16.36. Despite these figures, it was not enough to earn a further contract and James returned for a fourth season with Lancaster in 1899. It was a successful year with the ball in hand, particularly against the Millom CC batsmen with home and away bowling figures of 8 for 31 and 6 for 55. And it earned him further call-ups for Somerset during 1899, at Gloucester in June and at Old Trafford and Hull on the northern tour in July. There would be no further matches for Somerset. His four appearances yielded a batting average of 9.85 and 16 wickets at 15.50 with a best bowling return of 6 for 40. In fact, there would be no further matches for any club in England due to his dalliances with a young lady named Ruth Casson.

In December 1899, Ruth sought damages from James at Leeds Assizes for breach of promise. James had met the young dressmaker in Blackpool in 1895 and wooed her with tales of being 'well-to-do' and due to inherit from his father who was supposedly a farmer in Taunton. Promises of marriage had led to intimacy with James probably fathering Ruth's daughter Violet in January 1898, though no father's name is given on her birth certificate. After being told of a second pregnancy in June 1899, James returned to Taunton at the end of the cricket season and broke off contact. The judge found for Ruth, awarding her £75 damages and maintenance payments of five shillings a week (25p). A second daughter Maud was born in January 1900. Both girls would grow up with the surname Tyrrell taken from the man that Ruth married in 1902.

James needed to be found before Ruth could receive any of the judge's compensation and perhaps James saw a way out of his tricky situation by disappearing off to South Africa with the West Somerset Yeomanry. He was part of the 25th West Somerset unit of the 7th Battalion of the Imperial Yeomanry that sailed to South Africa, arriving on 23 March 1900, to reinforce the regular Army in the Boer War. One of his officers on the troopship was Lieutenant H.T. Stanley **[86]**. Unlike the unfortunate Henry Stanley, James was not a casualty of the War and, like most of his unit that did survive, he joined the Pretoria constabulary once the city had come under British civilian control. As one young yeomanry soldier from Somerset wrote home, 'there are a lot of our chaps joining the police and it is as well to be earning 7 shillings [35p] a day in the police as 1 shilling and 5 pence [7p] in the Army'.

Many unattached men made a life for themselves in South Africa long after the War ended in 1902, and James was aware of what awaited him back home. He was still in South Africa in 1905, though by this time he had left the police, and he is recorded as 'the old Somerset cricketer' scoring 106 and 65 not out for Wonderfontein in two matches against Belfast, Transvaal. And in 1909, he married a widow, Harriett Urie Angus, in Bethal, Transvaal. In May 1912 he acquired a dairy farm known as Goedehoop, in the Trichardt area of Bethal. Harriett died in 1919, aged 38, and in December 1921, James married a young woman from Cape Province, Evelyn Florence née Watts. They had a daughter Avril in 1927 but she would never know her father. James was already terminally ill and died in a nursing home at Trichardt three months later, on 25 August 1927, aged fifty-five. Avril died in 2003 possibly not knowing of the skeletons in her family cupboard and unaware that she had stepsisters leading parallel lives in Britain.

LEONARD CHARLES BRAUND [121]

It was not difficult to find images of Len for his biography in VOL.1. There are a sizeable number taken over his long professional career with England, Surrey, and Somerset spanning twenty-five years from 1896 to 1920. There are at least six known postcard images of him posed at the wicket some of which have become rare and collectable. But this image is a fresh one, having been obtained recently at auction and it shows him in best Sunday clothes during his early days of cricket with Surrey. It is such a fine image and would have been used had it been available.

The biography in VOL.1 touched on his days at Surrey and speculated on his reasons for moving to Somerset but one hundred and twenty plus years later it still makes no obvious sense. Len, the son of a successful artist specialising in portrait painting had lived in affluent Richmond since the age of three, had been educated at the British School in Richmond and had played his early cricket for Richmond CC. And he was just making a name for himself in the Surrey 1st XI having played in the last five matches of the 1898 championship in which Surrey finished fourth. So why did he leave for the county that finished bottom? Why did he significantly lessen the chance of international selection by moving to an unfashionable county? And why miss two championship seasons serving a period of residential qualification?

He played just four first-class matches in 1899, three against Australia for various sides and the other for Somerset against Oxford University. In Somerset's match against the mighty Australians, the Somerset supporters had a taste of what was to come when he opened Somerset's first innings with C.A. Bernard **[102]** and scored 82 in a first-wicket partnership of 152 runs. He spent the rest of the summer playing for local clubs like Taunton CC, playing the occasional match for London County CC and he also had a spell coaching at Winchester College.

A player's residential qualification was often open to confusing interpretation and Somerset, impatient to see young Len play for them in the championship decided to test the waters. They risked playing him in the match against Middlesex on 4 June 1900 and the subsequent appeal from Middlesex was upheld by MCC. There was an amusing incident in the match which Len would often recall. He was no-balled when he hadn't let go of the ball. He held it aloft challenging the umpire's decision, but the extra run was given. Unable to play championship cricket for the rest of the season, Len played a full season of first-class cricket for London County and W.G. instead.

Len never commented on his reason for moving to Somerset. It is unlikely that the twenty-three-year-old was persuaded by money. He was still living at home with his parents, had no commitments and Somerset would not have offered him more than Surrey anyway. He would also have had no doubts about a future with Surrey as he was confident of his ability and worth. And there was no rift between the two parties to explain his Surrey departure although at times over the seasons 1896 to 1898 he must have been frustrated by his lack of 1st XI cricket.

A clue might just lie in a comment in *Cricket: A Weekly Record of the Game* dated 29 December 1898. It stated 'Braund played useful cricket [for Surrey] in the West and if it is true that he is qualifying for Somerset, the cider county can be congratulated on a good catch, while Surrey can afford to lose him with good grace'. Put simply, no-one, least of all Surrey, realised how exceptional he would become and the comment about playing useful cricket in the West may also be a clue to why he signed for Somerset.

It was Surrey's penultimate championship match and maybe the Taunton crowds and the ground's febrile atmosphere appealed to the young man of bohemian upbringing. Despite not getting a wicket on a perfect batting surface he could not have failed to be impressed by the spirit in which Somerset played their cricket (a swashbuckling century from W.N Roe **[26]** and a stylish one from L.C.H. Palairet **[68]** may have helped). And perhaps Len was amused by the comical last half hour of play in which Len kept wicket and stumped G.C. Gill **[108]**. It was a final passage of play which the newspapers noted could not be taken seriously.

It is an interesting theory that one match changed the direction of his first-class career and perhaps that last half hour of play was the deciding factor as Len was never one to take cricket too seriously. R.C. Robertson-Glasgow **[246]** recognised this lack of seriousness when in *More Cricket Prints*, he wrote 'When he is inclined to speak on cricket he speaks with long wisdom and a humour that has little respect for persons, and none at all for averages, records, and clumps of figures'.

A PERFECT THOUGH NOT A FULL-BLOODED ACTION
Braund jumps in to drive. Wrist-work is obvious in the pick-up of the bat

Len was another player to feature in the *Land & Water* article of 1920 and this posed photograph taken by E.H.D. Sewell is included here because most of Len's images are of him at the wicket with ball in hand. Sewell's comments that went with the photograph are also included.

Len was granted a benefit in 1908 and naturally enough chose the Surrey match at Bath. The in-swing of W.T. Greswell **[188]** had accounted for the Surrey openers, Hobbs, and Hayward, by the time 21 runs were on the scoreboard. And then, as so often happened to Somerset beneficiaries the weather gods intervened, and rain took hold of the match. There was three hours of play instead of three days and Len netted next to nothing. He was heard to say, "let there be no more benefit matches if you please". Years later he said that he refused another benefit because he had lost money on the first!

Len bowed out of first-class cricket with impressive career statistics. He had played 432 matches, including 23 for England, and 281 of these matches were for Somerset. He had scored over twelve thousand runs for the club, which included 13 centuries, scored at an average of 25.40. He took 684 wickets for Somerset at 28.00 and both his highest score and best bowling figures were for Somerset. His best bowling of 9 for 41 (15 for 71 in the match) was made in 1902 against Yorkshire in their only defeat of that season. And his highest score of 257 not out was made in 1913 against Worcestershire at New Road. By 1913, some of the magic had gone out of his bowling and he was being picked primarily for his batting. He had lost his length and some of his ability to impart spin which meant his bowling was often punished.

At the end of his playing career and after a brief spell coaching in Cambridge, he became a first-class umpire in 1923. In a long umpiring career spanning sixteen seasons, he officiated in 374 first-class matches including three Test matches (in 1926 and 1928 at Lord's and 1929 at Headingley). This candid photograph of Len was taken during a break in play during a championship match at Kettering in 1928. He retired from umpiring in 1938, forced by poor health which resulted in the loss of a toe. This was followed in October 1843 by the amputation of a leg from the hip down and this prompted Dick Palairet, who was president of Somerset at the time, to set up an appeal for Len, beginning with a £21 donation from the club.

Len bore his illness with great stoicism and, typical of the man, he wrote cheerfully from his hospital bed to wish his admirers at Somerset well, assuring his friends and supporters that he would soon make a full recovery.

The recovery would turn out to be much longer than he expected. Len had to spend nine months in hospital by which time the Somerset appeal had raised £250. And there were further operations to endure before he had to lose his other leg in May 1946. When Herbert Sutcliffe heard the news of his second amputation, he started a national appeal for Len and one of his other old England teammates Phil Mead of Hampshire (Phil had become blind that same year). The fund would eventually close the following year having raised the sum of £6,671 (equivalent to over £300,000 today).

Len lived another nine years and could often be found in the Lord's pavilion sat in his bath chair. "Not bad, to have a reserved seat on wheels" he would exclaim, without any hint of self-pity. He died in Putney on 23 December 1955, aged eighty.

OSWALD MASSEY SAMSON [125]

Oswald was born in Taunton on 8 August 1881. He was the youngest of three sons born to Charles and Mina Samson. His father ran an architectural practice in Hammett Street, Taunton and was also the Bath and West Diocesan surveyor for more than twenty years.

Charles was originally from Kent and educated in Hertfordshire. After qualifying as an architect, he came to Dunster where he was responsible for the restoration of Dunster Castle and Dunster Church. When this project ended, he set up his practice in Taunton and moved his family to Staplegrove Road. His two eldest sons, Charles jnr and Harold, were sent to Chard Grammar School where they excelled academically. They were both excellent cricketers and played locally - Charles jnr for Norton CC and Harold for Taunton CC – the latter also going on tour with Moonlighters CC (Harold's close physical resemblance to Oswald can be seen on page 99).

Oswald was sent to a school in Dorchester where he showed such early academic promise that he was entered for and gained a scholarship to Cheltenham College in September 1895 when aged fourteen. He won various prizes and medals while there, played for the cricket 1st XI of 1899 and gained a mathematical scholarship to Hertford College, Oxford. He did so well at Oxford that the University awarded him a Mathematical Exhibition in 1901,

and he left Oxford with a double first in the subject.
He made his debut for Somerset in June 1900, aged eighteen. It was a single appearance that year against his University, and he scored 23 runs in his only innings. He played in the same fixture the following year and also made his championship debut against Kent in July 1901. By this time, he had played in various university trial matches but failed to earn a regular place in the side or obtain a blue in either 1901 or 1902. In 1903, he played for the University against Somerset and in a couple of other early University matches without much success and it seems he was quite fortunate to be selected for the Varsity match based on his university form.
His selection was undoubtedly swayed by his maiden and only century for Somerset against Gloucestershire at Gloucester the week before the Varsity team was announced at the end of June 1903. He had been asked to open the Somerset innings in place of Lionel Palairet who was one of four missing regulars in a weak Somerset team, and he produced a patient, if unspectacular, innings of 105 runs. As a measure of how the innings was crafted, he was missed when on 63 having been at the crease for two hours, fifty-five minutes. But it was good enough for the University and Oswald's score of 32 not out towards the end of Oxford's second innings set up a challenging total which Cambridge could not match.

This close-up of Oswald in cricket attire is taken from a Montague Cooper team photograph which has never been published before. The full team photograph can be viewed on page 228. It is a particularly sharp image, taken during the match against Surrey played on 20-22 August 1903 when he had finished university.
He played for Somerset in most of the July and August matches

of 1903 but failed to build on the century at Gloucester. After a run of very average scores, he was moved down the batting order, and by the time of this match against Surrey, he was propping up the innings at number ten in the batting order. After this match he played no further first-class cricket for five years while he forged a career as a schoolmaster at Rugby School and played club cricket for Rugby CC.

He was persuaded to play for Somerset in 1908 during the summer vacations. It was an arrangement that continued until 1913, but he never managed a repeat of the patient century achieved in 1903. His highest score during his second spell at the club was 66, made in 1912 against Worcestershire. He finished his Somerset career with a batting average of 18.62 from the forty-five first-class matches he played.

Oswald never married and up to the time he moved to Rugby he had always lived at home with his parents. On reaching sixty in 1906, his father retired and moved with his mother Mina to Rugby, leaving their son Harold to take over the running of the architectural practice which now had offices in Bridgwater as well as Taunton.His parents moved to Hillmorton Road, Rugby which was a short distance from the school and its boarding houses. Oswald stayed at his parent's house until he was called up for war service in 1917 when this photograph was taken. Fifteen years after his *annus mirabilis* of 1903, his life ended on 17 September 1918, aged thirty-seven.

Lieutenant Oswald Massey Samson of the Royal Garrison Artillery died from his wounds sustained during the Somme battles of the Final Hundred Days. He had been serving with the 143rd Heavy Battery Unit which was equipped with four 9.2-inch howitzers designed to wreak havoc beyond the enemy lines. Oswald is buried in the Communal Cemetery Extension at Péronne, a small town situated on the banks of the Somme River in the east of the Somme Department of Picardy.

WILLIAM HYMAN [127]

William, known as Billy, made thirty-eight appearances for Somerset between 1900 and 1914 but he is best known for his triple-century scored for Bath Association CC (the predecessor to Bath CC) on 12 July 1902. It was against Thornbury CC on the 'Ship' ground near Thornbury. Dr E.M. Grace captained the host team which contained the Gloucestershire bowlers A. Sellick **[164]**, Teddy Spry, and Arthur Paish. There was a brief mention of Billy's innings in VOL.1, but it was so extraordinary that it deserves greater coverage.

The match began with no warning of what was to unfold. Bath batted first and scored 124 to which Thornbury replied with 85. Bath's second innings began at 4.35 pm and when stumps were drawn at 6.25 pm the score was 461 for 6 wickets; Billy was on 359 not out. Despite having the Gloucestershire bowling trio, E.M. stubbornly continued with his lob bowling throughout the one hundred and ten minutes of carnage. Billy hit thirty-two sixes, all off E.M. It should not have been a surprise to the Thornbury bowlers as Billy's 130 against them a few weeks earlier must have been fresh in the mind.

Gwynfor Lloyd Williams (G.L. Williams **[410]**), captain of Bath CC, wrote a monograph of Billy's innings for his club's centenary brochure of 1959 which was published in the *Daily Telegraph*. It impressed the cricket collector and writer Irving Rosenwater so much that he asked for a copy and Gwyn sent Irving his original manuscript. It includes the following passage:

A report of the match states that the ground was about the same size as North Parade and that the tremendous score was only possible because E.M. Grace used six balls. No sooner was one ball in the air going over the boundary than another followed, then another and another. After Hyman reached his first hundred , the doctor is said to have remarked "I'll bowl him out or break my arm". He did neither. After the second hundred had been passed someone asked the doctor to change the bowling . "No fear" he answered "he is just beginning to nibble. When the team returned to Bath and told the great news, it was considered so fantastic that it was not believed. The final comment came at the end of the scoresheet with the laconic statement that no bowling analysis was kept of the second innings! A photograph of the Bath side of 1900 shows Hyman to have been of average height, about 5' 6", and the possessor of a magnificent moustache. The secret of his hitting, as with all the great hitters, must have come from superb timing and not from great physical strength.

The photograph mentioned by Gwyn is shown below:

Back row L-R: E.E. Chappell (scorer), W. Swain, G.T. Short, S.W. Rowse, T. Taylor, E.J. Twinning (umpire);
seated L-R: ***W. Hyman [127]****, E. Grant* ***[122]****, H. Wood (Capt)* ***[161]****, J. Thomas* ***[132]****, A.E.B. Freeman* ***[171]****;*
seated on ground L-R: W.F. Lowe, A.H. Beezer ***[124]***

Billy is seated far left holding his bat. He was also a decent footballer, considered one of the finest goalscoring forwards that Radstock Town, the place of his birth on 7 March 1875, had ever produced. He resisted many overtures to sign professional terms and played frequently for Somerset AFC captaining the side on many occasions. He also played for Bath City during the time he was a schoolmaster at South Twerton School. The 1921 census shows that he had left Bath by this time, with his second wife Winifred and young son Geoffrey, and was teaching at the Wesleyan School in Chapel Street, Pelsall, Staffordshire. He retired to St Austell, Winifred's birthplace, and died there on 11 February 1959, aged eighty-three It was a shame that he did not live long enough to take part in the centenary celebrations and enjoy the attention he would have received from the recollections of this truly epic innings.

ALFRED EDWARD BAILEY [128]

VOL.1 assumed Alfred's birth was not registered having failed to find an entry for him. Further research reveals his birth was registered under the surname Evans, the son of Eliza Evans, with no name given for the father. His birth certificate shows that Alfred was born in Norwood on 13 March 1871, *not* 14 March as recorded in VOL.1. The confusion appears to have occurred because the latter date is specified in the 1939 census.

Eliza was living with a bricklayer, John Bailey, and Alfred was their second son. During the next few years, the sons and three additional siblings that followed adopted the Bailey surname. John Bailey died in 1880, aged thirty, before Eliza and John had chance to legitimise their union, and Eliza was left to bring up five children under the age of eleven. The 1891 census finds her still in Norwood working as a charwoman with her two eldest sons working as bricklayers to supplement their mother's meagre income.

Little is known about his cricket in Surrey except that he played colts, club & ground, and 2nd XI matches for his home county during the early 1890s. In 1892, he managed just one appearance for the 1st XI, and this was against Essex, a minor county at the time. There was an appearance for the prestigious Lord Sheffield's XI in 1894 against South Africa which may have caught the eye of Somerset. And by the mid-1890s, he was playing regularly for Taunton CC and other local clubs, presumably to achieve a residential qualification for Somerset. He appeared in an early-season trial match in May 1896 for a Sam Woods' XII and played in various club & ground matches during the next couple of seasons. In one match, against Bedminster CC in July 1898, the *Bristol Mercury* reported that Alfred was still qualifying for the county which if correct confirms that Somerset were not in any hurry to sign him as a professional. Somerset's reluctance to commit to Alfred was because resources were already stretched to the limit with Messrs Lewis, Braund, Robson, Gill,

and Cranfield on the payroll. It would be another two seasons before Alfred made his first-class debut on the northern tour.
Meanwhile he had professional engagements with Ashton-under-Lyme and Rochdale before he was asked to play two championship matches against Lancashire and Yorkshire at the end of June 1900. He was used sparingly as a bowler in both matches and against Lancashire was taken off after one over which included three no-balls. It is possible that nerves had got the better of him (he had bowled 4 no-balls in the Yorkshire match) but no-balls do seem to be a feature of his bowling, described by one reporter as being 'left-handed, varying pace and pitch very judiciously.'
Alfred would drop further down the list of professional bowling options after F.P. Hardy **[138]** was awarded a contract in 1901, and another four seasons would pass before he was called upon again. Somerset began the 1905 season with A. Bucknell **[120]** as professional bowling cover on a match-by-match basis before turning to Alfred. He was selected to play against Yorkshire at Harrogate, and although he only took one wicket for a century of runs, he kept his place for the next match against Hampshire. And on a pitch that suited his bowling, he opened with Ernie Robson and took seven wickets to Robson's one. Alfred played a further three championship matches that year taking his season's tally to 29 wickets at 15.31 runs apiece. It was enough to earn a full-time contract for the following season.
Alfred played every match during the 1906 season. He took 65 championship wickets at 26.59 runs apiece which included a dream start in the opening match against Warwickshire at Taunton. He took 5 for 59 and 6 for 6 in the match and the *Somerset Standard* remarked that he had bowled an irreproachable length making the ball turn and giving the batsmen no chance whatever. Alfred made a habit of dream starts to the season because in 1907 he achieved his best figures in the opening match against Yorkshire, taking 8 for 46 in the Yorkshire first innings.
The photograph on the opposite page, was taken during the match, and he is likely holding the match ball. The postcard image was obtained after publication of VOL.1 but a head and shoulders close-up was included in VOL.4. This book allows this superb image to be shown in its entirety. The vehicle in the background was owned by Henry Murray-Anderdon who a few years earlier had traded in his pony and trap for a chauffeur-driven Daimler. No doubt John Brice who took the photograph had deliberately posed Alfred in front of the car

in deference to the honorary secretary. On the reverse of the postcard, it states that it was published and sold by 'Brice Picture Post Card Specialists of Taunton'. Four subjects are known to have been in the postcard series (the number held by the MCC library, A.E. Lewis **[119]**, W. Montgomery **[169]** and A.E.M. Whittle **[177]** are the other three). John Brice had a newsagents and stationers in Bridge Street close to the County Ground and he had been at the County ground to cover the presentation to Sam Woods following his resignation as captain. It was mentioned in the *Taunton Courier* that he took several photographs of the players while the ceremony was in progress and had picture postcards on sale early that evening. It is hoped for John Brice's sake that Alfred's postcard was in immediate demand after his performance against Yorkshire because his postcard would have a short life on the shelves of the Bridge Street newsagents.

Alfred could not repeat his bowling achievement against Yorkshire and a run of poor performances led him to be in and out of the team. And before the season had ended, the local newspapers were announcing that he had ended his association with Somerset to take up an engagement with Dunfermline CC. He was club professional there for two years, taking 217 wickets in total, which earned him two call-ups for Scotland. One was against the touring Australians in June 1909 when the visitors were on the brink of defeat at the end of the 2-day match. They were teetering on 147-7, needing a further 56 runs, and

Alfred had contributed to the Australian woes by clean bowling Charles Macartney and Albert Cotter.
After Dunfermline, he had a season with Uddingston CC in South Lanarkshire where he was only slightly less successful with 97 wickets during the season. Somerset were not quite done with Alfred. He made two further appearances in August 1911 - against Gloucestershire at Bristol and Worcestershire at Taunton - before calling an end to his professional career and opening a tobacconist shop in Catford. He had taken 129 first-class wickets for Somerset in total at 25.55 apiece. Alfred later moved to Swale in Kent where he ran another tobacconist shop. He died there on 1 August 1950, aged seventy-nine.

HARRY CHIDGEY [129]

Harry Chidgey at Bournemouth in 1919

In the late Victorian and Edwardian eras, Somerset were blessed with a trio of amateur wicketkeepers - Messrs Newton, Wickham, and Martyn – the subject of the iconic photograph which was used on the cover of VOL.1. These three fine wicketkeepers limited Harry's chances of selection because he could not afford to play as an amateur like the other three. And while the above trio's contributions have been feted, Harry has largely been overlooked. Yet Harry's ratio of catches and stumpings to matches played is on a par with Newton and far better than the other two. And he held the record for the most stumpings in an innings (four) in Derbyshire's first innings at Bath in 1919, although it has been equalled by several Somerset wicketkeepers that have followed since. Harry, however, has been denied this record, as according to CricketArchive, the dismissal of S.W.A. Cadman was a catch rather than a stumping despite every newspaper, including the *Bath Chronicle and Weekly Gazette* whose reporter was at the match, recording it as a stumping. The official scorebook also has this method of dismissal.
Harry played ninety-eight matches for Somerset over

a period of eighteen seasons from 1900 to 1921, taking 134 catches and 56 stumpings. Most of his appearances were before the First World War. He appeared in ten of the championship matches played in 1919 and the *Taunton Courier*, mentioned that Harry's services were to be retained in 1920. But ominously for Harry, it mentioned that M.D. 'Dar' Lyon **[237]**, 'a promising wicketkeeper now at Cambridge', had been registered. Dar Lyon was an excellent bat, unlike Harry who was a confirmed number eleven, and Dar's amateur status made him a much more attractive proposition for Somerset. Harry was not selected in 1920 and Dar Lyon played in two-thirds of the matches, scoring a century on debut, and finishing the season with an average of 27.50. Dar played fewer matches the following year, preferring to concentrate on Cambridge cricket, but Harry was only selected if there was no amateur alternative. Somerset had an abundance of amateur keepers to choose from and four of them - M.L. Hill **[261]**, F.E. Spurway **[241]**, T.C. Lowry **[252]**, and S.L. Amor **[185]** - played for Somerset in 1921.

Harry's last appearance for Somerset was against Warwickshire at the County Ground in August 1921. The club had generously granted the match as his official benefit, but it was yet another occasion ruined by the weather with a delayed start on day one and a result by the end of day two. Harry was not out without scoring in both innings and left with a first-class batting average of 6.91. Yet Harry was a prolific run scorer for his local club Flax Bourton CC where he had first played for the 1st XI in 1893 and continued as a player until well into the 1930s.

As his VOL.1 biography states, he never strayed far from Flax Bourton except to play or umpire cricket. He was elevated to the first-class umpires list in 1925 and officiated for two full seasons. His was one of eight names put forward to umpire the Test matches against Australia in 1926 and he was lucky enough to be selected, by ballot, for the Fourth Test. The following year he threw in his lot with the Bristol & District Umpires Association citing 'business reasons' for his withdrawal from the first-class panel. His business according to official documents was rate collecting.

He died on 16 November 1941, aged sixty-two, at North View, Flax Bourton, a bungalow and quarter acre garden he shared with his mother. Death had never been far from his door. His first wife died in 1909, his only brother Bert, a promising young cricketer, was killed on the Somme in 1916, his father who had kept *The Angel Inn* in Flax Bourton for forty-seven years, died in 1921, his second wife died in 1925 leaving him with two young boys, his brother-in-law (father of A.E. Waters of Gloucestershire) died in 1930 and his mother died at North View in 1935. He treated all these personal disasters with great stoicism.

HENRY MARTYN [131]

Henry was the son of the Reverend William Waddon Martyn and Maria Andrew née Lawrence, the daughter of Northmore Lawrence, a Cornish magistrate and one-time mayor of Launceston. The Waddon Martyns had served the Church of England for four generations, administering pastoral care in the border areas of Cornwall and Devon. His father had eventually settled as the rector of Lifton, where the family had long held the living, and Henry was born there on 16 July 1877. He was William and Maria's seventh son and eleventh child.

Henry was educated at Lifton Primary School and Exeter Grammar School where he gained a reputation as a forceful and combative batsman. It was enough for the Devon County side to select him to play in the match against Dorset at Weymouth on the day of his seventeenth birthday. He was a late replacement after the Devon team were forced to make several last-minute changes. There was nothing to celebrate on his birthday as he was out for a duck in his only innings. And it is unlikely that he kept wicket as he had come relatively late to the discipline.

He had only donned the gloves in his time at school when a life-threatening illness rendered him unable to field or bowl. J.G. McCormick, his captain in the school 1st XI at the time, claimed responsibility for persuading Henry to keep because he couldn't afford to do without Henry's batting. It was an instant success and Henry took to it 'like a duck to water' according to McCormick.

Henry went up to Exeter College, Oxford and took part in the Freshers' and Seniors' trials but failed to make the University XI in 1897 or 1898.

An image of Henry, on the opposite page, is from a photograph of players that took part in the Seniors' trial of 1898. It was taken on the steps of the pavilion in The Parks. Henry was in his second year, and this was one of several trials which featured players on the fringes of the University XI. The *Oxford Chronicle* reported that taking this photograph had delayed the start of the match and the photographer must have struggled to marshal the twenty-four aspiring cricketers into some sort of order. Included among them was one young man who would have no difficulty breaking into the Oxford team, B.J.T. Bosanquet. He had yet to perfect the googly, but his batting and fast-medium bowling was enough to ensure that he would play for the University XI and obtain his blue in 1898. Henry Martyn was not so lucky. He failed to make an impression in the trial, and it would have taken something exceptional to dislodge the highly experienced keeper, R. W. Fox, a triple blue from 1896 to 1898.

After Fox left Oxford, Henry was able to take his place and earn his blue in 1899 and 1900. He was far from the finished article as a wicketkeeping and in the 1899 Varsity match he let through 19 byes in Cambridge's first innings although he did take a difficult catch to dismiss Gilbert Jessop and he stumped a future Somerset captain John Daniell. Henry worked as a teacher after leaving university. A family friend, the former Somerset joint-secretary Thomas Spencer, had found him a job at his newly established school in Wraxall, near Long Ashton. It meant his availability was limited and he played just nine matches for Somerset in 1901 and 1902. He was however able to play more regularly thereafter having decided that teaching was not for him. Although his wicketkeeping had seriously improved he was sometimes played for his batting alone when Arthur Newton or Archie Wickham declared themselves available.

Sam Woods reckoned he was good enough to play for England just as a batsman and rated the young cricketer highly. His enthusiasm for Henry's batting may well have been influenced by his recollection of the match against the Australians at Bath in 1905 which he mentions in *My Reminiscences*. Though his memory failed him on some counts, he was correct about Henry saving the game. He scored a defiant not out century (the only one of his first-class career) after Australia had declared on 609 for 4 and enforced the follow-on. Sam had been impressed when he asked Henry where he would like to bat, thinking he would need some recovery time after a day and a half in the field, and Henry replied "First, of course, I generally do".

Sam had picked Henry for the Gentlemen against the Players as early as 1899, and he made a further six first-class appearances for the Gentlemen and Gentlemen of England during his short first-class career which was over far too soon. He made the 1906 season his last because his bachelor days were about to end, and he had no alternative but to declare his cricket innings closed and find full-time employment. The last match of the 1906 championship season was against Yorkshire at Bath on the 27-29 August.

It was the usual comprehensive defeat for Somerset with Rhodes and Hirst dominating the match. Left to score 524 to win the match, Somerset capitulated during the morning session of the third day, dismissed for 134 with Henry, fifth out, having contributed 23 runs.

It was a blessing for Henry that the match was over by lunchtime as he had a train to catch and his wedding to attend in Crediton the following day. He married Mabel Gunnora Gurney, the only daughter of the Rev W.B. Gurney, rector of Poughill, in a ceremony officiated by one of Henry's elder brothers the Rev Robert Waddon Martyn. And that was effectively the end of his first-class career for Somerset although he made a single reappearance in 1908 to honour a promise made to Len Braund that he would play in his benefit match against Surrey. He played 74 first-class matches for Somerset and finished with a respectable batting average of 24.86.

Henry was a huge loss to Somerset, not so much behind the stumps as Somerset had other options in Wickham, Newton and Chidgey. It was Henry's ability to contribute crucial runs that was sorely missed as he was easily the best batsman when compared to his three contemporaries.

If Somerset saw no merit in Henry keeping wicket there were plenty of respected judges that did. John Arlott, in a 1981 article, selected him as the best English wicketkeeper not to have played for his country. And Plum Warner described him as the 'most brilliant amateur wicketkeeper in the country'. This remark was made in a 1905 article, and many suggested that it was only the superior batting of Dick Lilley that kept him out of the Ashes Test series in 1905. That same year, he was immortalised in a pastel drawing by Albert

Chevalier Tayler which appeared in part V1 of *The Empire's Cricketers*.

The rare photograph shown here is by George Beldam and was used by Chevalier Tayler to produce his drawing, although Tayler chose to have Henry removing the left-hand bail.

One hundred and twenty years on, it is difficult to justify these high opinions of Henry as a wicketkeeper. His career victims average (to overall wickets taken in the matches played) is inferior to all three of his contemporaries and the Somerset keepers that came after him. It suggests the perception of his wicketkeeping was based on style rather than substance. He was tall and his upright stance, always standing up to the fastest bowlers of the day, must have made him an imposing and intimidating presence behind the stumps. Add to that the long arms and legs, the fast hands and extravagant manner, and it is easy to see why Henry caught the eye of so many of his peers.

One innings in the Gentlemen v Players match at Lord's in 1906 is a perfect example of his style. There was no faster bowler on the circuit during the early 1900s than Neville Knox of Surrey, reputed to bowl at up to 95 miles per hour. Henry kept to him and there was talk of the Players fearing for their safety against Knox's bowling. There was astonishment that Henry stood up to Knox who took fifteen wickets in the match, eight of them bowled or lbw. And Henry had no dismissal to his name, letting through 25 byes in the match, but who can tell how much his standing up contributed to Knox's wickets.

After his brief spell as a teacher, Henry appears not to have needed any employment to sustain his bachelor lifestyle and on 30 August 1906 when asked by the registrar in the parish church of Crediton for his rank or profession he replied 'gentleman'. However, it seems that his resources did not stretch to supporting a wife and a household on Haines Hill, Trull Road, because he would soon be describing himself as a commercial traveller. But the title deceives, for he was working as a salesman for E.S. & A. Robinson and for his close friend Foster Robinson who did most to turn the paper bag firm his grandfather had established in 1844 into an international conglomeration. The Robinson family was a great supporter of West Country cricket and were renowned for being able to field complete teams of talented cricketers named Robinson. Some would play cricket for Gloucestershire and others like T. Robinson **[42]** and C.J. Robinson **[55]** played for Somerset.

Foster Gotch Robinson was later chairman of the company and was knighted for his efforts. He and Henry were at Exeter College together, where they played cricket for college and university in 1900. Foster later played as an amateur for Gloucestershire between 1903 and 1923, captaining the team after the Second World War. Foster was a very good and supportive friend to Henry, and he was best man at Henry's wedding. Henry may have worked for Foster as a commercial traveller, but this was clearly not a normal employer/employee relationship.

Henry was thirty-nine years old when he joined the Somerset Light Infantry as a lieutenant in September 1916. He arrived in France the following April and was pitched into some of the fiercest fighting of the War. On 25 July 1917, just after the Somerset Light Infantry went over the top during the Battle of the Scarpe near Arras, Henry was admitted to a field hospital suffering from neurasthenia. Some versions of the condition were referred to as shell shock, but the clinical diagnosis refers to locomotor disorders, twitching, trembling and paralysis as symptoms. When he returned to England a month later, it must have been a terrible shock to friends and family to see this once confident, self-assured man reduced to a nervous and physical wreck. He was treated at Trefusis House, Falmouth, used by the Red Cross as a military hospital, but it is not known how long he was there.

Henry would not have been able to continue his former employment, but his old friend did not desert him. The 1921 census has Henry and Mabel living in Chilbolton, near Stockbridge in Hampshire where Henry was working as a water bailiff for 'F.G. Robinson of Chilbolton'. It seems that even this less than challenging job proved too much for him. In 1925, the couple who never had children, moved to Dawlish where Henry died on 8 August 1928, aged just fifty-one. Mabel was at his side. Henry's war disability was not the cause of his death, certified as (a) sclerosis of the liver and (b) cardiac failure. But its primary cause suggests his experience at Arras had a profound effect on the last decade of his life bringing it to a sad and premature end. In different times and circumstances, he would have played cricket for his country.

PETER RANDALL JOHNSON [133]

Randall Johnson was born in Wellington, New Zealand on 5 August 1880. His father George, a triple cricket blue at Cambridge, moved to New Zealand in 1861 to practice as a barrister. He met Randall's mother Lucy Russell while he was a councillor to the Legislative Council, the upper parliament for the National Assembly of New Zealand. Lucy was the daughter of Lieutenant Colonel Andrew Hamilton Russell, the Minister for Native Affairs in the Assembly. He had been a career soldier, granted a commission by the Duke of Wellington, before settling in New Zealand.

Randall and his two sisters were born in New Zealand before his father retired and returned to Devon. Randall was educated at Eton College and was in the Eton XI in 1897. He went to Trinity College, Cambridge in 1898 and obtained his cricket blue in 1901, his final year at college. Even at Eton he was known for his dapper appearance. He trained as a barrister and was called to the bar in June 1894 but would in time find stockbroking more to his liking. Christopher Hollis in *Oxford in the Twenties* would later remark 'he was always faultlessly dressed; it was his habit to drive up to a match arrayed in top hat and morning coat. He would say to his fellow players "Just been doing a spot of work" as he changed into his flannels'. Had he not needed to earn a living, he would undoubtedly have played a Test match on the 1903/04 tour of Australia with P.F. Warner. It was well known that he had been invited to tour

Randall at the Oval in 1920. E.H.D. Sewell captioned this photograph: AN ENIGMATIC STROKE - the original intention is defensive, but this stroke may easily develop into a scoring push or a glance. His position makes the latter seem more plausible

but could not spare the time. As it was, he did tour America with Bosanquet in 1901, with Lord Hawke to Australia and New Zealand in 1902/03, and with MCC to New Zealand in 1906/07.

Randall played 275 first-class matches during a long cricket career which lasted from 1900 to 1927. Somerset had the benefit of 229 of these matches and his relatively modest batting average for Somerset of 25.82 belies his true worth to the county. Apart from the early and last couple of seasons, he was rarely out of the top two in the averages. He scored seventeen centuries for Somerset and was unlucky not to have got another two at Bath against Sussex in 1910 when he ran out of partners in both innings on 98 and 96 not out. Randall hit Worcestershire for 163 on two occasions, but his highest score came in 1908 during an impressive successive scoring run of 164 and 131 against Middlesex, 117 and 19 against Hampshire and 31 and 126 against Kent.

During the First World War, Randall lost no time enlisting as a lieutenant with the 8th Devonshire Regiment, serving in Mesopotamia where he was wounded, and ending the War with the rank of major. After the War and despite having to earn a living, he played five full seasons of cricket before his appearances tailed off. In his last two seasons, 1926 and 1927, the trademark fluency had all but deserted him, and he averaged just 13.42 with the bat in sixteen appearances. There had been just one innings, against Surrey at the Oval in June 1926, which brought back memories of better times. Set an implausible 402 runs to win the match, Somerset were 88 for 5 when Randall came to the wicket and he was 117 not out when the innings closed, just 77 runs short of the target.

There was no better assessment of Randall's batting quality than the one provided by H.J. Channon, who was the cricket correspondent of the *Taunton Courier* and would later recall that 'His off-drives were superb. Like Lionel Palairet before him, his head was right over the ball when he drove, and almost simultaneously the umpire was signalling another beautiful four.'

Randall at the County Ground towards to end of his cricket career. This rare postcard photograph is thought to have been taken in 1924

Randall married Effie Hamilton-Gell in 1905 and they had two sons and two daughters. Effie was the daughter of the vicar of Clyst St Mary in Devon and the couple made the village their family home when not at their Warwick Square town house used by Randall when working in the city.

Both of Randall's sons went to Eton College. The eldest son Philip went off to Hawkes Bay, in New Zealand, to work. And it is no coincidence that descendants of Randall's maternal grandfather, Lieutenant Colonel Russell, had extensive farming interests in the area. These included the ownership of the huge Tunanui Station in Hawkes Bay and parts of the station are still owned and run by the Russell family to this day. Philip was married in New Zealand and later moved to Australia where he pre-deceased his father. The younger son Kenneth was in the Eton XI that played Harrow School at Lord's in 1932 and later followed his father into stockbroking. His elder daughter Elizabeth married Alick Goold, a stockbroker who was an Oxford rugby blue and former Liverpool and Lancashire rugby player. His younger daughter Dora became a Lady after marrying the 6th Baronet of Buxton.

Randall retired to Clyst St Mary but was not blessed with good health in later life. As his health declined, he needed a wheelchair to get around, suffering from what was assumed to be arthritis but which was later diagnosed as muscular dystrophy. Kidney failure was the cause of death, on 1 July 1959, aged seventy-eight. It is not clear why his death occurred at the *Bedford Hotel*, Sidmouth, seventeen miles away from the family home in Clyst St Mary, but it is assumed his illness was unsuited to homecare.

GEORGE WILLIAM JUPP [135]

George Jupp was born in Axbridge but later lived in Clevedon where his father was the Great Western Railway's station master. The family hailed from Sussex where the Jupp surname proliferated in club cricket. In later life, George would claim to be the second cousin of V.W.C. Jupp, the Sussex and England cricketer, though he could only have been the remotest of many times removed cousins at best.

The images used in VOL.1 were taken from his Scottish playing days, so it is pleasing to present this close-up of him taken at Quantock Lodge in September 1894 which was the year he left to work in the Edinburgh Department of Works. George is eighteen years old in this photograph and must have already been known to the Somerset authorities for him to be playing for the Moonlighters CC team at Quantock Lodge. Details of George's childhood years were difficult to find and the biography in VOL.1 concentrated on his adult life in Edinburgh. VOL.1 repeated Wikipedia in claiming that George was educated at Uppingham School, but it is now clear that he was educated locally at the Merchant Venturer's School in Bristol otherwise known as the Colston's School. By this time, he was playing cricket for Yatton CC having first shown promise as a

thirteen-year-old for his local club Clevedon CC. And in 1893 he had appeared for Somerset Club and Ground against a Radstock and District XI where he had a decent partnership with the Somerset professional F. Bolus **[82]**. George also played football for Clevedon FC.

After his move to Edinburgh in 1894, he became one of Scotland's foremost cricketers, playing for Carlton CC and making eleven appearances for his adopted country mainly against the touring sides of Australia, South Africa, and West Indies. His highest first-class score of 56 came in his last match against the Australians in 1912. He played for Carlton from 1894 to 1910, captaining the team for several seasons and heading the batting averages in most of these seasons. His best was 1900 when he scored 1,500 runs, and it was probably news of the achievement by this Somerset-born cricketer that prompted his old county to select him for a match at Old Trafford in July 1901. Four more matches in 1906 and 1907 completed his five appearances for Somerset in which he could never repeat his club form. He finished with a batting average of 11.00. George had regularly headed the bowling averages at Carlton but was asked to bowl just 18 balls for Somerset which went for just one run.

George was a talented sportsman, a gift that would be inherited by his daughter Nancy. At the age of six, she would accompany her father around the Longniddry Golf Course in Edinburgh with her four cut-down clubs. Seven years later in 1934, she was with her family in Stoke Poges supporting her older sister Rhoda who was entered in the Girls' National Golf Championship when it was decided that Nancy might as well play in the week-long event. Nancy was the youngest competitor in this prestigious event which attracted entries from the World's best young female golfers. Nancy had never had a handicap, was 4ft 6in tall, and had to use full size clubs. This was her

GIRL GOLF CHAMPION

Miss Nancy Jupp, the 13-year-old Longniddry girl, being congratulated by her father, after winning the Girls' Golf Championship at Stoke Poges, yesterday.

first national competition and she proceeded to overwhelm her opponents in the early rounds prompting the British press to christen her the 'wonder girl' and praise her near-perfect golf. In her first-round match, her drive from the twelfth tee travelled 280 yards to set up a birdie and complete her victory by 7 and 6.

With Rhoda out of the competition, Nancy won her semi-final and final against girls who were five years older, and she became the youngest and smallest champion in the history of what is now called the Girls' Amateur Championship. Her win was heralded as sensational, but Nancy was later quoted as being 'fed-up' with all the fuss and bother. She didn't care for the limelight and never competed again.

In later life her passion for the game would take her around the world as a golf writer and editor of golfing magazines. This led to Nancy directing golf tournaments, her first major tournament being the 1964 US Open. By the time she retired in 1987, Nancy had organised fifteen US Opens and four PGAs as well as numerous non-majors. She had organised the 1977 US Open at Southern Hills Country Club in Tulsa and returned there to direct the 1982 PGA tournament. And it was in Tulsa that she decided to give up her nomadic lifestyle. Never married, she died there in 2013, aged ninety-three.

George would not live to see his girls reach womanhood. He retired from the HM Office of Works, Edinburgh in 1935 having worked his way up from office boy to principal in charge. But unfortunately, he had precious little time to enjoy retirement. He died in Longniddry on 6 July 1938, aged sixty-two. His death was unheralded in the county of his birth but was very much lamented in Scotland. *The Scotsman* called him one of the most popular cricketers who ever played in Scotland and one of the most successful with bat and ball.

LIONEL HUGH MAJOR [150]

Despite an extensive search, it was not possible to find an image of Lionel for VOL.1. This can now be rectified by the inclusion of this family photograph:

The photograph features six cousins, the sons of Charles and Ernest Major who were manufacturers of bricks and tiles in Bridgwater. Lionel (top right) is with his two older brothers, Gerald (top left) and Charles (middle). They were the sons of Charles Major and the other three were sons of Ernest.

Lionel was born in Burnham-on-Sea on 21 August 1883, but as the business in Bridgwater prospered, the family moved to 'Maplehurst', Wembdon, where the above photograph was taken. Lionel's eldest brother Charles took holy orders and when War broke out served as an army chaplain, dying in Germany in 1919. Gerald was always destined to take over his father's interest in the business which left Lionel to forge a career of his own. On leaving school in 1902, he worked in the business until 1910 but, perhaps unfulfilled, decided to emigrate to British Columbia in Canada. Up to this point, his club cricket had

been with Bridgwater CC where he often teamed up with his cousin Charles Oswald Major who is shown bottom right in the family photograph.
Perhaps it was inevitable, given Sam Woods' links with Bridgwater, that Lionel would be given a chance to play for Somerset. His single appearance, against Sussex in 1903, was not a great success. He batted at number 10 in both innings making scores of 6 and 11. Perhaps Sam had a conscience about dragging the young man all the way to Hastings because he brought him on to bowl when Sussex had all but won the match inside of two days. It resulted in a surprise bowling return of 2.4 overs, 2 maidens, 1 for 5. He made a much greater impression playing cricket for Victoria BC. His stay in Canada lasted a dozen years, but four of them were taken up with the First World War.
Much was made in VOL.1 of his brief experience of trench warfare in April 1915, as a lieutenant with the Canadian Expeditionary Force. He was in the thick of the Second Battle of Ypres and the fighting around St. Julian when the Germans first employed chlorine-gas. When the Canadian forces were withdrawn on 3 May 1915, its casualties during thirteen days of fighting totalled almost six thousand including a thousand dead. It was all too much for Lionel who was diagnosed as suffering from shell shock the day after withdrawal. He spent much of the following year hospitalised and then recuperating at the homes of

various relatives in Bristol, Devon, and London. Lionel returned to light duties in Canada in April 1916. His powers of recovery must have been extraordinary because this photograph shows that, by August 1917, Lionel had risen to the rank of lieutenant colonel and was commanding the 2nd Depot Battalion of the British Columbia Regiment at Willows Camp in Oak Bay, Victoria. The photograph is in the collection of the British Columbia Museum. Lionel remained in Canada until the mid-1920s, and facts about his later life in England are covered in some detail in VOL.1. Without the knowledge of his later service with the 2nd Depot Battalion, it was suggested in the biography that Lionel had embellished his war career even to the point that he requested his rank should be included on his gravestone. In the light of this additional information, the perception of Lionel's war service must be reappraised. Lionel died in Exmouth Hospital on 25 June 1965, aged eighty-two.

ERNEST ARTHUR GRESWELL [155]

The father of Ernest Greswell and his younger brother William (W.T. Greswell **[188]**) was *not* William Henry Parr Greswell, the son of William Parr Greswell, both noted authors, historians and men of the cloth, vicars of Doddington and Kilve, respectively. It is unfortunate that VOL.1 sourced the family connection from CricketArchive without questioning its accuracy. The mistake was almost certainly made because William Henry Parr Greswell was a well-known local cricketer having played for the Gentlemen of Somerset. He had even played in the 1875 match at Sidmouth and was present at the meeting which led to the founding of the county club. But W.H.P. Greswell was the uncle of Ernest and William. Their father was Charles Herbert Greswell.

Charles, known as Herbert, was working as an engineer when he married Edith née Tatham in Tamil Nadu, India in 1881. Edith was born in Kandy Sri Lanka, the daughter of a civil servant in the country then known as Ceylon. Charles and Edith had three sons and a daughter all born in India. Ernest was born in Cuddalore in the Tamil Nadu State of India on 8 June 1885, and four years later, his brother William was also born there. Cuddalore is a town situated on the south east coast of India, south of Chennai, and in the days of the British Raj, was an important port for the export of tea, sugar, rubber, and spices.

The boys were sent to England for schooling, initially to live with their grandparents in Kilve, but later they lived with their parents after they had returned to live in the nearby village of Holford, near Williton. The third son, Jack Ewart Greswell, died in Holford in 1894, aged seven. The family would later move to Wayfield, Bicknoller where Edith died in 1913 and Herbert died in 1926. Ernest's life is well covered in his VOL.1 biography and need not be repeated here. He died in Minehead on 15 January 1962, aged seventy-six. An updated biography for William is included on page 139.

ARTHUR SAMUEL SELLICK [164]

Arthur was a journeyman professional cricketer and coach all his adult life. He played six first-class matches for Somerset in June and July 1905 but was never selected again. He had little chance to use his 'late stroke', the caption used in this image, taken from an article on a Gloucestershire XI in a 1904 *Black and White Illustrated Budget* magazine. The image included in VOL.1 was poor by comparison with this one.

There was just the one score in double-figures in his ten innings for Somerset and he left with a batting average of 4.00. And surprisingly, he was asked to bowl just six overs during his brief stay. His first county, Gloucestershire, got more out of him than Somerset as a top-order batsmen, but Arthur never made a fifty for either county.

Yet at club level, he was a prolific run-scorer and wicket-taker and was much in demand. In 1906, he played as a professional for Nether Stowey CC but would also turn out for the Imperial Tobacco XI. He was then engaged as the professional at Westbury United CC and held that position from 1907 to 1910. He had an exceptional season in 1908 and was presented with an inscribed marble clock recording his 1,000 runs and 100 wickets which including three hat-tricks. Wiltshire CC called on his services while he was at Westbury and he would play fifty-eight matches for the county, his last appearance coming in 1926.

As with his first-class counties, the half-century eluded him, but he was selected principally for his bowling. It was the county connection which led to him being appointed as coach and groundsman at the County Ground in Trowbridge as

well as gaining a lucrative engagement as Trowbridge CC's professional.

He had opened a sports shop while in Westbury and he continued that business in Trowbridge, adding tobacco to the list of goods sold. His last shop was in Roundstone Street, and he lived above the shop with his wife Francis Olivia and their two daughters. The business was advertised in the local press, and it seems to have prospered. The First World War intervened, and although Arthur's war records have been destroyed, he must have served his country because when the advertising returned in 1919 it had the added note that the recently demobbed Arthur was now 'open to receive orders for laying out pitches, tennis courts, bowls greens, etc'.

And Arthur's cricket continued as before. During the early 1920s, he played for Bath and Lansdown as well as Trowbridge, and it was common for him to play for and against Lansdown in the same season. He also played regularly for Wiltshire during this period and was very successful with ball in hand. In the seasons 1920 to 1925 he took 70 wickets at 19.14 apiece for Wiltshire. In addition to all this, he coached the boys of Monkton Combe School for which he received a silver inkstand in recognition of his services. On the face of it, Arthur was leading a satisfying and prosperous life, but all was not well at home.

Arthur had developed an infatuation for Mrs Ellen Fricker, a woman separated from her husband and two children. By March 1926, Arthur had deserted his wife, sold the sports business and was living with Ellen at a house in Bath owned by her mother. Matters came to a head in September 1927 when Olive, as she was known, applied to the courts for maintenance of their two children. His divorce and the protracted maintenance claims which dogged Arthur for the rest of his life are well documented in VOL.1.

The acrimony was enough for Bath to terminate Arthur's services and Wiltshire no longer selected him after 1926, although this may have been more to do with his move to Bath and his diminishing bowling powers. Meanwhile Arthur had a year on the first-class umpires list in 1929 (not 1919 as recorded in VOL.1) and even had another spell playing and coaching Westbury United. He and Ellen eventually moved to the South East where Arthur was employed as a groundsman for various employers including the BBC and London Transport. In 1939, he and Ellen were living at Malden Coombe in Surrey where his occupation is stated as 'head groundsman', and as late as 1950, aged seventy-two, he was still playing cricket and working as a groundsman at the Old Rutlishians Sports Ground in Merton. Arthur died in Carshalton on the 16 January 1958, aged seventy-nine.

WILLIAM MONTGOMERY [169]

The lack of bowling options in 1904 was the reason for Somerset's rash decision to recruit Bill Montgomery under the noses of the Surrey authorities. It happened during the match against Surrey at Taunton on 22-24 August 1904. Bill had been at Surrey for eight years with few opportunities for 1st XI cricket. He had played in just six championship matches before 1904. But he had played in the three matches prior to the Taunton fixture and was perhaps miffed at being replaced by a leg-break bowler even though it was the better option on the slow, rain-sodden wicket which would not have suited Bill's right-arm fast bowling.

Bill was most likely at the County Ground as twelfth man when his move to the West Country was sealed. He was aged twenty-six, newly married with a baby on the way, and naturally looking for more security than Surrey was prepared to give him. Somerset however were prepared to offer a three-year contract while he qualified by residence. As Bill was selected to play for Surrey's remaining championship matches in late-August, it suggests that his county was in the dark about Bill's impending move, and they were apoplectic when the news broke. The Surrey authorities were no doubt still smarting from losing Len Braund to Somerset a few years earlier and although Bill was not in the same league as Len, they refused to play Somerset in 1905.

The blame for Somerset's perceived act of treachery was laid at the feet of Somerset's Honorary Treasurer, Gerald Fowler **[60]** who had to excuse himself at the Somerset AGM in 1904: He was reported as saying:

A great many things had been said by Surrey concerning Somerset and concerning myself, but I have behaved in a perfectly straightforward manner and the Somerset committee know all the facts. I have not written to the papers because I do not approve of discussing matters of that sort in the Press as doing so leads to more ill-feeling. There is no doubt that Surrey are very annoyed at present, but I hope in the course of time they will get over it and Somerset will once more be able to play them again.

It would take Surrey three more seasons to 'get over it'. Surrey felt that Somerset, by not approaching them beforehand, had broken rule 7 of the laws of county cricket and had reported the matter to MCC. This came to nothing as it was determined that Bill had approached Somerset, not the other way around. Meanwhile, Bill wintered in Bath and became the professional at Lansdown CC in 1905, duly qualifying for Somerset. In the end, it was Surrey president, Lord Alverstone, who offered an olive branch and a 'chance to bury the axe'. Matches between Somerset and Surrey resumed in 1908, by which time Bill had been released after playing just ten matches for Somerset taking 3 wickets at 35.66 apiece. He had one first-class half-century to his name scored at Bath in 1907 against Warwickshire.

This recently unearthed Brice postcard photograph of Bill was taken at the back of the Priory Barn in 1907. It was Bill's last season with Somerset before giving up the game for the security of work as an electrician

Somerset finally returned to the Oval in June 1908 only to be thrashed by an innings and 204 runs with J.N. Crawford scoring a career-best 232 in Surrey's first innings. After a short spell as a professional at Chippenham, Bill played in minor county championship cricket for Hertfordshire and Cheshire and the odd match for Wiltshire while working as an electrician. He came back into cricket late in life when he coached at Oundle School, Peterborough, a position he held for seventeen years. He died in Peterborough on 14 November 1952, aged seventy-four.

JAMES MAXWELL [173]

Jimmy Maxwell played just ten matches for Somerset between 1906 and 1908, and in consequence seems to have managed to avoid too many requests for an autograph because his is one of the rarest to obtain. VOL.1 used Jimmy's signature from the 1911 census return, but his autograph from 1908 has since been found. As it is quite different from his signature, the autograph is shown here:

Jimmy, the son of a travelling draper, was born in Taunton on 13 January 1883. He attended the Independent College, later to become Taunton School, playing cricket for the college and local clubs such as Taunton Press and Wilton. His first match for Taunton was in 1899 against Bridgwater when Taunton were bowled out for 57, with G.C. Gill **[108]** taking 7 for 27, and Jimmy was bowled by Tom Kelway for 4 runs. It was a baptism of fire for the sixteen-year-old at this higher level of cricket but by the early to mid-1900s he was playing regularly for the Taunton 1st XI as well as maintaining his links with Wilton. His fast but somewhat erratic bowling in this company was especially impressive. Jimmy made his Somerset debut in the first championship match of the 1906 season, at the County Ground against Warwickshire beginning 17 May. It took the newspapers by surprise as he was not on the team sheet, and he only played because of the last-minute withdrawal of E.S.M. Poyntz **[163]**. Jimmy probably owed his selection to living a few hundred metres from the County Ground. But it would have also been swayed by his performance in the match for Taunton at the County Ground against the Somerset Stragglers the previous Saturday when eight of the cricketers that featured in the team against Warwickshire were playing, including the captain, Sam Woods.

Jimmy took two wickets in that match and on debut the following Thursday he was asked to open the bowling. His opening spell proved wicketless, but he finished the innings with 1 for 43. He was not asked to bowl in the second innings and scored a duck in his only innings. He retained his place and played a further seven matches during the season, but his 12 wickets were taken at a cost of 50.41 apiece. He did manage to score 67 not out against Gloucestershire at Bath in mid-June, his one and only half-century, scored in three-quarters of an hour, included 'a big hit to the tent'.

He had played on a match-by-match basis in 1906 and his performances were never enough to persuade Somerset to grant him a contract in 1907. Jimmy moved to Swansea CC where he replaced another fast bowler, Ernest Gill of Leicester who was the brother of G.C Gill **[108]**. Towards the end of the season, the *Cambria Daily Leader* reported that 'There has been no more popular professional fast bowler connected with the Swansea club than J. Maxwell of Taunton who takes his benefit today'. His performances for Swansea in the 1907 season were enough to secure a five-year contract with improved remuneration.

He was recalled by Somerset for the two matches on the northern tour against Lancashire and Yorkshire at the end of June 1908. He had little opportunity against the mighty Yorkshire but in the match against Lancashire at Liverpool he took 5 for 63 in Lancashire's first innings which helped to bring his Somerset bowling average down from a shade over 50 to a shade over 40. There would be no further appearances for the county, probably because Somerset would not have been able to match the wage which Swansea were prepared to pay him.

During his time with the Welsh club, he also played fifty-two minor county matches for Glamorgan between 1909 and 1914, averaging 26 with the bat, including three centuries, and taking 165 wickets at 13.73 apiece. He also played three matches for South Wales against the Australians in 1909, the Indians in 1911, and the South Africans in 1912. His performances for Glamorgan suggest that Somerset could have got more out of Jimmy had they persevered with him.

The First World War put an end to Jimmy's professional career, but he continued to play cricket locally throughout the 1920s, mainly for Taunton Deane and Taunton Thursday. As explained elsewhere, the latter club suited tradesmen who could not get away for Saturday matches. Towards the end of the decade, these sides would include Jimmy and his son, James Maxwell jnr. The availability of material from the 1921 and 1939 censuses sheds new light on Jimmy's work and family life. In 1921 he was living in Sydney Terrace, Taunton with his wife Violet and their son and daughter both born pre-War in Swansea. He was working as an outfitter for William Hare's drapery store in East Reach in 1921 but by 1939 had returned to his father's trade as a travelling draper. Jimmy, a widower for twenty-eight years, died in Taunton on 27 December 1967, aged eight-four.

ALBERT EDWARD MARK WHITTLE [177]

Bert's autograph is as rare as Jimmy Maxwell's and another example of where the 1911 census return signature was used in VOL.1. His markedly different autograph is included below.

And this superb photograph of Bert has also surfaced since the publication of VOL.1. It will bring back memories for older Somerset supporters who as young autograph hunters would hang around the practice nets at Taunton, now the car park to the right of the main gate. Bert's biography in VOL.1 records that he played for Warwickshire before signing for Somerset, but it missed the fact that the club could have signed him at least nine years earlier when young Bert was in his prime.

Bert was born in Bedminster on 16 September 1877 and was therefore residentially qualified to play for Somerset. Additional research shows that Bert had appeared in an early-season trial match in May 1898 where he opened the bowling and took three top-order wickets before finishing with a haul of 6 for 57. The *West Somerset Free Press* suggested that his right-arm medium pace bowling had plenty of variety in pace and pitch. A missed opportunity for Somerset. And it was not as though the 20-year-old was an unknown having been a regular Bedminster CC allrounder for several years.

It seems likely that he attracted interest from Warwickshire when he was living in Birmingham where he was on Aston Villa's books. Somerset's loss was confirmed by the *Taunton Courier* in June 1899 when it stated that he was going to Warwickshire and would be a professional for Olton CC while qualifying by residence. Somerset had been upstaged but would have been able to make a counteroffer had they wished. But they had signed G.C. Gill **[108]** the previous season and would not have had the resources to employ both. It is questionable whether they could even afford George Gill since he would soon receive a better offer from his native Leicestershire which Somerset could not match.

Bert played sixty first-class matches for Warwickshire between 1900 and 1906, averaging 24.07 with the bat, including twelve fifties and a top score of 104. In addition, he took 56 wickets at an average of 35.91. Curiously, he only played a single first-class match against Somerset during his time with Warwickshire but that was enough to remind the Somerset authorities of what they had missed. He took 3 for 40 in Somerset's only completed innings (the wickets of Johnson, Woods, and Lee) and he scored 71 not out to set up a declaration in Warwickshire's second innings. Somerset just managed to hold on for a draw.

Bert's figures for the twenty-nine matches he played for Somerset between 1907 and 1911 pale by comparison. He had a significantly inferior batting average of 18.84 and he took just 8 wickets at an average of 51.25, but by then he was into his thirties and past his best.

The VOL.1 biography will remind the reader that, after retiring from first-class cricket, the pressure of running a business in Bedminster and providing for a wife and five children became too much for Bert. His life ended tragically on 18 March 1917 at the Dorset County Asylum, aged thirty-nine.

STANLEY LONG AMOR [185]

Stanley was born in Bath on 22 July 1887, the son of Arthur Amor and Alice Jane née Long. Arthur worked in the family building and construction business in Bath which had been set up by Alice's father. In time, Stanley would become a director of the firm and hold several other directorships within the city. But it is as a sportsman that he will be most remembered.

He was an underrated wicketkeeper batsman who was a Bath CC stalwart, captaining them for thirty-five years and later becoming the club's president and chairman. He was first mentioned as a player in 1903 when he played for Bath Association 2nd XI as a fifteen-year-old, and by 1905, he had become a regular for the Association 1st XI (Bath Association CC became Bath CC in 1913). Stanley was appointed captain of Bath in 1914, replacing another Bath stalwart, H. Wood **[161]** who had played one first-class match for Somerset in 1904. VOL.1 mentioned that Stanley stepped down in 1930 but this was a typing error and should have read 1950. He was in his sixty-first year by this time and continued to play occasionally for the 1st XI after he had relinquished the captaincy.

"HOW'S THAT, UMPIRE?"

S. L. Amor: a quick stump off a fastish ball

Stanley played twenty-six first-class matches for Somerset between 1908 and 1930, and almost half of these were played at the Recreation Ground, Bath. He had few opportunities to bat but kept wicket competently when asked to play. He held 26 catches and made 21 stumping and he was very proud of the fact that he had stumped Jack Hobbs twice. One of these occasions was at Bath against Surrey in 1920 off the bowling of Jack White so it is no surprise to find Stanley among the players featured in the *Land & Water* article. This rare and clearly staged photograph from the article is shown opposite. A.E.S. Rippon **[222]** is the hapless batsman.

VOL.1 needs correction. Stanley did *not* die on 7 August 1965, the date shown in the CricketArchive database. The date appears to have been taken from the National Probate Office record and is a clerical error. Further examination of this official record should have revealed that the date could not possibly be correct because the date of probate (28 May 1965) is earlier than the date of death. Stanley died in his home city a year earlier than has been recorded. He died, on 7 August 1964, aged seventy-seven.

WILLIAM TERRITT GRESWELL [188]

William, known as Bill to family and friends, was born in Cuddalore in the Tamil Nadu State of India on 15 October 1889. As explained previously on page 129, William Henry Parr Greswell was *not* the father of Bill or his elder brother Ernest (E.A. Greswell **[155]**).

The boys' father was Charles Herbert Greswell, always known as Herbert. He was a decent club cricketer (playing with another brother, Arthur Ernest Greswell, for Nether Stowey CC) before moving to India to take up employment as a civil engineer. The boys' mother was Edith née Tatham the daughter of a civil servant in Sri Lanka, then known as Ceylon, and it is likely that the family's tea interests in Ceylon came from her side of the family. Bill and Ernest were educated at Repton where they both made the cricket XI, but it was Bill that excelled at the sport.

Bill made the school XI in his second year at Repton and held his place throughout his time there. By 1908, he had discovered that he was able to swing the ball into and away from the batsman, a rare ability at this time which was amply demonstrated by his 14 wickets for 77 runs in the school's innings victory against Malvern. In all matches for the school that season he took 59 wickets for 12 runs apiece. And in the summer holidays he took 15 wickets for 120 runs while playing for the Gentlemen of Derbyshire against Uppingham Rovers.

Bill's brother Ernest had first played for Somerset in 1903, aged eighteen, while still at Repton. He played twelve times for the county before he was lost to Somerset cricket when he left England in January 1911 to pursue a career with the Indian Forestry Department. Bill first appeared for Somerset in 1908 after leaving Repton and played in all five August matches, taking 22 wickets at 28.27 apiece. In only his second match he took 7 wickets for 42 runs in Hampshire's second innings of 128 to secure a much-needed Somerset victory. The county had clearly happened upon a talented cricketer but were aware he was required to work in Ceylon. Somehow, they convinced his father, now retired and living in Bicknoller, to postpone his move to the island until October 1909.

His unusual bowling action, described as leaning back at something in the order of a 45-degree angle, was mentioned in VOL.1. It was this action that enabled Bill to achieve prodigious in-swing. Two photographs of this action are known to exist as they appeared in *From Sammy to Jimmy* by Peter Roebuck, but the

originals are not to be found in the Cricket Museum. One original photograph has surfaced since the publication of VOL.1 and is shown opposite. It would have been included had it been available in time. Taken at the Oval in 1922, it was in the private collection of Jack MacBryan. As a contemporary of Bill's, Jack would have been in a good position to appreciate his unorthodox style.
Somerset got the most out of Bill in 1909 during his seventeen appearances for the county. In the match against Middlesex at Lord's he surprised many of his teammates who were unaware he could bat by scoring a century in seventy-five minutes. He also took 9 wickets in the match suggesting the Middlesex batsmen had a problem with Bill's swerve because two were out lbw and the rest bowled. It produced a rare Somerset victory, just one of four, in 1909. And in the match against the Australians at Bath, he took four Australian wickets for 11 runs in 13 overs causing panic in the Australian ranks, set just 68 to win the match. They scraped home by two wickets. It was probably his tender age that counted against an England call-up against the Australians that year.
Bill also managed three other first-class matches in 1909. Two of them were for H.D.G. Leveson-Gowers XI at Eastbourne against the two Oxbridge XIs. In the match against Cambridge, he took 13 wickets at just over 13 runs apiece. His other first-class match was for the Gentlemen against the Players at Scarborough in September. A month later he was off to Ceylon for what was widely referred to as an initiation into tea planting. Although always being described as a tea planter, there is no evidence that he was ever involved in the physical production of tea or rubber in which his family had interests. In official documents Bill always referred to himself as a broker.
Bill was only supposed to be away for a year to learn the business, but he did not return to England until 1912. Meanwhile he had played a great deal of cricket in Ceylon and in 1911 alone he took a record number of 232 wickets. Somerset welcomed him back in 1912, which was undoubtedly his best season in English cricket. He took 132 first-class wickets at 17.78 and Somerset were the beneficiaries of 104 of these wickets which included thirteen five-wicket and four ten-wicket hauls. Then it was back to Ceylon and no further first-class cricket until after the First World War.
During the War, Bill served as an officer in the Somerset Light Infantry, reaching the rank of major. He was seconded to the Royal Engineers and mentioned in despatches in 1918 for 'gallant and distinguished service in the field'. He returned to Ceylon after war service and resumed his non-first-class

cricket career there. In October 1920, he was picked for the Ceylon team to play in a one-day match against the England side headed for the Ashes series of 1920/21. He took the first four wickets to fall as the England side held on for a draw. Bill later wrote that J.W.T. Douglas, the England captain, asked him when he was coming back to England saying that Bill would get into the Test side if he did. He did return in 1922 and played twenty matches for Somerset but a finger injury hampered his progress. Even so, he took 86 first-class wickets at 19.60 apiece during the season.

There were no Test matches in 1922 and he was not selected for the 1922/23 tour of South Africa. It is not known whether he made himself available, but he was back in Ceylon by the time the tour took place. He continued to achieve phenomenal bowling success in Ceylon. S.P. Foenander, the country's official historian, records that Bill took 961 wickets at less than 8 apiece between 1909 and 1923, followed by 110 wickets at 7.30 in 1924. His best overseas bowling figures in a match were 16 for 45. Bill did not return to England until 1925, a few months after having the satisfaction of inducing another feeble and embarrassing performance against his bowling from an England touring side on its way to Australia. In the Columbo stopover, Bill took 8 wickets for 38 runs dismissing the tourists for 73 runs. Although Bill was in England for the whole of the summer, his business commitments prevented him playing outside of London and Somerset. Ten first-class matches, three for MCC at Lord's and seven home fixtures for Somerset, were all he could manage, supplemented by several appearances for the Somerset Stragglers. Then it was back to Ceylon and once there he lost no time in taking 11 wickets for the Europeans against Ceylon.

Bill returned to the UK permanently in 1926 which was probably prompted by the death of his father Herbert whose extensive interests in West Somerset and overseas needed to be settled. He played two full seasons for Somerset in 1927 and 1928 and his bowling was as good as ever, belying his thirty-seven years. It prompted *Wisden* to remark that he 'seemed just as good as when last in England, his swerve and accurate length invariably troubling batsmen, especially when a new ball was in use.' His best bowling analysis in England came almost at the end of his first-class career, in 1928 against Hampshire at Weston-super-Mare, when he took 9 for 62, thanks to G.R. Hunt **[118]** who held five catches in a leg-side trap.

Somerset would have preferred much more from Bill, but he made himself unavailable for the 1929 season and played just twice more for Somerset in 1930. In his last appearance against Sussex in May 1930, when aged forty, he opened the bowling with Arthur Wellard, taking 3 for 36 from his 24 overs in Sussex's only full innings (compared with Arthur's 3 for 90). There is little doubt that Bill would have achieved greater cricket honours and be recognised as one of Somerset's greatest cricketers had he been more available.

In later life, William became president of Somerset from 1962 to 1965. All biographical sources have William dying in Bicknoller where he lived at his home, Weacombe House, and this 'fact' was repeated in VOL.1. But this is *not* the case. Further research shows that he died of coronary thrombosis some ten miles away, at Halse Manor Hospital in Halse on 12 February 1971, aged eighty-one.

BERT FRANCIS MORGAN [192]

The biography included in VOL.1 is of the wrong man. Bertie Francis Morgan born 6 December 1885 at Finsbury Park, London was *not* a professional cricketer and never played for Somerset. The real Somerset cricketer was Bertie's cousin, Bert Francis Morgan, born two years later.

The error is regretted as the *Somerset Cricketers* series has always challenged archival sources by thorough research. But in this case, too much reliance was placed upon the dates of birth and death which are shown in the CricketArchive database. And the database is a confusing mixture of both cousins because it has Bertie's date of birth and Bert's date of death. The mistaken use of Bertie's date of birth can be excused because Bert's birth was never registered. It is only since the 1939 census returns were published (not available at the time of researching VOL.1) that Bert's birth date can be categorically confirmed as the 25 December 1887.

Excuses can therefore be made for the error, but more diligent research should have raised alarm bells. It would certainly have identified that Bertie had no cricketing provenance whatsoever and was a stonemason all his working life whereas Bert had inherited a fine cricket pedigree. His father, James Morgan, was on the ground staff at Lord's when Bert was born. His parents, James and Fanny Caroline were non-conformists, a possible reason for not registering Bert's birth, but it could also be a case that as Bert was born on Christmas Day, his young parents (eighteen and sixteen) put off registering the birth until after the holidays and subsequently forgot to do it. There is no marriage registration for James and Fanny, and this may also have been a reason for not bothering to involve officialdom in their son's birth.

If any doubt remained over the identity of the Somerset cricketer, it was finally resolved by the discovery of an obscure entry in a Lancashire League review which mentioned 'Bert Francis Morgan' being 'cradled in cricket, the son of James Morgan, head groundsman of the Wimbledon Cricket and Lawn Tennis Club, born not far from Lord's'. However, the exact location can never be confirmed in the absence of a birth certificate. In the 1911 census, Bert records his birthplace as Paddington, another document has it as Maida Vale.

Bert was indeed cradled in cricket. His father, born in Sevenoaks, Kent, is known to have been involved with Kent and is recorded as a professional for 'Players of Kent'. When Bert was four years old, his father accepted a groundsman's job at Wimbledon Cricket and Lawn Tennis Club. James would later become head groundsman at Wimbledon. According to *The Wimbledon Club 1854-2004, A Sporting Scrapbook* by Stephen Chalke, James Morgan remained at Wimbledon until after the First World War before he and Fanny emigrating to Australia. While at Wimbledon, the cricket square was reckoned to be second to none and James kept the ground as if it were his own garden. He was a good enough cricketer to play for the cricket club when needed and is known to have scored two centuries during his time there.

Bert Morgan's father, James, umpiring a Wimbledon CC match in 1908

It was inevitable that Bert would follow in his father's footsteps and indeed was employed by Wimbledon as an assistant to his father. He was playing for Surrey Club & Ground at the age of fifteen and a year later was assisting

Surrey's 2nd XI. Thereafter, he played for Middlesex 2nd XI and for various local club sides as a groundsman/professional.

It is said that Bert received offers from Surrey, but it was Pelham Warner who recommended Bert to Somerset. Bert served his residency qualification as the professional at Lansdown CC in 1907 and 1908 with Somerset paying half of Bert's wages. It was an arrangement that suited both clubs. He was a prolific wicket-taker while at Lansdown, capturing over 250 wickets in the two seasons he was with the club. He was a left-arm, medium to medium-fast-paced bowler who batted right-handed. In the Somerset club and ground matches of 1909 he scored 764 runs and took a remarkable total of 124 wickets at 9.00. But despite these numbers, admittedly against lesser opposition, it seems his captain John Daniell had little confidence in his young bowler, preferring the more experienced bowlers at his disposal in the shape of Ernie Robson, Sam Woods, and Talbot Lewis.

Bert played just six first-class matches for Somerset and was not given much of a chance to prove himself as a bowler. He was given a total of 8 overs in his first two matches, against Hampshire (in 1909) and Yorkshire (in 1910). And in the remaining four matches played in 1910 he was demoted in the batting order and used sparingly as a bowler. Little wonder that he was left with a batting average of 5.72 and just 2 wickets to his name, at a cost of 175 runs. It is a sad indictment of Somerset's treatment of professional bowlers when viewed against Bert's subsequent development as a bowler. It was a huge opportunity missed by the club.

It is not clear whether Bert was released by Somerset or left of his own accord but in 1911 he accepted a three-year contract to play as the professional for Tunstall CC in the North Staffordshire League. In one of those seasons, he was the only player in the League to take over a hundred wickets and there were many outstanding performances during his time there. For example, against Burslem in 1912, he took nine wickets at 8 apiece, seven clean bowled, and he caught out the tenth. He was still living in Wimbledon at the time and lodging in Tunstall during the season. It was here that he met Dorothy Edith Wilkinson, a London-born girl who was working as a cashier at the local cinema. They married at Wollaston Register Office in 1912. Dorothy lied about her age and the fact that her father was deceased, suggesting that she married Bert without the consent of her parents.

Tunstall would most certainly have re-engaged Bert but with a wife to support

This extremely rare postcard was produced by E. Hawkins and Company, of Preston Road, Brighton. The photograph would have been taken about 1909 when Bert was still playing for Somerset

he sought more lucrative engagements in the Lancashire League to supplement his wages from the Staffordshire minor county club. He was at Ramsbottom CC in 1914, where he took 88 wickets at 8.12. The First World War years were filled with a brief sojourn in South America and service in France and Belgium with the Coldstream Guards.

After the War he was invited to play first-class cricket for Middlesex, but he had to decline because of his lucrative employment with Staffordshire and with Werneth CC in Oldham. Bert was the archetypal journeyman cricketer, a fact remarked upon by Plum Warner when he said that Bert could have played for England 'had he not been a rover'. His willingness to go where the most money took him, without regard for first-class cricket, recalls another of the same breed, England bowler S.F. Barnes who was Bert's teammate at Staffordshire. It requires little imagination to picture them comparing contractual terms.

Bert played for Staffordshire in the two seasons before the First World War often bowling in tandem with Barnes or taking on strike bowler responsibilities when Barnes was committed with England and elsewhere. Bert was invariably overshadowed by the great man when they played together. For example, in July 1913 they skittled Northumberland out for 91 in the space of 26 overs with Bert taking 2 wickets from his 13 overs and Barnes finishing with 8 for 19. It is little wonder that Staffordshire were the leading minor county at the time. And when the minor counties championship returned in 1920, Bert was re-engaged for the 1920 to 1923 seasons when not required by Werneth CC.

In the 1920 and 1921 seasons, when Staffordshire were first and first equal in the championship respectively, he played in sixteen of the twenty matches taking 78 wickets at a shade over 14. Sid Barnes did not return to the county of his birth until 1924 and someone had to make way for him. Belying his forty-nine years, Barnes took 7 for 12 in his first match back. Bert played one last match for Staffordshire a few weeks later taking two wickets as against the twelve taken by Barnes. In 47 matches for Staffordshire, Bert took 223 wickets at 13.89, in contrast to Barnes who took 1,376 wickets at 7.99 in his 177 matches for the County.

It helped that minor county matches of two-day duration were scheduled during the week allowing Bert to play league cricket with Werneth on a Saturday. Between 1919 and 1922, he took over 100 wickets a season for the club in all but the last season when matches were badly affected by rain. Never one to stay too long at any club, it was time for him to move on, and well before the end of the 1922 season, the newspapers were reporting on his imminent move to Todmorden CC. He had a full season at Todmorden in 1923 followed by a move to Rawtenstall in the Lancashire League for the start of the 1924 season. The move proved to be short-lived.

Rawtenstall issued a statement in early June that the club had taken the decision to release Bert and were seeking a replacement for the rest of the season. There was no further explanation, but his release could not have been due to his on-field performance as Bert had started the season brightly with two '5-fers' in the opening matches. It is more likely that there was some sort of altercation during what proved to be Bert's last match in the Lancashire League against Nelson on 24 May 1924. The match had begun well for Bert by removing Nelson's opening bat and having the Lancashire and Australian cricketer, Ted McDonald, caught and bowled for 3. But Bert was unable to complete his overs, perhaps through an injury that he had sustained two weeks previously, and this may have caused some resentment within the club. In the event, it had no bearing on the result as the match was abandoned to rain at the halfway stage. There would thus have been plenty of time for an altercation to develop in the bar afterwards, perhaps fuelled by alcohol, if Peter Roebuck' assessment of Bert is correct (see below).

It is quite clear that Bert's sacking was unplanned because Rawtenstall had to settle for a temporary replacement from the Lancashire 2nd XI for the following Saturday's match. Bert wasted no time in looking elsewhere for a new employer which in the circumstances meant a move away from the Lancashire League. That same week, Bert placed a situation wanted advert in the *Athletic News*:

> **BERT MORGAN, Staffordshire, Lancashire League, and Central Lancashire League, Seeks Engagement immediately; full time or match pro.; left-hand bowler, right-hand bat; expert groundsman.—Wheatholme-street, Rawtenstall, Lancs.**

This advert led to his move to the Northeast and an engagement with Wallsend CC for the rest of the season.

The electoral rolls suggest that his wife Dorothy did not move with him, and the marriage could well have been over for some years before his move away from Lancashire. Living with an itinerant and frequently absent cricketer who clearly had issues with employers could not have been easy for Dorothy and the marriage probably never survived the traumatic death of their only child Edna to tuberculous meningitis during the summer of 1921. And it probably didn't help that Bert was of no great support to Dorothy when the seven-year-old was rushed to the Royal Infirmary in Oldham while Bert was taking 6 for 43 for Staffordshire against the Kent 2nd XI in Leek. Bert was allowed to absent himself from the remainder of the match and made it to the hospital where the little girl died a day later.

After two seasons with Wallsend, Bert moved to Normanby Hall CC in the North Yorkshire & South Durham League for the following two seasons before moving back across the Pennines to Dick, Kerr's CC (now BAC/EE Preston CC) in 1928. He was there for three seasons and set a league bowling record in 1929, taking 111 wickets at 4.90, which is never likely to be broken. He followed this with 93 wickets in 1930, only being denied another century of wickets by the weather which decimated the last two matches. He then moved to Castleton Moor in the Central Lancashire League, initially on a one-year contract but newspaper reports suggest that he was re-engaged in 1932.

This most nomadic of cricketers then returned to the Northeast in 1933 to become the groundsman and professional at Billingham Synthonia Cricket and Bowls Club in County Durham. He was still playing regularly and taking wickets throughout the rest of the 1930s. For example, at the club's AGM in 1935, he was presented with an inscribed ball for taking 7 for 8 against Darlington.

Bert had turned fifty-two by the start of the 1940 season but still found the strength and fitness to play every match that year. The 1939 census has Bert living with a woman twelve years his junior, calling herself Florence Morgan, though there is no marriage registered for the couple. This would be his last full season for Synthonia, but he turned out for the club on the odd occasion afterwards and maintained the wickets and bowling greens until his retirement in 1949. Bert died of cancer in the Stockton and Thornaby Hospital, Stockton-on-Tees on the 25 February 1959, aged seventy-two.

VOL.1 used Bertie's signature from an official document which is significantly different from Bert's. This is Bert's signature taken from the 1921 census return:

Bert played for a phenomenal number of clubs with employment lasting one or two years, three at the most, until he was in his late forties when his services were less in demand and job security was the priority. It suggests that some of the moves during his professional career were driven by an uncompromising attitude towards his employer. His time at Somerset remains the only blemish on a successful career, and it will never be known whether his lack of success at Somerset was due to Bert Morgan's character flaws as Peter Roebuck suggests. Roebuck described Bert in *From Sammy to Jimmy* as 'a difficult man with a fondness for brown ale and free speech'. This is pure speculation on Roebuck's part as there is no documented evidence of inappropriate behaviour at Somerset or elsewhere. Furthermore, Bert was barely twenty when he first arrived at Somerset. Too young to have developed a drink problem but perhaps not too young to perceive the injustice of Somerset's amateur ways when he was clearly not given a fair chance to perform. His later performances, week in week out, do not suggest unreliability either. Plum Warner described him as a rover, but this could be Plum's diplomatic way of showing displeasure at a professional chasing the money and lacking loyalty to his club, especially to Plum's own club, Middlesex, which had shown some early interest in Bert's availability.

A difficult man or just a downtrodden and mistreated worker? He should be given the benefit of doubt and his memorable contribution to league cricket history should be celebrated.

JOHN CORNISH WHITE [194]

"THE STOGUMBER DRIVE--"

As Somerset calls it' J. C. White completing a very effective and safe stroke for an off break pitching either on the leg stump or outside the off stump

John, always known as Jack, was born on 19 February 1891 at Woodlands Farm, in Holford, a small village in the Quantock Hills Area of Outstanding Natural Beauty. The family subsequently moved to Escott Farm in Stogumber. Most action photographs have Jack as a bowler, so this photograph taken from the *Land & Water* article of 1920 is unusual. It comes with the caption 'THE STOGUMBER DRIVE', described by E.H.D. Sewell as 'completing a very effective and safe stroke for an off-break pitching either on leg stump or outside the off stump'.

Jack resigned as captain of the club at the end of the 1931 English season after five years of doing the job. It came after several years of intense cricket and gruelling travel on the international stage, beginning with the Ashes tour of 1928/29 and ending with the tour of South Africa in 1930/31. Sandwiched between these tours were four home Test matches, three of which he captained. Modern international cricketers complain of burn-out, of too much cricket, and would surely not have coped with the schedules their predecessors faced in the 1930s. For example, Jack had bowled over 1,300 overs during the 1928 domestic season and almost immediately left for Australia where he bowled a further 870 overs. On his return, he bowled 1,560 overs in 1929 - 22,593 balls bowled in the space of eighteen months!

The 1928/29 tour was also a severe test of endurance when compared with its modern equivalent, with more matches played, rudimentary accommodation, negligible communication with family back home, and the lengthy travel durations. On Jack's tour of Australia, it took over three weeks to reach Perth and the journey from Perth to Sydney could take three days of railway travel. Jack had left for Australia on 22 September 1928 and returned on 22 April 1929 to a hero's welcome at Taunton station. The mayor, mayoress, and various local dignitaries were there to greet him as were his three younger children, most of his Somerset teammates, and a large crowd of well-wishers. His father and two brothers, all farmers, were also at the welcoming and were no doubt relieved to see him after seven months of minding Jack's farm in addition to their own. Jack would have little time to attend to the myriad of matters needing his attention as the start of the 1929 championship season was just three weeks away.

The 1930/31 tour of South Africa was no less arduous than the Australian tour, lasting almost five months, and in the circumstances, Jack could be forgiven for passing on the burden of captaining Somerset and for reigning in the amount of cricket played. Almost immediately, it was announced in local and daily newspapers that he was a 'shoo-in' for the vacant position of Somerset secretary. As the rumour gained momentum and the nomination was proposed, Jack White found it necessary to refute the story. *The Western Daily Press* edition of 19 December 1931 carried an interview with him in which he denied any knowledge of, and responsibility for the nomination and in further remarks he made it clear that his resignation as captain was because he needed to devote more time to his farm, Yarde Farm in Combe Florey.

In the past, his tightly-knit farming family had covered Jack's absences, but his two brothers had their own farms to run - Fred in Highworth, Wiltshire and George in Washford – and his father, Thomas, now in his mid-sixties, had his hands full with Escott Farm in Stogumber.

From 1932 onwards, he appeared in fewer than half the county's matches, and mostly at home venues requiring less time away. In his last two seasons, 1936 and 1937, his appearances dropped even further. By this time, he was relying on the accuracy of flight and guile, without spinning the ball appreciably. It was a far cry from the Taunton Schoolboy who in 1909 had set out to model his bowling on that of his mentor Ted Tyler. His final match was at Weston-super-Mare in August 1937 when he reached the total of 2,350 first-class

wickets after he had taken the first of his five wickets in Glamorgan's second innings. His Somerset bowling record of 2,165 wickets and 185 five-wicket hauls will never be beaten.

Despite his farming commitments he still found time to play cricket for local clubs including the Somerset Stragglers. He would also attend his old school to coach the boys and he was a regular in the Stogumber village nets where he would sometime place a half-crown on the stumps encouraging the lads to bowl him out.

Field sports remained a strong interest, though it cost him the loss of his left eye in 1938, and for many years he was secretary of the Quantock Staghounds Hunt. His eldest son John was killed in 1943 while serving as a wing commander in the Mediterranean and his other son Tom followed him into farming. John and his wife Agnes also had two daughters. He continued to take a keen interest in Somerset affairs, serving on the executive committee and its cricket committees, culminating in his appointment as the club's president in the autumn of 1960. He had little time to savour the honour as he died on 2 May 1961 at Yarde Farm, aged seventy.

Other honours followed, not least the dedication of a pair of wrought iron gates which had the initials 'J.C.W.' as a centrepiece in the form of an impressive monogram. They were placed at the main entrance to the County Ground in St. James Street and Agnes White was the guest of honour at the unveiling on 1 May 1963.

When the club widened the main entrance in 2017, the gates were replaced with ones of more modern design emblazoned with the wyvern logo and 'JCW' at the centre. The old gates are safely stored on the ground and the club are exploring the areas where they could best be displayed.

JAMES BRIDGES [203]

Jim styled himself J.J. and occasionally J.F. Bridges, perhaps to add more gravitas to his name in the scorebooks, but the reality was that he was born plain James Bridges in Timsbury on 28 June 1887. He was always known as Jim to family and friends.

Jim made his debut in the championship match against Hampshire beginning 11 May 1911 and came away with creditable bowling figures taking 2 wickets in each Hampshire innings for the combined total of 41 runs. During the seasons 1914 to 1926 he was an ever-present member of the side save for missing the first half of the 1921 season following a motorbike accident. It seems he did not learn his lesson because two years later, on his way to play in the Yorkshire match at Taunton, he lost control of his bike near the East Brent police station and was thrown into a deep ditch. Trapped under the motorcycle, he was in grave danger of drowning but for the timely assistance of P.C. Bull. After a bath and the loan of a suit from the policeman, he made his way to Taunton and the match.

J. F. BRIDGES' SHORT JUMP
Which he makes prior to his stride of delivery. The whole attitude foreshadows much body work in his action

Jim was one of the players featured in the *Land & Water* article of 1920. The action photograph taken by E.H.D. Sewell during the match against Surrey at Bath is shown here along with Sewell's comments. By 1927, Jim was playing sporadically for the county, primarily because he had lost much of his pace off the pitch. And he would have understandably considered the match against Derbyshire at the County Ground at the end of July 1928 to be his last match for Somerset. It wasn't

Jim in his debut season of 1911 at New Road, Worcester

a great ending to his long county career, he went wicketless in the first innings and was not asked to bowl in the second.

A year later, an injury to Arthur Wellard forced Somerset to call upon him for one last time. The late call-up was not so surprising as he was having an exceptional summer for Weston-super-Mare CC (he topped the bowling averages that year with 104 wickets at 6.15 apiece). His last match was at Fry's Ground, Bristol against Gloucestershire, and Jim opened the bowling in both innings. He bowled 21 overs for a miserly 39 runs but didn't take a wicket. There was a bizarre moment during the match when Jim had to leave the field. It seems that Jim was not the only accident-prone member of the family. Mid-way through the match he had to rush away when his five-year-old daughter Daphne fell over the balustrade at the family home in Atlantic Terrace, Weston-super-Mare. Happily, Daphne recovered from her injuries.

Jim had made 214 appearances for Somerset, taking 685 wickets at 25.59 runs apiece. He continued to play for Weston-super-Mare 1st XI right up to the Second World War, captaining the club between 1932 and 1935. In May 1938, against the mighty Bath CC he played alongside his son Peter who was tried as an opening bat. Peter opened with L.C. Hawkins **[295]** and against Bath's powerful bowling line-up he stayed for 95 minutes scoring 20 runs. The *Bath Chronicle* remarked that the seventeen-year-old would make a good cricketer, but he never achieved a higher level of cricket.

Jim played for the Gentlemen against the Players twice, in 1922 and 1924. It is odd that he remained an amateur throughout his first-class career as Jim had to work all his life. Playing cricket only remained viable thanks to the support he received from his hard-working wife and children. Although Jim's key dates of birth and death are correct in VOL.1, some mistakes were made identifying the personal details of his adult life. Mistakes easily made, given the commonness of the name and the confusion he created by adopting a middle initial. The family details are accurate up to the time he left Timsbury as a young adult to work as a male nurse in Medway. Jim did marry a local girl in Medway, but she was not Annie Mabel Connell.

Jim married Margaret Isabel née Read, in Medway, in 1909 before returning to Timsbury where their daughter Dorothy was born in 1913. Margaret died the following year, aged twenty-nine, leaving Jim responsible for his baby daughter. He remarried in Bristol in June 1915 while he was stationed as a staff sergeant in the Royal Army Medical Corp at Colston Fort in Bristol. His second wife was Katie née Dunkerton, the daughter of a Knowle blacksmith. In time, young Dorothy would be joined by four stepsisters and a stepbrother. After the First World War, Jim worked as an insurance inspector for the Motor Union Insurance Company while supporting Katie in the running of a boarding house in Claremont Crescent, Weston-super-Mare. They remained in the town and by the late thirties they were running the *Cavendish Hotel* on the corner of Regent Street and St James Street just off the sea front. Their two eldest daughters, Dorothy and Florence, were assisting in the running of the hotel which was a popular watering hole when the Weston cricket festival came to town.

Some corrections to VOL.1 are necessary. Jim died of a stroke in Hackney on the 26 September 1966 (*not* the 29 September 1966 as recorded in CricketArchive), aged seventy-nine. Also, the biography presumed that Jim and his family had moved to the South East to live because his death was recorded in Hackney. However, this may not have been a family move. The electoral rolls for Hackney record him living in an unconnected household since at least 1958 and without his wife Katie. Katie, who had been living with her daughter Constance in Weston-super-Mare, died two years after Jim.

ARCHIBALD YOUNG [207]

Tom on debut for Somerset at New Road Worcester in 1911

Archibald, known as Archie in his younger days but later universally known as Tom, was the son of George Young, and Zillah née Stone, who was the daughter of a gamekeeper living on a farm in Broomfield, near Bridgwater.

George and Zillah were married in Bathwick where George earned a living as a coachman. Tom was the eighth born of their nine children consisting of six boys and three girls. Tom was born in Bathwick on 6 November 1890 and George died when Tom was twelve years old whereupon Zillah and her younger children moved to Widcombe, Bath.

Tom attended Bathwick School and from there he was employed by Lansdown Cricket Club as a 'ground lad' where he was expected to assist with the upkeep of the ground and act as a ground bowler to club members and their sons. His breakthrough came in 1910. Bert Morgan **[192]** had been Lansdown's professional while qualifying for Somerset and he was replaced by Claude Spencer of Berkshire in 1909. Spencer was not available in 1910 because of family illness and the Lansdown committee agreed that Tom should be appointed the club professional. This ancient and prestigious club must have had some confidence in the nineteen-year-old ground lad. Or perhaps it was a financial expedient as it was a less than generous offer of 18 shillings a week up to the start of the club's season on May 1st and thereafter £1 a week during the season.

Given the close association on and off the ground between Somerset and Lansdown it was inevitable that Tom was soon attracting the attention of the county club. He made his debut as a batsman against Worcester at New Road in late August 1911 being out for a duck in his very first innings, but he made amends in the second innings with the second highest score of 36. He played in the subsequent final two matches, but his four innings yielded just 33 runs. Somerset would not call upon him again before the First World War.

With nothing forthcoming from Somerset and poor wages from Lansdown, it was reported that he had accepted an offer in 1912 from Britannia Works CC at Gainsborough, Lincolnshire which also included a job in the locomotive factory. Later in 1914, it was reported that he was doing well playing cricket in South Wales although there are very few reports outside of playing for Senghenydd CC in the Amber Valley. Other reports confirm that he was in Wales long enough to have qualified for Glamorgan.

Tom joined the Army in November 1914 as a lance corporal and was part of the British Expeditionary Force in France and Belgium. He wrote home to his mother in December 1915 mentioning the severe weather they were experiencing and asking her to 'put a letter in the Chronicle and ask the good people of Bath if they could send us a football'. Tom, who had been a very good footballer as a goalkeeper for Bath City Amateurs, wrote that his company were in the battalion final to be played on Christmas Day 1915, but they had no football to practice with. The *Bath Chronicle and Gazette* duly published the request, but it is not known whether it met with any success. Tom survived the War unscathed although he suffered, as did many millions of men, from the long-term after-effects of mustard gas poisoning.

Tom played his club cricket for Bath CC immediately after the War. He also played two matches for Somerset at the Recreation Ground but runs eluded him. Not so for Bath where he topped the batting averages in 1919 with 751 runs at an average of 50.00 per innings which included three centuries. He was not selected by Somerset in 1920 and it was mid-June 1921 before John Daniell asked him to play again. The match was against Derbyshire at the Recreation Ground. It is odd that up to this point Daniell had never asked Tom to bowl as he must have been aware that he was a regular wicket-taker at Bath. The *Bath Chronicle and Gazette*, remarking on the fact that five Bath players would be playing in the Derbyshire match, questioned why he had never been asked to bowl. The newspaper concluded 'this time it is pretty certain his bowling will be tried'. And it was – for one over costing 4 runs.

From this time onwards he became a regular member of the Somerset side, and perhaps because of the confidence placed upon him, his batting improved by leaps and bounds. He scored his maiden century in 1923 against Glamorgan at the County Ground and narrowly missed completing 1,000 runs in the season. The following year he made a career best 198 against Hampshire, fittingly at Bath. And during this innings, he, and M.D. Lyon **[237]** hit a two-hour double-century partnership which had John Daniell exclaiming "I have never seen two finer hitting innings in the course of my experience".

However, it would still be a while before his bowling was taken seriously. And yet in the twelve years between 1922 and 1933 he took 380 wickets for Somerset at 25.58 apiece. It included a best bowling return of 8 for 30 against Derbyshire at the County Ground in 1930 when the visitors were comfortably placed on 59 for 2 wickets in their second innings and batting out for a draw. Tom was brought on and ran through the last eight wickets to have the side all out for 107 and achieve an unlikely victory. 1930 had been one of his best seasons for Somerset. He had scored 1,219 runs (the most in any season) and taken 71 wickets at 18.00 apiece. He had also played for Bath whenever possible and helped the club go through the season unbeaten.

Moreover, 1930 had been his benefit year with the associated local friendlies and promotional events. Typical of these events was a cinema night attended by the Somerset and Hampshire players who were playing at the County Ground. The audience was treated to a showing of the film burlesque about 'limitless' Test Matches, written, directed, and produced by M.D. Lyon **[237]**. It was said to have produced much merriment and Tom was £26 richer by the end of the night which he described as a 'great success'. It was also a great achievement to get Tom on his feet for a thankyou speech as he would usually decline in favour of a more outgoing teammate.

As for his official benefit match, there are so many examples in Somerset's history of benefits ruined by rain or ending prematurely and Tom's was no exception. He had chosen the Sussex match at Bath at the end of July 1930, a game interrupted by rain throughout when no play was possible on the final day, and the ground collections suffered as a result. His benefit year still yielded a very welcomed £750.

It must have been a gruelling year for Tom, and it may have contributed to his admission to the Winsley Sanatorium for Consumptives at Limpley Stoke, near Bath in January 1931. He was admitted after a chest x-ray revealed the early signs of tuberculosis. He was at Winsley Chest Hospital (known by that name at the time) for several weeks, and doubts were expressed that he would ever be fit to play cricket again. It was the start of a long and lingering terminal illness which was fought bravely.

Tom in May 1933, his final year of a long professional career with Somerset, the gaunt look of a man far from well

It would have been a major cause for concern if this key allrounder had been unavailable, but miraculously, Tom was present for the opening match of the season on 6 May. He did miss nine matches in 1931, mostly because of a thigh strain, but he still managed to score 1,185 runs at 34.85 and take 40 wickets at 20.95 apiece. Tom soldiered on for two more seasons, retiring at the end of the 1933 season. There had been a punishing schedule of eight matches that August which must have taken its toll. In the first four of these matches he scored a century, against Glamorgan, and took 16 wickets at 25.25 apiece, but there was an ominous contrast in the last four matches when he managed just 4 wickets at 77.75 apiece.

His condition deteriorated after his retirement and the family even moved to Odd Down on the outskirts of the city for the sake of Tom's health. It was to no avail and during a last stay at Winsley towards the end of March 1936 he asked to return to the city so he could be close to his wife Violet, whom he had married in 1922, and their three young children. He was transferred to Bath hospital where he lay seriously ill. A friend was quoted as saying that he was his usual cheerful self and talking about cricket right up to the end. Many of his old teammates came to visit him, including Jack and Frank Lee who made a special trip from London to be at his bedside three days before his death on 2 April 1936, aged forty-five.

The official cause of death was pulmonary tuberculosis. Contrary to previous reports that have him dying at home, he was never well enough to leave hospital. His old county captain R.A. Ingle **[268]** (who was also Tom's solicitor) was with him at the last and remarked at his funeral "Tom was one of the finest players that ever played for Somerset. Given better health there was no limit to the eminence in the game he might have achieved. There was no better stroke player in first-class cricket. He was a pleasure to watch". Various cricket matches and social events were organised after his death with the proceeds going to his widow.

Tom's funeral was held at St Philip's Church, Odd Down but he was interred in the cemetery of St James' Church, Bath. It proved to be an unfortunate choice and Tom was not left to rest in peace. The churchyard was severely damaged in the Bath blitz during the Second World War and his remains were re-buried in the Lyncombe and Widcombe cemetery during the 1960s.

JOHN CRAWFORD WILLIAM MacBRYAN [208]

John, always known as Jack, was born in Box on 22 July 1892, the son of Henry Crawford MacBryan and Eveline Ada Truman, the daughter of a wealthy East Indies merchant. Henry was a psychiatric doctor who ran the lunatic asylum at Kingsdown House, which was once the residence of Judge Jeffreys, but in Henry's time it went by the colloquial name of the 'Box Mad House.' Jack was the eldest of four boys and one girl, a production line that ended when Eveline died in 1902 giving birth to the youngest sibling Gerard. Henry who remarried the following year, was an enlightened member of his profession who advocated the humane treatment of his patients allowing them unrestrained freedom of movement. As his family also lived in the main house it must have been a very unconventional upbringing for the children. P.G. Woodhouse was supposed to have based his famous loony doctor Sir Roderick Glossop on Henry. The three eldest boys excelled at most sports. Jack was at Exeter School and would go on to represent Somerset at cricket, golf, hockey, and rugby. Edward, was in the Oundle XI and XV, played rugby for Bath and cricket for Wiltshire. Reginald, the third son, was in the Cheltenham College XI, played for Lansdown CC and was in the Sandhurst XV. All four boys were sent for military training. Despite Jack's preference for a medical career, he went to Sandhurst as did Edward and Reginald. Gerard, always the odd one out, in many senses, went to the Royal Navy College in Dartmouth.

Gerard was too young to participate in the First World War, but the others were involved from the outset. Jack and Edward were in the Somerset Light Infantry. Jack was wounded and taken prisoner at the battle of Le Cateau on 26 August 1914 and spent the rest of the war as a POW in Holland. It almost certainly saved him from being killed in later battles. Edward was wounded at Ypres in May 1915 and sent home to recover. He returned to the front a year later and two months after that, in July 1916, was reported missing presumed dead. Reginald, who had joined the King's Own Scottish Borderers in 1917 was also wounded and spent some time in the military hospital at Whitechapel. Philip Eade in *Sylvia, Queen of the Headhunters*, a book about the debauched life of Sylvia Brett, the wife of the Rajah of Sarawak, recounts that when Jack returned in 1918, he found Kingsdown House in a dilapidated state. His father, having succumbed to drink had failed to collect the patients' fees. Jack soon discovered that Gerrard had plotted against him while he was away, and within a week of arriving home, he was thrown out of the house and subsequently disinherited. It is hard to tell how much of this story is true. Jack's father was a functioning member of Somerset's Bath area committee until 1932 although abstinence was not a requirement of membership. However, if true, it would have made for some awkward moments when Jack was playing in subsequent Bath festivals.

Gerard duly inherited Kingsdown House. He was clearly madder than most of his father's patients and was later described as the Rasputin of Sarawak having ingratiated himself with the royal family while he was employed as the Rajah's private secretary. It had been with the encouragement of the aforementioned Sylvia. He believed himself to be the rightful successor to the Rajah and became increasingly delusional. There were various manic episodes including arriving at parties naked believing he was invisible, barking on all fours believing he was a dog and carrying a black box everywhere he went which he claimed could blow up the world. Despite his undeniable charm, intelligence, and wealth, Gerard lived in cheap Hong Kong hotels as a down-and-out recluse towards the end of his life in 1953 and he either died by his own hand or starved himself to death. The authorities could not decide on the cause of death by the time he was found.

With such early life experiences in the 'Box Mad House' and German prison camps, it is no wonder that Jack spurned close friendships and was seen by many as standoffish and unsociable. His cricket was his way of expressing himself – tough, uncompromising, and combative.

He played his first match for Somerset in late August 1911 against Lancashire at the Recreation Ground in Bath while he was down for the summer from Sandhurst. The future Somerset opener was asked to bat at number eight and scored 19 runs in each innings, the second of which was the highest score in Somerset's paltry innings of 89. It was perhaps a portent of what was to come with Jack often critical of his teammates' tendencies to bat flamboyantly and without concern for the interests of the team. That was never Jack's approach. He had been on Somerset's radar for some time and had played on the County Ground two years earlier, aged seventeen, for Lansdown against a Somerset Stragglers XI which included seven Somerset cricketers, among them Jack White and John Daniell.

Jack played occasionally for Somerset in the years before the First World War as much as his commitments to Sandhurst and the 1st Battalion of the Somerset Light Infantry allowed. None of his twelve pre-war appearances, which included a highest score of 65, suggested a stellar cricket career. After the War, he resigned his commission and went up to Jesus College Cambridge where he played for the University XI in 1919 and 1920, narrowly missing his blue in his first year and getting it in his second. This was also the year when Jack won a hockey gold medal at the Antwerp Olympics and the year he made his first century for Somerset. It was against Hampshire at Bournemouth and his

109 runs came in three hours, twenty minutes. It was a typical MacBryan innings. The newspapers reported that 'At times he drove hard, and played cleverly to leg, but for the most part he contented himself with defensive methods. His figures included eight 4s'.

From Jack MacBryan's private papers – always neat and tidy in dress and at the wicket, never flamboyant

Jack's best cricket came during the three seasons 1922 to 1924 when he scored 1,457, 1,831 and 1,608 runs respectively at an overall average of 36.54. It was the middle season that first attracted the attention of the England selectors. Chosen for the Rest in the second Test trial against England he scored 80 and withstood the England bowlers for nearly three hours and 30 minutes. He also had decent scores for the Gentlemen against the Players and the Uncapped against the Capped. It would in time lead to his call-up for the 4th Test Match against the South Africans in 1924. It was somewhat fortuitous as he was chosen to replace Jack Hobbs who was dropped for refusing to make himself available for the 1924/25 Ashes tour. And it was frustrating for Jack that the Old Trafford rain famously prevented him from batting, bowling, or fielding in the match. He was also picked as one of the *Wisden* Cricketers of the Year after the 1924 season.

Wisden described him as 'essentially a steady batsman' and added 'He is neat and finished in style without being in any way spectacular, and so far from being obsessed, like many of the moderns, by on side play he gets a good proportion of his runs by cutting, this alone making him good to look at'. It was a huge disappointment for Jack that he was not selected for the Ashes tour of 1924/25. His hopes were raised when the MCC approached him by letter to ask if he was available to tour and Jack wrote back in the affirmative. The MCC were probably keeping options open as it was still in the balance whether

Hobbs would tour. But Jack took his rejection badly and it would rankle with him for the rest of his life. He did manage a tour that winter playing in ten of the fourteen first-class matches played by S.B. Joel's XI in South Africa, scoring two centuries, and averaging 26.62 per innings.

Jack never repeated the rich vein of form achieved in the mid-1920s and played his last match for Somerset in June 1931, against Essex at the County Ground. He had played 156 matches and scored 8,372 runs at an average of 31.00 including 16 centuries.

As well as the Bill Greswell action photo taken at the Oval in 1922, Jack commissioned several of himself in action. This one, demonstrating his wide stance at the crease, is the best of the series:

In later life Jack corresponded with Ted Francis, the secretary of the Somerset Wyverns, a supporters club formed by Somerset exiles in London and the home counties which no longer exists. Ted wrote to Jack in 1976 more in hope than expectation. Ted Francis hoped that Jack might be persuaded to divulge some juicy anecdotes for his newsletters. After all, the man had played with Somerset legends like Sam Woods, Len Braund and Jack White. He had also played in some historic matches such as when Jack Hobbs made his 100th first-class century at Bath in 1923 and his 126th and 127th first-class century at Taunton to equal and pass W.G. Grace's record. Ted Francis made initial contact by sending him a birthday card and introducing himself as the editor of the Wyvern newsletter. Within a few days Ted received a brief reply and could never have imagined that over the course of the next seven years he would receive over sixty long and revealing hand-written letters. In time, the pair would become good friends and Ted would visit Jack, always a convivial host, for dinner at his lodgings or at restaurants in London.

Jack gave Ted several of his mementoes, including the photographs included here. The letters show that he did not enjoy his time with Somerset. There was no love for his captain John Daniell, and he was not reticent in giving his opinion of fellow players. He describes J.C. White **[194]** as selfish and over-bowled while Jack all but calls him a coward (harking back to the First World War when White's farm commitments gave him exemption). But his greatest distain was reserved for his fellow Somerset amateur P.R. Johnson **[133]** who he blamed for spoiling his chances of going to Australia. The reference in VOL.1 to Jack calling Randall Johnson an 'overrated popinjay' is in the letters. It was most probably motivated by jealousy. Randall's classical and elegant batting style was certainly something to envy, and Randall's success as a stockbroker was in direct contrast to Jack's experience in the City.

Not all teammates were treated to his caustic tongue. He hero-worshipped Sam Woods. Some content is controversial, for example, one passage talks about John Daniell's efforts at shielding the ball from his opposing captain, Percy Fender, because Jack White had been picking the seam with his fingernail. When Ted died, the sixty letters, plus another ten letters between Jack and other Wyvern members, were put up for auction in 2018. There was some fierce bidding for the letters, but eventually the lot was secured by the Cricket Museum.

Most of the letters are rambling and repetitive due to Jack's failing memory, not surprising given his age at the time of writing. An edited and much précised summary of all seventy letters has been produced for the Cricket Museum. Jack had a stock of stories and anecdotes which are often repeated in the letters and will be recognised by devotees of Somerset cricket history. Many appear in David Foot's fine book *Cricket's Unholy Trinity*, which has Jack as one of the triumvirate. David Foot acknowledges Ted Francis for his help loaning the letters and there are passages in Foot's book taken word for word from the letters.

Jack was a prolific embroiderer ever since he developed the skill while a POW.

There is an image of him in *Cricket's Unholy Trinity* presenting a framed copy of an embroidery done to commemorate the 350th anniversary of his old school, Exeter. It was taken just before he died and shows him at home in trademark dressing gown with the Headmaster and Bursar of Exeter School. He also produced an embroidered Wyvern which he had framed and presented to the Somerset Wyverns. A working copy was found amongst the letters but all efforts to trace the whereabouts of the original, which was believed to have hung in the Wyvern pavilion on the County Ground, have failed.

Jack had had his fair share of bad luck during his long life. The chorus girl he married soon tired of him, and his stockbroking business was not a great success. By the time of his correspondence with Ted Francis, he was living out his life in Cambridge lodgings owned by a companion, Mrs Cecil Mackay. He died there on 14 July 1983, just short of his ninety-first birthday.

MANEK PALLON BAJANA [209]

M. P. BAJANA, THE DELHI CRICKETER

At the beginning of a fast-footed off hit. The elbow action promises that the ball will be kept well down

Manek was in his last season playing for Somerset when he played against Surrey at Bath and was the subject of this rare photograph featured in the *Land & Water* article of 1920. The reference by E.H.D. Sewell to Manek being from Dehli is inaccurate. It was typical of the lazy and often racist references overseas cricketers had to endure. In Manek's case it was manifest in the way locals would ignorantly call him 'Banana' or 'Pyjama'.

And Manek was not even spelt correctly as he wrote his first name as Maneck in all official documents. He has an extensive entry in Wikipedia, but it contains very little information about his early life and just has him 'born in India'. And there is also very little about his adult life outside of cricket even though he spent it almost entirely in England.

And some sources still refer to him as Prince Bajana though there is nothing at all to suggest that he had any India royal blood or was even from a high caste. His name may conjure memories of the Raj - maharajas, palaces, and untold wealth - but this was far from the reality of Maneck's short life. The name Bajana comes from the Indian feudal state of that name in Gujarat, North West India. His family were Parsees, descended from the original Persian emigrants who followed Zoroastrianism. Maneck clearly took his religion seriously because in the 1911 census he wrote 'Zoroastrian' in the 'NATIONALITY' column. Informatively, he wrote Mora, Suvali, in the 'BIRTHPLACE' column. This traces his birth to the village of Mora, near Surat in Gujarat State, a mere 600 miles from Delhi! Furthermore, it discounts a royal birth as Mora would not have been a suitable place for such an event.

Some historians and writers have furthered the belief that Maneck first came to Somerset's attention in 1911 after he had scored a century against them during the Indian Tour of the British Isles. But Maneck was already well known to John Daniell and other Somerset cricketers who had played with him in India in 1909. By this time, Maneck was employed by the Maharaja of Cooch Behar (now Koch Bihar) in West Bengal who went to great lengths securing the services of the best native and overseas cricketers for his team.

Modern-day cricketers are not the first to benefit financially from the Indian continent's passion for the game. Over the years many top names were employed to play and coach for the maharajas during the English winters including the likes of Jack Hobbs and Herbert Sutcliffe. The Maharaja of Cooch Behar employed the Somerset trio, John Daniell, Talbot Lewis, and Ernie Robson in 1909 and Maneck was one of the home-grown players. All four cricketers appeared in the Maharajah's side that overwhelmed Calcutta at Eden Gardens in December 1909 and it must be presumed that one of the Somerset trio, probably Daniell, persuaded the young man to come over for the 1910 English season. In addition to playing for the Somerset Stragglers in 1910, topping the club's batting averages with 54.30 and scoring a century against Sidmouth, he appeared for a variety of local clubs including Taunton CC and Taunton Deane CC.

The dapper Maneck Bajana at the County Ground, Taunton in 1912

Prince Kumar Hitendra Singh Naraya **[195]**, who was studying at Cambridge, was also playing cricket in Taunton with Maneck in 1910, and perhaps this is why Maneck came to be regarded by the British public as a high-born prince by his association with a real one. Prince Naraya was the youngest son of the Maharaja of Cooch Behar and his future lay firmly in India. Not so Maneck, whose manners and impeccable dress were those of a committed anglophile. He decided to stay in England after the 1911 tour and as far as can be ascertained he never returned to India for any length of time if he returned at all.

He played fifty-one first-class matches for Somerset between 1912 and 1920 while he was based in London and playing club cricket for Shepherd's Bush CC. He also appeared for the Indian Gymkhana which played in the Middlesex premier league at the beginning of the First World War and later played in Gymkhana's more prestigious fixtures at Lord's, against MCC for example. Maneck was more inclined to play matches of this kind than the mundane club matches. VOL.1 intimated that he returned to India in 1920 but this was not the case. By this time his English-born family were firmly based in London where he had met and wooed a young English girl called Emma Tryphena Hicks. She was nine years his junior. Tryphena, as she preferred to be named, came from Clapham, the daughter of a Royal Navy paymaster. She worked as a cashier in a central London drapery store which is probably where they met. Maneck got her pregnant and they had a daughter Ruth in June 1914. Nine months later they married at Paddington Register Office. They set up home in St Stephen's Square, Paddington where their son Harold was born. Maneck is mostly described in official documents as of independent means, and he was known to be in partnership with a Turkish-born antique and art dealer post-war and until 1920 when the partnership was dissolved.

His independent means together with any earnings from employment could not have stretched very far judging by his family's living conditions. Their accommodation in St Stephen's Square was a rented, four-roomed tenement in a large, multi-occupied, Paddington property that was home to four families. It was a far cry from his days employed by the Maharaja, and it refutes any idea that he had huge inherited wealth as was presumed by his association with Indian high society.

Maneck's home was still the same four rooms when he died in the Mildmay Mission Hospital in Bethnall Green on 28 April 1927. It had been a long and painful illness and he was just forty years old when he died of colon cancer. Tryphena was left £750 in Maneck's Will, hardly a princely sum. She never remarried and died in Paddington in 1955. Her children would later emigrate to the United States and Canada.

LANCELOT EDWARD SETH WARD [216]

Lancelot was generally known as Seth, a name used by successive generations of the Ward family in honour of his namesake, Seth Ward, Bishop of Salisbury (1671-1689). Seth's father was the Rev Percival Seth Ward, the son of Seth Charles Ward, the clerk of records in the High Court of Chancery. Percival married Annie née Trueman a year before his ordination in 1866, and after curacies in Farnborough and Aylesbury, he was appointed vicar of St Mary's Church, Apsley End, Hertfordshire in April 1875. By this time, the couple had produced three sons and two daughters. Seth, the sixth and last child, was born

on 7 August 1875, a few months after the move to Apsley.
VOL.1 had no image of Seth, and despite further attempts to locate one, nothing has been found to put a face to his name. The photograph below, shown here courtesy of Hertfordshire Archives and Local Studies, is as close as it has come to finding an image. Taken in 1895, it features Seth's parents and his brother Charles Melville Seth Ward taking tea in the garden of Apsley vicarage. It does not feature Seth, but at least it offers a view of where he spent his childhood years.

Seth and his three brothers inherited their father's love of sport, especially cricket and association football and they all played both sports for Rickmansworth, West Herts and Apsley. Seth was also a talented athlete, demonstrated at his first senior school, Oak Vale, Berkhamsted, when at the annual sports day, aged fourteen, he came first at long jump, pole vault, throwing the cricket ball, and an event referred to as the 'donkey race'. He was sent to Felsted School to complete his education and was in the cricket and football 1st XIs of 1891 and 1892. The school archives at Felsted, like every other archival and military source, holds no image of Seth. Football was the sport at which Seth showed most promise. He was said to be a protégé of Arthur Dunn, the Corinthian FC and England international, who at the time was teaching at Elstree School not far from Apsley. There is nothing to confirm that Seth was a Corinthian. However, he did play for the Crusaders and the Wanderers, both prominent clubs in the early days of the Football Association. The Wanderers were the original holders of the Challenge Cup, the predecessor to the FA Cup.

Seth joined the Bucks Militia on leaving school and, three years later, passed the competitive examination of militia subalterns to earn a commission in the 2nd Battalion of the Oxford and Bucks Light Infantry. His first overseas posting was to the North-West Frontier of India in 1897, in response to an uprising by Pathan tribesmen along the border between India and Afghanistan.

The Tirah Memorial to the 62 officers and men of the 2nd Battalion Oxfordshire Light Infantry killed during the Campaign. Erected in Oxford. (Drawn by Oxford Journal artist 7 July 1900)

The fighting, which lasted from October 1897 to May 1898, was known as the Tirah Campaign, and was at its bloodiest in the area around the Khyber Pass where Seth's battalion was engaged. He received several commendations for his part in the Tirah Campaign.

Seth's battalion remained in India for another five years while he found time to play cricket for Punjab CC and reputedly an All-India XI. But before the battalion's eventual return to England, Seth was seconded by the foreign office to British East Africa in 1902. He was sent to serve with the reformed King's African Rifles (K.A.R), which had five battalions covering the British East African protectorates of Uganda, Somaliland, and Nyasaland (the Republic of Malawi since 1964). Seth was posted to the 4th Battalion (4 K.A.R.) based in Bombo, Uganda, which was responsible for protecting British interests in Uganda. More specifically, the 4 K.A.R. was charged with the security of the Ugandan Railway, a British state-owned company which had built a railway line from the port city of Mombasa to the Kisumu terminus on the eastern shores of Lake Victoria. Other duties of the 4 K.A.R. included keeping the peace amongst the various warring tribes and dealing swiftly to quell any challenge to British rule. They were met by what was colloquially called an 'expedition'. The one against the Nandi uprising in 1905/1906 was a particularly bloody affair for which Seth received several medals and clasps. The Nandi lost thousands of men, their spears being no match for the British rifles and seven-pounder guns.

The battalions of the K.A.R. were made up of native Askari troops led by seconded British officers and the officer composition of each battalion was flexible, providing reinforcements across British East Africa where and when it was needed. During the next twelve years of service in Africa, Seth fought with 5 K.A.R. in Somaliland against 'The Mad Mullah' and with 2 and 3 K.A.R. in Nairobi before returning to 4 K.A.R. in 1913 as its commanding officer with the rank of Lieutenant Colonel.

His time in Africa was not always confrontational. In 1911, the then Major Seth Ward led a party of 2 officers and 112 Askari to confront what was described by the Governor as an 'outbreak of hysterical mania on the part of the Akamba tribe in an area near Nairobi which was populated by European woman and children. The matter was settled without force and described by the Governor as 'a fine example of the protective and preventive function exercised by the mere presence of disciplined troops'. The report was possibly embellished to counteract British government moves to make economies in the size of the K.A.R. Several battalion companies were disbanded or withdrawn during the period 1911 to 1914.

All this would change on the outbreak of World War One by which time the the remaining battalions of K.A.R. were scattered across the region in far-flung outposts of British East Africa. Seth was charged with taking command of all units of the K.A.R., and, along with other British Army reinforcements, the K.A.R. were engaged in fighting the German army across the border between British and German East Africa, the latter area now made up of Burundi, Rwanda, and Tanzania.

Seth remained in Africa until 1915 by which time he seems to have held a strategic planning role. In late 1914, Major General Arthur Aitkin landed a British-Indian force at the German East African port of Tanga where they were overwhelmed by the Germans. Aitkin suffered 850 casualties and lost guns, and equipment before a hasty re-embarkation. Seth seems to have had some hand in the preparations because it is reported that before launching this disastrous assault, Aitkin had gone to Mombasa 'to confer with the Governor, Brigadier General Stewart, and Lieutenant Colonel Ward.'

Seth was recalled to England to serve with the Royal Field Artillery. He was given the rank of acting brigadier-general and during the remainder of the First World War saw action in France and Flanders whilst in charge of several artillery brigades. He was twice wounded in the process. He was awarded two DSOs, in 1916 and 1918, and he was mentioned in despatches six times for his exceptional service during the War. Seth retired from the army soon after hostilities ended with the rank of lieutenant colonel.

A year before the War, Seth had a period of extended leave during the summer of 1913 and he based himself in Eastbourne, the scene of many Ward family holidays when the boys would play cricket for Eastbourne CC. He played several matches for the club whilst he was on leave. VOL.1 may have been harsh on the assessment of Seth as a cricketer for he also made several high scores (the highest being 80 against Old Wellingburians) for Sussex Martlets in late August. Seth's appearance for Somerset against Kent in May 1913 was less successful, scoring a 0 and a 3 in his two innings. He played two more first-class matches for Somerset in 1920, when aged forty-four and well past his best. These were back-to-back matches against the universities, more than likely when the county was short of players. He reached double figures just once in his five innings for the county and was left with a first-class batting average of 3.60.

Thereafter, the call of Africa was too much for Seth to resist. In March 1924 he accepted the position of ADC assisting the newly-appointed Governor of Nyasaland, Sir Charles Calvert Bowring, for which he would be awarded a CMG. Seth had planned one last visit to England to coincide with Bowring relinquishing the governorship on 30 May 1929. He then intended to retire before the appointment of a new governor and settle in Nyasaland at a tea estate he had recently purchased. But the plans were ruined by an illness which forced him to cancel his passage home at the beginning of June. The illness was diagnosed as stomach and bladder cancer, and he returned to England for treatment a month later. He ended his days at St. Thomas's Hospital, Lambeth, and died there on 27 August 1929, aged fifty-four.

Seth's beloved sister Mildred was the beneficiary of his estate and received his medals, decorations, and citations. These have passed through successive generations and now reside with his great-nephew.

N.B. Seth's obituary states that he was never married and his Will, signed at St Thomas's Hospital a fortnight before his death, makes no mention of a wife or child. Yet numerous websites, including CricketArchive and Wikipedia, claim that Seth was the father-in-law of Argentinian cricketer Frederick Francis Keen. Keen, however, was married to Margaret Oswald née Brown, born in Argentina in 1916, the daughter of James Brown, a rancher in Mar Del Plata. The veracity of this claim is therefore open to doubt, yet it is such an extraordinary one to make if not true, that reservations remain. Margaret Brown's mother Lilian was in Bournemouth during the summer of 1915 with husband James and two small children, and she was in England to give birth to a third child before returning to Argentina where she had Margaret in 1916. Seth was in England in 1915, before his posting to France, so it is therefore theoretically possible, if highly implausible, that Seth was Margaret Brown's biological father.

LESLIE PHILLIPS MARSHALL [218]

Leslie was very close to his younger brother Alan (A.G. Marshall **[225]**) because they were born in India then packed off to board at Taunton School. Both were intellectually gifted as well as being fine sportsmen. They were born fifteen months apart in Salem near Madras (Chennai) but their parents, the Reverend George Charles Marshall, and Mary Phoebe (known as Minnie) née Phillips, were working as missionaries much further south in Parvathipuram, Andhra Pradesh.

Leslie made four appearances for Somerset in 1913 and 1914 while studying medicine at Cambridge before cricket and studies were cut short by the First World War. He served in France from November 1915 as a captain in the West Yorkshire Regiment for which he was awarded a Military Cross in 1918. He was discharged with shrapnel injuries to his leg and buttocks, and it probably saved him from the usual fate suffered by junior officers at the front. After the War ended, Leslie and Alan returned to Cambridge to continue their respective studies. With parents still overseas (they eventually retired to Burnham-on-Sea) they had no home base in England. The 1921 census shows the affinity they had for their alma mater as they were both down from college and staying at the school as visitors. Alan would soon return to the school permanently as its science teacher.

After qualifying as a doctor, Leslie worked at various London hospitals which is where he probably met his future wife Catherine Mary née Hext. Catherine

Leslie Marshall as he appears in the photograph of the Quantock CC team that toured Scotland in August 1937

was also a doctor working in London, including a spell as the assistant medical officer at the Maudsley Hospital. By the time of their marriage in 1931, Leslie was a GP in the Taunton practice of Marshall, MacGregor, and Shore, first living in Staplegrove Road then moving to Blagdon Hill where they lived out their lives.

Leslie continued to play local club cricket in Taunton and for Somerset Stragglers throughout the 1930s and he regularly featured in Taunton School fixtures where as late as 1937, aged forty-four, he was still dominating matches with bat and ball. He made seven further appearances for Somerset between 1919 and 1931. His final match against the New Zealanders at Bath was his best performance, twice improving his best score with 29 in the first innings and 37 in the second.

Every effort was made to find a decent cricketing image of Leslie in VOL.1 without success, so it is pleasing to include one here. His good friend Fred Elam, a master at Taunton School and a teammate at Taunton Deane CC, started a touring side to play during the summer holidays and it was too much for Leslie to resist. The touring side, comprising masters and old boys of Taunton School, called themselves the Quantock Cricket Club. The first week-long tour visited Yorkshire in 1934 followed by Lancashire in 1935 where six matches were played. Further tours were arranged for Sussex in 1936, Scotland in 1937 and Kent in 1938. Always arranged for the last week in August, there were more serious matters to occupy the players in 1939. The tour survived the Second World War but only just, visiting Sussex in 1948 and Essex in 1949. By this time, Leslie had confined his kit to the loft. He died in Taunton on 28 February 1978, aged eighty-four.

N.B. The photographs of Quantock CC, a team lost to the mist of time, were in an album kept by Edward Roy Nesfield and sold at auction in 2020. His image can be found in the photograph included on page 179. It is worth recalling Edward's influence on Somerset club cricket. He was a useful allrounder, captaining the 1st XI at King's School, Worcester and playing three matches for Worcestershire after the First World War before his move to Somerset as a land agent. He managed Lord Carnarvon's estates around Dulverton and Colonel Herbert's residence at Pixton Park. Edward played his club cricket for Minehead and was a key playing member of the Somerset Stragglers throughout the 1920s and 1930s. He was a regular tourist for Quantock CC and the Devon and Somerset Wanderers and in 1933 came close to selection as an amateur for Somerset. He lived at 'Wickets' in Bridgtown and was an active member of the community for sixty years being responsible for the revival of Bridgtown CC, renowned for its pretty, sloping ground in the Exe Valley.

PHILIP ARNOLD FOY [234]

The biography in VOL.2 paints a colourful picture of Philip's adult life spent in South America. The main image used in the biography was of him in later life, but this photograph is a rare example of him in action.

P. A. FOY BOWLS A "NO-BALL"

A. C. MacLaren's master in the Argentine here shows how at the instant of letting go it is possible to bowl a ball without having one foot on the ground behind the crease. N. A. Knox has also been known to do this

It was taken during the match against Surrey at Bath in 1920 which featured in the *Land & Water* article by E.H.D. Sewell. The mention of A.C. MacLaren refers to him clean bowling the great batsman twice (it was *not* a pair as assumed in VOL.1). It occurred while Philip was playing for Argentina in 1912 during the series played in Buenos Aires against the MCC tourists. These matches were deemed first-class and in all such matches for Argentina he took 31 wickets at 16.41 and achieved his best bowling figures of 7 for 84. Sewell's mention of the 'NO BALL' refers to the 1884 code requiring the bowler to deliver the ball with one foot on the ground behind the bowling crease, and within the return crease.

Philip may have only briefly lived in Axminster, where he was born on 16 October 1891, but his Somerset credentials were strong – his GP grandfather Henry Foy was born in Taunton and lived above his practice in Middle Street, a cricket ball's throw from the County Ground. His father Arnold, a telegraphy superintendent, was posted to St Vincent, Cape Verde within the year which is where Philip's brother and sister were born. This was followed by a posting to Brazil where the parents soon realised it was no place to bring up children. His mother Mary returned to England with her children in July 1897.

The two boys were sent to Hadleigh House School where Philip's precocious sporting ability was soon recognised. In a school match against St Catherine's School, Littlehampton, aged eleven, he opened the batting scoring 89 of his school's 203 runs and took 5 for 0 to have St Catherine's all out for 2 runs (both leg-byes). The boys then went to Bedford Grammar School where Philip was in the 1st XI in 1908 and 1909. He retained his links with the school well into the 1930s playing for Old Bedfordians in Argentina.

Somerset would have dearly loved to have had Philip for more than one season. They had the First World War to thank for even that small mercy because he would not have returned to England otherwise. He was a much-decorated war hero, thrice mentioned in despatches and awarded an MC, and after the war he decided to stay on and take the associate examinations of the Institute of Civil Engineers. He clearly had time to spare because he played in almost all of Somerset's first-class matches during the 1920 season. He took 47 wickets at 21.59 apiece with his best bowling figures of 6 for 68.

His examinations passed by September 1920, he went back to Argentina and never returned, save for three months in 1930 after his mother's death. She died in May 1930 and was buried in St Peter and St Paul's churchyard, North Curry. Philip returned in July 1930 to sort his mother's affairs and accepted one last invitation to play for Somerset against Glamorgan in August.

To the likes of Arthur Wellard, Somerset's opening bowler in the match, Philip would have been regarded as some privileged amateur depriving a fellow professional of his appearance fee. And if Arthur was unaware of Philip's past reputation, his performance in the match (out for a duck in his single innings and 3 overs, 0 for 12) would have confirmed Arthur's opinion of amateur entitlement. Philip returned to Argentina where he died, a bachelor, in the British Hospital, Buenos Aires on 12 February 1957, aged sixty-five.

GEORGE EDWARD HUNT [247]

George's date of birth was *not* 30 September 1896, the date recorded in all official sources. Further research has confirmed it could not have been correct because his brother Willie was born just sixteen days after this date. Nor was he born exactly a year earlier as stated in the 1939 census. His true date of birth was 30 September 1894, and it should come as no surprise that, while sticking to the day and month of birth, the wily professional coming late to county cricket would knock a couple of years off his age. Arthur Wellard was a prime example of this practice. Would it have made much of a difference to the Somerset authorities had they known he was approaching twenty-seven years of age on debut in 1921?

George's birthplace was correctly recorded as Pill. The village is situated on the southern bank of the Avon, near Easton-in-Gordano a few miles from Bristol docks. It is easy to imagine George's father James Henry Hunt, a former seaman born in Pill, making his daily trip by small boat down the river Avon to the docks where he worked as a pilot. James married Eliza Thomas, also born in Pill, who was the daughter of the Bristol and Cardiff pilot, William Thomas. James and Eliza had nine children, two of whom died during childhood and a third, the previously mentioned Willie, was just twenty years old when he was killed in France in 1917. George was the third-born child, and fifteen years later Hubert (H. Hunt **[334]**), known as Bert, was the last.

George was the archetypal bowling pro; never complaining about workload and playing through the aches and pains of the daily grind. Not playing meant not being paid. In July 1927 (*not* 1937 as stated in VOL.2) a missed match ended a run of eighty consecutive matches. In his 233 first-class matches between 1921 and 1931, all played for Somerset, he took 386 wickets at 32.87

and his batting was decent enough to score a century and eighteen fifties. The century came at Clarence Park in 1928 against Glamorgan.
By 1931, approaching thirty-seven in real years by then, he was losing pace and his place to the younger duo of Wellard and Andrews. George took on the job as professional at Kilmarnock CC and held it until 1934 when he recommended his replacement, his younger brother Bert. George continued to play locally for Lodway CC until moving with his wife Maud and son George to the Redcliffe Bay area of Portishead.
In 1937, after Weston-super-Mare CC got wind that George was living just up the A38, the club offered him employment as the professional coach and groundsman at the North Parade ground. And for the next three seasons it gave Weston the best club bowling attack in the West Country outside of county cricket with George teaming up with the two Jims, J. Priddy **[319]** and J. Bridges **[203]**.
By this time, George's bowling had morphed from medium-pace to slow right-arm, but he continued to bamboozle the local club cricketers. In 1938, at the North Parade ground, he scored 174 against Bath CC and then proceeded to bowl them out for 66. George took 5 wickets and the rest fell to the two Jims. And in 1939, it must have been greatly satisfying for George to take 4 wickets against a full Somerset XI when the county side played Weston in a benefit match for his good friend Arthur Wellard. In what was most likely his last match for Weston on the 28 August 1939 against Yeovil CC he took 7 wickets which included the wicket of son George. George jnr, was making up the numbers for Yeovil, batting at number eleven and was clean bowled by his father for a duck.
It was not the last cricket match that George played. Although there is no evidence that he was with Weston after the Second World War, he was persuaded to make a cameo appearance at Kilmarnock CC's centenary match in 1952 when Len Hutton was a guest player.
VOL.2 repeated Peter Roebuck's claim in From *Sammy to Jimmy* that George was a carpet salesman after retirement but there is no evidence that this was his means of supplementing his professional cricket wages and there is no mention of this occupation in his obituary. The obituary states that after a life of professional cricket he worked as a builder and decorator. George died at home in Valley Road, Redcliffe Bay, after a short illness, on 22 January 1959, at his real age of sixty-four.

REGINALD ADDINGTON INGLE [268]

Reggie's mother Maria Taylor, a vicar's daughter, was packed off to Penzance where she discretely gave birth to him on 5 November 1903. It had been six and a half months since marrying Reggie's father Frank Seaton Ingle, a Bath solicitor. Presumably, she delayed her return to Bath until it would not have entered the vicar's head to question the unusual size of his infant grandson. Reggie was educated at Oundle School and was in the 1st XI for his last two years at school in 1921 and 1922. During the summer vacations he would play for Lansdown CC, and it was during the summer of 1921 that he first attracted Somerset's attention. The Somerset Stragglers put out a strong XI at the County Ground to play Lansdown that August. Several Stragglers were current Somerset players and Arthur Newton, keeping wicket, had a close-up view of the seventeen-year-old Reggie. Reggie opened the batting for Lansdown and batted soundly for his 84 runs. Messrs Woods and Daniell would doubtless have been taking note in the pavilion. The photograph below was in the album belonging to E.R. Nesfield, referred to on page 175, and is included here because it has a fine early image of Reggie playing for the Somerset Stragglers.

*Reggie Ingle is standing second from left. The Rev A.J. Hook **[109]** is seated in the central captain's position and A.S. Bligh **[265]** is seated on the ground left. E.R. Nesfield is seated far left*

Reggie went from Oundle to Jesus College, Cambridge. He played 8 matches for the University 1st XI during his last two years at college but never got beyond a score of 29 and finished with an average of 9.20. It was never enough to earn him a blue.

Reggie on debut against Essex, walking out after lunch on Day 3 with partner Jack MacBryan

Reggie was playing for Incogniti at Sidmouth when he was summoned to play against Essex at the County Ground, beginning 22 August 1923. The match was badly affected by rain, and it was not until the end of the second day that Somerset batted. Overnight at 24 for 1, Somerset had collapsed to 65 for 5 when Reggie went out to bat. He coped with the drying wicket where others had failed, scoring 54 in a 97-run partnership with Jack MacBryan. They were the only ones to reach double figures in the innings, Jack ending with a century. And when Reggie was out, the Essex players joined in with the crowd in clapping him all the way to the pavilion.

Reggie kept his place for the last two championship matches, but there was to be no repeat of his debut innings, his four innings yielding just 10 runs. He played for Somerset against his University at Fenners in 1924 when he made scores of 50 and 35, but it was still not enough to earn a blue. Somerset persevered with the young man when he returned to Bath for the summer, and it was to be the beginning of a lengthy career in which he played 309 times for the county between 1923 and 1939. As a batsman, his first-class batting average of 18.75 is unexceptional. Yet he often made runs when most needed, notably his two centuries in a match against Middlesex in 1928, and twice he reached a thousand runs in a season. His best year was in 1932, his first as captain, when he scored 1,083 runs which included three of his ten first-class centuries.

He remained as captain for the next five seasons and several pre-war professionals nominated him as the best amateur captain they had played under. And this despite Reggie having to discipline and drop two professionals, after some unreported social indiscretion on a northern tour. He was known to treat professionals and amateurs with the same courtesy, and he was uncompromising in the way he led the team. There was one interesting quote from him following the bodyline controversy on the 1932/33 Ashes tour. Asked about a daily newspaper's statement that the county captains had come to a gentlemen's agreement not to employ the tactic, he responded with "I have entered no agreement. If Somerset had the bowlers, we should do it ourselves". Reggie would no doubt have continued to lead the county after 1937 but for some manoeuvring behind the scenes which caused animosity between him and the Somerset authorities. The hard feeling would fester for several decades until an olive branch was offered with the award of honorary life membership in 1977. The official reason for his resignation was pressure of work from his legal practice in Bath, which makes good sense. And the animosity could not have been so terminal as he played eleven matches for the county in 1938 and 1939. Some were played under the leadership of his successor, E.F. Longrigg **[279]**, and others were captained by Reggie when Longrigg was unavailable. Interestingly none of these matches were at the County Ground, which fuelled the claim of animosity between the parties. Nine were at the Bath and Weston festivals and two were at Bournemouth, when he was doubtless taking advantage of the location to give his wife Pip and their three children a seaside treat. There was never a chance that Reggie would return to first-class cricket after the War. He lived a long life, dying in an Oakhill nursing home not far from his Timsbury home. He died on 19 December 1992, aged eighty-nine.

WALTER THOMAS LUCKES [269]

Somerset have always had decent wicketkeepers, but few have been as good as Wally behind the stumps. He ranks second behind H.W. Stephenson **[367]** in the total number of dismissals in a career for Somerset (827 victims) and there is little doubt that he would have surpassed Harold Stephenson's record if he had not missed eighty-two matches because of ill health during the middle part of his career, between the 1929 and 1932 seasons.

This candid photograph of Wally, wearing a Bridgwater CC blazer, was taken in his back garden before the start of his Somerset career. It was one of his personal photographs

Wally was born in Lambeth, London on 1 January 1901. He first played for Somerset in 1924 but it was not until 1927 that he was engaged professionally when taking over from the amateur M.L. Hill **[261]**. He played in most of the 1928 championship matches but worrying bouts of severe fatigue were the first signs that all was not well with Wally's health. Mr A.F. Davey, the Somerset secretary writing in the 1929 annual report, spoke of how he had suffered a 'break down in health' before the start of the 1929 season calling it 'a severe blow for the side'.

It was also a severe blow for the young man himself and in the event, he missed the first two-thirds of the 1929 season while various tests were conducted. In 1930 he only managed to play in six of the early championship matches before breaking down again and he took no part in 1931 when it was reported that Wally was diagnosed as suffering from a strained heart. His doctors had advised that he should not subject himself to any continuous strain such as playing county cricket.

Somerset had managed his absence in 1930 by calling upon A.G. Marshall **[225]**, F.L. Pratten **[309]** and A.H.S. Clark **[308]** among others but it was far from satisfactory. The county's annual trial for young hopefuls in late April 1931 became, according to the *Western Mail,* 'SOMERSET'S SEARCH FOR A STUMPER' involving not two but three wicketkeepers. K.G. Harvey, late of Blundell's School and on the staff at Wills in Bristol, kept for Reggie Ingle's XI and was said to have made a favourable impression. Fred Pratten and Jack Andrews alternated for J.C. White's XI. The trial was inconclusive and the Somerset committee decided they could make do with Fred Pratten. Meanwhile, K.G. Harvey (more of Kenneth Harvey on page 235) tried his luck with Gloucestershire and C.J. 'Jack' Andrews, from Weston-super-Mare and the brother of W.H.R. Andrews **[305]**, went on to play seven first-class matches for Hampshire.

But the strategy failed when Fred Pratten, well known for his club-level batting at Midsomer Norton CC, was unable to match the runs that Wally would have scored. Somerset were forced to re-engage F.S. Lee **[297]** from late June. They had let him go at the end of the 1930 season and, as well as opening the innings, he was given the gloves for most of the remaining season.

In total, Wally missed 69 championship matches during these three seasons. It did not stop him playing cricket for his beloved Bridgwater CC, nor did his weak heart stop him from scoring a century in July 1931 against a strong Bath CC XI which included eight first-class cricketers. Thanks almost entirely to Wally's century, Bridgwater beat Bath in the last over, the Bath club's first defeat since 1929. Wally followed this with a half-century against Taunton CC in August.

And his illness did not prevent him from coping with the excitement of getting married in September 1931 to Winifred Anne Norman, a local girl who lived along the Wembden Road. That winter he was scoring goals for Bridgwater Hockey Club and the following spring he turned out for Bridgwater in May and June 1932. But it was not until the fourteenth championship match of the 1932 season that Wally returned to the fold in the match against Leicestershire on 6 July 1932. There was no fuss or fanfare and barely a mention of his ill health save to say that he would play regularly 'if his health permits'.

And did he play regularly! Thereafter he missed just one of the 214 championship matches up to the end of the 1939 season and that was not on account of a strained heart. This was when he received a blow to the head while batting against Glamorgan and as a precaution missed the next match against Essex at Colchester in July 1936. It is a remarkable achievement for someone with a heart condition. He continued to play for Somerset after the Second World War, topping the first-class wicketkeeping list in 1946 with 75 catches or stumpings. And he played on until Somerset found a suitable replacement in Harold Stephenson. Wally played his last match for Somerset against Cambridge in June 1949.

R.C. Robinson-Glasgow writing in the *Tatler* was one of the first with news of his retirement:

With as little flourish as he kept wicket for Somerset, Walter Luckes has retired from the first-class game in his forty-ninth year. Bowlers know most about a wicketkeeper and down West we rated Luckes very high indeed. Apart from the catches he snapped up, his dry comments between overs, on mankind and the conduct of fate, cheered and tickled his companions.... In his early times Luckes was no mean batsman, but a weak heart caused him to sink to a position not far above the extras where many a bowler, expecting a rabbit, found a tiger.

Somerset gave him a testimonial in 1950, for which he received £1,800. Then in 1951, the club somewhat surprisingly announced that fifty-year-old Wally was registererd to Somerset for the 1951 season and would be available 'on a part-time basis'. They were perhaps fearing an England call-up for Harold Stephenson which never came and conseqently Wally was never needed. He worked for the South Western Electricity Board at Bridgwater and lived the rest of his life with his wife Winifred at Quantock Road, Bridgwater. Wally was an octogenarian when he died despite the much-publicised heart condition. He died on the 27 October 1982, aged eighty-one.

CECIL LEACH [271] and ESMÉ THOMAS LANCELOT REED HAYWOOD [275]

Occasionally a gem of a photograph surfaces which has such clarity that it would have added to or replaced several of the images contained in VOL.2. The photograph of the team (opposite) that played Cambridge University on 24 to 26 June 1925 is no exception and it would have been particularly useful for close-up images of some of the lesser lights that that appeared in this match. Cecil Leach and Tom Haywood were not qualified to play for Somerset by birth and their treatment in this regard was as different as their backgrounds and positions in life. Cecil, from Littleborough in Rochdale, the son of a cotton weaver and a Lancashire League professional, who was in his thirty-first year, needed to serve a period of residency before being allowed to play championship cricket. He was part-way through this requirement while being employed by the Ashton Gate Brewery and playing for Long Ashton CC.

Standing L-R: J. Bridges, ***C. Leach****, R.W. Draper, R.F. Trump (scorer), C.C.C. Case,* ***E.T.L.R. Haywood****, J.W. Lee;*
seated L-R: M.L. Hill, J.C.W. MacBryan, P.R. Johnson, R.A. Ingle, G.E. Hunt

Tom Haywood, on the other hand had a father who was a solicitor and a mother from a wealthy land-owning family. And he had the full set of initials. He seems to have had no barrier playing in his debut championship match a fortnight earlier. Tom was a Cambridge University undergraduate at the time and appears to have earned his selection as a top-order batsman through his links with the Somerset Stragglers. If there was any residency qualification at all, it may have had something to do with his divorced father's second wife who hailed from Chard. His championship debut had been against Sussex at Horsham, and it must have been with that county's acquiescence as Tom was born in Worthing. Another example of there being one rule for the amateurs, and another for the professionals.

This photograph not only offers additional images of the pair who briefly turned out for the county. It also has the unique claim to be the only known Somerset team photograph related to the 1925 season. As the backdrop in the photograph clearly shows, the match was not played at Fenners as stated in VOL.2. It has been taken at the back of the pavilion at the Recreation Ground, Bath. The match ended in a comfortable victory for the University thanks to the batting of two future England cricketers, Edward Dawson and Kumar Duleepsihji, and the bowling of a future Somerset cricketer and Millfield headmaster, R.J.O. Meyer **[338]**.

Another lesser light featured in the photograph is R.W. Draper **[277]**. Bob was training to be a solicitor in Bristol and was a left-arm fast bowler for Bath CC, much later a stalwart bowler and captain for Lodway CC. He was making the first of his three appearances for Somerset. The young man dressed in civilian clothes in the above photograph is Reginald Frederick Trump who had only recently taken over from Somerset's long-time scorer, Scott McCaulay after he had left for business reasons. Reginald was employed as a clerk, or assistant secretary, by Somerset and as the club scorer during the summer months. He remained at the club until terminal illness forced his retirement in 1952.

J.W. Lee **[276]** was another debutant in this match. Like Cecil Leach, he was having to qualify by residency for the county. In Jack's case, he was playing as a professional for Lansdown CC and his contribution to Somerset cricket would be significantly greater than that achieved by the three lesser lights. It leads nicely into the next biography of the Lee brothers.

JOHN WILLIAM LEE [276] and FRANK STANLEY LEE [297]

There were three cricketing brothers. Henry, known as Harry, was the oldest and the most talented. When Harry made his debut for Middlesex, aged twenty, in 1911, John William, known as Jack, was nine years old, and Frank was six. The Lee family lived in Barrett Street, off Oxford Street at the time and it comprised parents, Henry, and Annie, the three sons, two daughters and a niece, all eight of them living in a two-up, two-down property. In due course, Jack and Frank followed their older brother to Lord's but were forever in his shadow (Harry played 402 first-class matches for Middlesex and had one Test Match on the 1930/31 tour of South Africa).

Jack made one first-class appearance for Middlesex in 1923 against Somerset at Taunton where in his only innings, batting low in the order, he was run out without scoring. Frank made two appearances for Middlesex in 1925. This was not a fair reflection of their abilities. It was just such a hard team to break into with their brother Harry and Nigel Haigh (a Middlesex regular and England Test player) opening the innings and then followed by such players as Jack Hearne, Patsy Hendren, Walter Robins and Gubby Allen.

It was time to move on. Jack was first to leave for Somerset and after residential qualification made his championship debut in 1927. Frank followed two years later, coaching, and playing for Bath CC while qualifying, and making his championship debut in 1929.

Both brothers played throughout the 1929 season, featuring as middle-order batsmen with Jack usually given a higher spot. Jack, the allrounder, could also be relied upon to take fifty to sixty wickets in a season. There were no established openers with Messrs Rippon, Young, Longrigg, Northway and Ingle sharing the duties that year. It was much the same in 1930 although Jack occasionally opened with Tom Young. It was against Worcestershire in mid-June 1931 when the brothers were first asked to open together.

Frank had been released in 1930 but was re-engaged to solve a short-term wicketkeeping problem caused by the absence of Wally Luckes. This was Frank's first game back and no doubt it was the captain Reggie Ingle who had the bright idea to get him to open with Jack. It worked. In Somerset's first innings, they produced an opening partnership of 83 and Frank went on to make a fifty. Two games later they made a century partnership to set up a ten-wicket victory.

The brothers in close-up, Frank (left) and Jack (right), from a photograph of the team that played Worcestershire at Amblecote in 1933

The brothers continued as opening partners for the next four seasons, 1932 to 1935, during which both scored over 1,000 runs each season. At the end of the 1935 season, the club made the announcement that all the professionals would be retained except for Jack Lee who had accepted an offer to coach Mill Hill School, London. It has been claimed that Jack was using the offer to obtain a counteroffer from Somerset, but if that was the case the plan failed. He did play a few matches for Somerset in 1936 during the

August holidays which suggests there were no hard feelings.
The recently acquired press photograph of the Lee brothers, shown below, would have found a place in VOL.2. It was taken during a purple patch towards the end of the 1934 season when they scored 213, 119 and 146 in consecutive opening partnerships. Frank is on the left of picture, Jack on the right.
Frank continued to play throughout the seasons 1936 to 1939 and had his best season in first-class cricket in 1938, scoring 2,019 runs, including seven

centuries, at an average of 44.86. He returned for one full season after the war and featured spectacularly in Somerset's lowest innings score during his benefit year of 1947. It was at Bristol and a holiday crowd of 12,000 saw Somerset skittled out for 25 on a pitch that had lost its top. It would have been worse but for Frank's 17 runs scored before being bowled by the county's tormentor, Tom Goddard, who took 5 wickets in 7 balls.
Frank became a respected first-class, international umpire, living a short walk from Lord's. He died on 30 March 1982, aged seventy-six. Jack was less fortunate than his brother. He was killed in action in Normandy on 20 June 1944, aged forty-two.

HERBERT FRANCIS THOMAS BUSE [303]

There was so much to write about Bertie's life in VOL.2, that some aspects, such as his early life and his enormous contribution to Bath rugby and cricket, could not be given the coverage it deserved. There is now the chance to put this right.

His father, Francis Buse was a Welshman born in Aberdare who as a young man played rugby and rowed for Cardiff. He made a living as a commercial traveller, moving around the UK. He married a young woman called Bessie Bennett from Barton Regis and they had a son, Philip Henry Graham Buse, in 1897 while living in Manchester. But the union was mired in tragedy. Bessie died two years later in Bristol; and Philip would be killed in action on 5 November 1916, aged nineteen, while serving with the Worcester Regiment during the Battle of the Somme.

Bertie's father was remarried to Edith Watts while he was in Worcester, then returned to Manchester where the couple had a son and daughter. By the time Bertie came along, on 5 August 1910, the family had settled in Horfield, Bristol but then moved to Bath where Bertie spent his formative years. Francis died in Bath when Bertie was fifteen years old. And within a year of his father's death, Bertie had become well established in the Bath CC 1st XI, a team that could call on nine Somerset players.

His medium pace bowling was already displaying the accuracy and steadiness that would be a hallmark of his Somerset career. So much so that he was entrusted to open the bowling for Bath CC at the tender age of sixteen. In one match during the 1927 season, Bertie took 6 for 32 against Timsbury CC. The following year he played a key part in a Bath Area XI which won the inaugural Somerset County Cricket Club Knock-Out Cup. Bath Area had easily beaten a strong Bristol & District XI in the semi-final of the Competition thanks to the bowling of Bertie Buse and Victor Woodward, the two young Bath players in the photograph overleaf. The pair were even more destructive in the final at the County Ground, bowling twenty overs apiece and dismissing the Taunton Area XI for 68 runs. Bertie's figures were 5 for 22. Walter Whiting, the Bath Area captain, singled out Bertie for special praise at the presentation ceremony, and with performances like these, with and against established county cricketers, it was thus a matter of time before Somerset came calling. The photograph is taken from a scrapbook kept by Bertie:

L-R: C.H.C. Taylor (Secretary Bath Area cricket), V.L. Woodward (Bath CC), W.C. Whiting (Bath CC captain) and H.T. Buse. This newly created trophy is the Somerset County Cricket Club KO Challenge Cup which the Bath Area won at the County Ground on 12 September 1928

Bertie made his debut for Somerset in July 1929, a month short of his nineteenth birthday. It would have been a month earlier against Cambridge at Bath but at the last minute, in anticipation of a dead wicket, the offer to play was withdrawn. Mr A.F. Davey, the county secretary, took the trouble to write to Bertie. He wrote 'we are sorry to disappoint you, but it is no good you trying to bowl in your first match when conditions are dead against you.' It may have been something of a relief to Bertie who had intimated that he did not want to make his debut in his home city.

His debut against Surrey was a baptism of fire with Hobbs in imperious form scoring a double-hundred in Surrey's only innings of 555. Bertie opened the bowling with Arthur Wellard but after six tidy overs was mercifully spared from another spell. He acquitted himself well with the bat, scoring 16 and 21 in Somerset's innings and 158 run defeat, which was more than most of the team achieved. During the next seven seasons he was only called upon to play in twenty-five championship matches while he made his living working as a clerk for a Bath solicitor.

Somerset signed him as a professional at the start of the 1938 season. During the winters he kept himself fit playing rugby and table tennis, the Bath singles champion six years in succession in the case of the latter sport. He first played as full back for the Bath 1st XV against Devonport Services in January 1930. He would play regularly in this position or at centre for Bath throughout the 1930s and, in October 1934, he was selected to play for the Somerset XV against Hampshire.

There was further personal tragedy during the 1930s. Having lost his only step sibling during the First World War and his father in 1926, his brother John, known as Jack, died on 25 May 1932 from injuries sustained when his motorbike collided with a car at a crossroads in Sutton Waldron. Then his mother Edith died in 1939 after years of poor health. This was probably the catalyst for his marriage to a local girl, Elsa Kathleen Nash, in January 1940.

He continued to play for Bath CC during the war while working for the civil service in Bath and until he was called up to serve in the RAF in December 1942. There were no overseas postings and he managed to play charity cricket for teams like the RAF and London Counties. After the war he returned to Somerset better than ever and three of his best four seasons with the ball occurred in the post-war years.

Having played in every championship match during the 1953 season, he was probably expecting a better offer from Somerset than a one-year contract extension. This was rejected and the curtain was brought down on his first-class career which had spanned twenty-five years. He had played 304 matches for Somerset, taking 657 wickets at 28.77 apiece.

There were several highlights. Bertie himself recalled his 7 for 26 against Northamptonshire in 1949 and his 6 for 23 against Yorkshire at Bramhall Lane in 1951, both in a losing cause. His career best bowling figures of 8 for 41, also in a losing cause, was against Derbyshire in 1939. It is easy to recall Bertie's exploits with the ball and forget those with the bat. He was a very competent middle-order batsman who scored 10,238 runs at an average of 22.69 during his Somerset career, including seven centuries and forty-seven fifties. Four of his centuries came during the post-war years but his best score of 132 came in July 1938 against Northamptonshire at Kettering.

This is another photograph taken from Bertie's scrapbook. The scoreboard confirms that the photograph was taken during the morning session on the second day of the match against Northamptonshire on 5 June 1949. Bertie went on to make 42 runs in this innings mostly in partnership with Harold Gimblett.

Perhaps Bertie kept the photo to remind him that he almost brought off an unlikely victory single-handedly. Having helped his side set a modest target of 64 runs to win, he had Northamptonshire tottering at 58 for 8 before their captain, the ex-Surrey and England cricketer Freddie Brown, making his debut for Northampton, got them home by two wickets. Berties's 7 wickets for 26 runs was one of his memorable bowling achievements mentioned above.

His departure at Somerset in 1953 came after a gruelling benefit year of social events and cricket matches against local cricket clubs across the county. In addition, he had chosen the championship match against Lancashire at the Recreation Ground, Bath as his official benefit match with the expectation that he would get a decent reception in his native city.

It must be the most infamous benefit match in Somerset history. A match that was over in a day. The weather prior to the match had been dreadful and the wicket was in a poor state. A plan to relay the pitches had been delayed by a Coronation year festival and when the Somerset groundsman Cec Buttle arrived to lay out the square he found it had no grass and was covered in moss. Desperate measures were needed involving bulls' blood, cow manure and grass cuttings rolled in. The teams must have been slightly alarmed when arriving to find a red tinge to the surface of the wicket. Bertie had a decent spell of bowling, taking 6 for 41 in Lancashire's innings of 158, but the total proved more than enough to beat the sum of Somerset's two innings. Roy Smith remembered the day well:

We were 55 all out, I was the top scorer on 9 and had the misfortune to run out Harold Gimblett for nought. Poor Harold was out by a mile. Lancashire got 158 and we were out for 79. The game finished by 5.30 and I was home by 7pm. It was terrible for Bertie, but the public rallied, and Lancashire sent him a generous cheque. The pitch didn't have any live grass on it and when the ball hit it a piece of turf lifted. When Cyril Washbrook was batting, he didn't know if he should put it back or throw it away!

His benefit year still raised £2,814 but it could have been better had the weather been kinder and the batting stronger. What better way of summing up Bertie's bowling than to quote from Wally Luckes, writing in the benefit brochure:

His worth as a player is well known and of his bowling, I would write just this: While keeping wicket for Somerset I heard more tributes to Bertie's bowling from the batsman at the crease, than to the bowling of any other player.

In refusing the one-year contract

extension Bertie was safe in the knowledge that he had the security of a job offer and a new life in South Africa. He left for Cape Town with Elsa and their two sons on Christmas Eve 1953 where Bertie was to begin an appointment as the rugby and cricket coach at King Edward's School in Johannesburg and he remained there for the best part of ten years. He became a very respected coach at the school helping many young cricketers reach provincial standards. In 1960 he informed Ron Roberts, the writer of *Sixty Years of Somerset Cricket*, that he had a very good pupil in his charge, a seventeen-year-old named Bacher. This was Dr Ali Bacher, the Test captain and hugely influential administrator who did so much for South African cricket on the cricket board after the collapse of apartheid in the 1990s.

Mine host at the St. Peter's Finger, in Lychett Minster, near Poole

In 1964, on return from South Africa, he took over as landlord of a public house in Dorset before it was time to retire to the city he had served so well as an outstanding sportsman. In 1984, he and Elsa moved into newly built accommodation for older people sited in the grounds of the Royal United Hospital, Bath. Bertie and Elsa were one of the couples presented to Princess Anne when she came to officially open the home in 1984. Bertie died there on 23 February 1992, aged eighty-one. His beloved wife, Elsa, remained in Bath where she died on 22 October 2009.

ROY SMITH [373]

In his days as a maths and sports teacher, Roy had been the sporting inspiration for a generation of schoolboys at Huish's Grammar School, but few of them would have been aware of the cricketing achievements of this modest man. For that was in the past and nothing to boast about although in later life he found time to set down his thoughts on his ten years with Somerset. He titled it *Leather on willow: Somerset County Cricket Club 1947-1956*.

The forty-four pages of closely typed script shine a light on what it was like to experience the ups and many downs of being a 1950s professional cricketer. He wrote with humour and self-deprecation. Much of it is personal but there are some interesting reflections on his cricket career which began in 1947. Roy's reminiscences and all the photographs shown here are courtesy of his daughter, Jill Cowles.

His performances for Somerset Colts against Devon Colts in 1947, when he took a lot of wickets and scored runs (86 in the first match, 79 in the return), was enough to produce an invitation to go to Taunton at the end of August so they could see him bowl. He had to bowl to E.R.T. Holmes, the captain of the Surrey team playing a championship match at the time. Roy remarks "As I was wearing flat pumps, I had to put a penny down to mark my run up and I was so excited I forgot to pick it up at the end."

The trial was a success, and he was offered a job in the office helping Nigel Daniell the assistant secretary in the morning with net practice in the afternoons. His wage was £2-10s-0d a week. Roy's cricket career was interrupted by national service in 1948 and 1949 and his 1st XI debut was delayed until June 1949 against Cambridge at Bath. He was only called upon to bowl seven overs in the match and was caught behind off a leg glance for a duck in the first innings. Faced with a similar ball from the same bowler in the second innings he got off the mark with a four and made a creditable 40 runs. Roy remarks "I batted with Wally Luckes, and I scampered as many runs as I could get but was reminded by him, he was no youngster. He was nearly fifty at the time."

Although he did not play another first-class match that year, it was enough to earn a contract for the following season. In his reminiscences he talks of early April net practices, of the senior professionals' casual attitude to training and of trying to impress the Somerset captain S.S. Rogers **[366]**. He made his championship debut against Surrey in June 1950 at the Oval but was not asked to bowl and had moderate success with the bat. He played another six matches in 1950 but spent most of the season frustratingly as twelfth man. Roy remarks that the duty "lost its glamour after a time and the lowest point came at Edgbaston when I was asked to lay off money for a bookmaker. Tremmy was friendly with Len Creed, and he was putting money on horses for him. I told him very sternly that this was not part of my 12th man duties and that I would not do it." (Tremmy was M.F. Tremlett **[360]** and Len Creed was a member of Somerset's Bath area committee and later credited with bringing Viv Richards to the club). It was probably not the most sensible thing to refuse his future captain.

VOL.3 mentioned Roy's apprenticeship with Tottenham Hotspur. His reminiscences include a comment on receiving his first wages from Somerset: "I received my first cheque but as I did not have a bank account. I had to ask the Tottenham Secretary, Reg Jarvis to cash it. I felt very rich then even though it was about £12"

He was in and out of the 1st XI in 1951 and had few opportunities to bowl. As an outstandingly athletic fielder he was probably being picked for this reason alone. Matters improved in 1952 after an early spell as twelfth man when the non-smoker was amused to be asked by Len Hutton to get him twenty Players cigarettes. "I did so but smiled because at the time he was advertising Craven A!" Then unexpectedly he was told he was playing at Old Trafford. In his words "It was a dream come true" but the match did not go Somerset's way. Cyril Washbrook scored a double century and when Somerset batted Brian Statham clean bowled Gimblett, Stephenson and Tremlett. Roy wrote "Every time a different stump flew out of the ground. I had a quick dash to the dressing room to get padded up. I got stuck in and got thirty runs before I was clean bowled by Statham too. We had to follow on and I was promoted to number 4, I had scored 45 not out before the rains came."

He kept his place and a month later got his first fifty at Taunton against Essex as well as having Doug Insole stumped in both innings. Harold Stephenson made the first stumping but then had a bout of sciatica and Harold Gimblett made the second stumping. He played in the last two games to see if he could become Horace Hazell's successor (the forty-three-year-old's contract was not being renewed for 1953). During the last match of the season at Grace Road the Leicestershire coach told Roy he could get him a three-year contract if he was interested, as opposed to the one year offered by Somerset, but he decided to stay with Somerset. He remarked "Years later I wondered if I had made the correct decision".

1953 was the best season of his short career. In May at Northants, Roy put on 156 with Harold Gimblett before the latter was out for 151 and Roy's innings of 86 not out came to an end when rain stopped play. And a month later at Frome, the venue for the return match against Worcestershire, Roy achieved his first and only century of his first-class career. He wrote "We batted first, and it was not long before I was in. I batted steadily and had a stand of 125 with Bertie Buse. When I reached 98, I had to play a couple of maiden overs. Then I got a ball that I cut square from Jack Flavell and set off like a scolded cat. I was so excited that I was out a couple of balls later. I went into the dressing room grinning from ear to ear and Ben Brocklehurst awarded me my county cap." There was also the battling 77 not out against the Australian tourists, in late August, in a season that saw him score 1,146 runs at an average of 26.13. But his bowling had not kept pace with his batting improvement. In July, against Hampshire, he was taken off after two overs when Cliff Walker

got after him and according to Roy "the skipper wrote me off as a bowler after that and I hardly bowled again for the rest of the season. I was embarrassed and upset after being hit so severely."

In 1954, Roy was seen to be more of a batsman than a bowler and was asked to open the batting with Harold Gimblett. He admitted being disturbed by the idea as he had not opened in any cricket, and he had good reason to be concerned facing the new ball with opening bowlers like Trueman and Statham as opponents. His worst nightmare came in April against Yorkshire, facing Trueman with an hour left to play and a wicket perfectly suited to his bowling. Roy wrote "Harold was out for a duck, and I made 4, both out to Trueman. In the second innings I got fed up with ducking his bouncers and I aimed to hook but I was through the shot and felt the ball touch my right ear. The finger was up, and I was out caught behind for 3. Sam Pothecary, the umpire, apologised later but I was so shaken I didn't mind. It was the fastest bowling I ever faced. After this game Harold Gimblett retired from first-class cricket. I was sorry to see him go but I was disappointed because he got me to be an opening bat, reluctantly I must add".

The opening experiment was not a success. He scored 474 runs in the season at an average of 13.94 and took just 5 wickets in the 23 matches played. In May 1955, he scored 46 and 65 in the match against the RAF which kept him in the side for the matches against Surrey, Yorkshire and Nottinghamshire and then was told that he was being 'rested', and that he should get some runs in the second team. Later in the season Roy was picked for the match against Worcestershire which Somerset won without much of a contribution from Roy. He wrote "I must say I began to lose my enthusiasm for professional cricket, and I did not see any future for me. Bill Andrews had become the coach and frankly I did not rate him. I needed someone to put me on the right lines. I am not sure whether I needed a sympathetic approach or a kick up the backside. I received neither". It was his last first-class match and Roy recalls "I had an odd feeling of relief. I began to think of alternatives."

The alternatives included an application to St Luke's College, Exeter to train as a teacher. He had married Mary Rutt in 1954, the daughter of 'Ginger' Rutt the deputy headmaster at Huish's Grammar School in Taunton and with the encouragement of his wife's family he accepted a place at St Luke's starting in September 1956. The deciding factor was the appointment of Somerset's first professional captain, Maurice Tremlett. In Roy's words "I realised whatever

I did I wouldn't get into the first team. He didn't rate me very highly and as captain he would have a say in selection. When Somerset won the opening game [against Essex] I went to the dressing room to congratulate Maurice on the win. I was told it was a team game and I then realise there was little chance for me however well I did in the second team".

Roy wrote to the club stating he would not be seeking a new contract. The last words in his reminiscences are "I wanted to leave on my terms and not give them the chance to sack me. So ended my time with Somerset County Cricket Club." Roy had played 96 first-class matches for Somerset. His 173 innings had produced 2,600 runs at an average of 17.13 runs. His 19 wickets were achieved at 57 runs apiece. Roy's reminiscences would have been familiar to many professional sportsmen of that era. Precious little attention was given to a player's wellbeing or mental health, and it is a sad indictment of the Somerset leadership and coaching in the 1950s. In Roy's case, we are left to conclude that he would have been a better cricketer with the right sort of encouragement. But Somerset's loss was Huish's gain. Hundreds of schoolboys benefitted from his ability to demystify algebra and many of them, under Roy's caring and sympathetic guidance, were given the belief that one day they too could become a professional sportsman, whether merited or not.

Roy died at Weston-super-Mare on 20 September 2020, *not* 22 September 2020, the author's mistake when writing the obituary published in *The Cricketer*.

MERVYN JOHN KITCHEN [429]

Mervyn may be amused to learn that he is the 428th player to represent Somerset in first-class cricket. VOL.1 mistakenly has Cambridge University as his first match on 29 June 1960, but he made his debut against Middlesex a month earlier on 28 May 1960. F.J. Herting **[428]**, whose debut was against Gloucestershire a week later, therefore becomes the 429th player.

GEOFFREY CLAYTON [443]

When Geoff Clayton died on 19 September 2018, aged eighty, at the Holland Close sheltered housing facility in Delph, near Oldham, the Somerset CCC

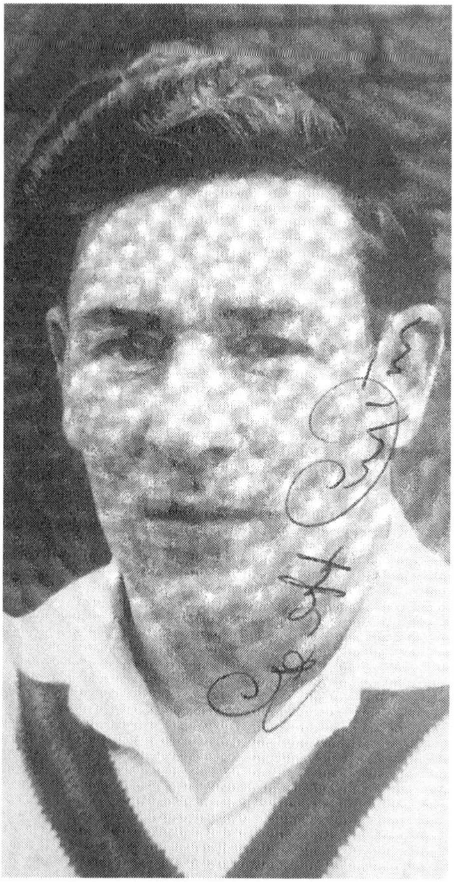

website included his VOL.3 biography as part of a tribute to the wicketkeeper who played for Somerset between 1965 and 1967. The reason he came to Somerset from Lancashire is well documented and it proved to be a great signing for the club which needed a replacement for Harold Stephenson. He played 89 matches for Somerset, taking 209 catches and making 33 stumpings, to average 2.72 dismissals per match. It is an average which far exceeds that achieved for Lancashire and ranks second behind R.J. Turner **[541]** on the list of all-time wicketkeeping averages for the club. Rob Turner is slightly ahead with a figure of 2.80.

The biography in VOL.3 states that he cut his teeth at Mossley CC, but thanks must go to Martin Lees for tweeting, @MartianKnees, that he started with Micklehurst CC, playing in the Saddleworth League.

Over one hundred and fifty people attended his funeral, which was part funded by Lancashire Cricket and the PCA, and the Club's chaplain Rev. Malcolm Lorimer and historian Keith Hayhurst spoke about his one-off character, surprisingly ecumenical in attending both chapels and church as well as being a regular at three public houses.

There were many stories told about Geoff and the church rang with laughter about someone who had no airs or graces. The number of people there was an indication of how much he was held in their affection.

ALEXANDER COLVIN AINSLIE [VOL.5, Page 1]

The Reverend Ainslie's fingerprints are all over the agreement to form a county club that followed the Gentlemen's match at Sidmouth in 1875. But despite a mention in VOL.1 and VOL.5, the man widely regarded as the founder of Somerset cricket has not received the coverage he deserves because he never made an appearance for the county that he helped set up.

Only a few basic biographical details were provided previously but given his contribution to cricket in Somerset this deserves to be rectified. And it provides an opportunity to unveil a photograph of Alexander which has appeared recently, courtesy of Messrs Robin Ansell, Allan Collier, and Phil Nichols, in *Secure the Shadow – Somerset Photographers 1839-1939*, published by the Somerset & Dorset Family History Society in 2018.

It is a carte de visite taken by William Morley, the same photographer who produced the Fullands cricket match image shown on page 217. The carte de visite would have been taken towards the late 1860s when William Morley established his business in East Street, Taunton and when Alexander was vicar of Corfe.

Alexander was born on the 14 July 1830 in Hammersmith, the son of William and Margaret née Colvin. He was one of eight children and the only one born in England while his parents were taking a break from his father's work in India. Their children were not the most robust and only two of Alexander's siblings, William, and Catherine, lived beyond childhood. His parents were of Scottish stock. His father was an independent merchant in Calcutta (Kolkata) and Margaret's father was also based there working for the East India Company. Alexander spent his first few years of life in India but had little recollection of their stay at Ballygunge, near Calcutta. Margaret and the children returned to London in 1835.

The return was most probably due to concerns over the health of the remaining children. Alexander was a delicate child and there were worries that he would suffer the same fate as most of his siblings. When Alexander was seven years old, he was sent, along with older brother William, to a small private boarding school in Lewes Crescent, Brighton, in the belief that the sea air would be good for the boys' health. It was here that Alexander acquired his love of cricket, attending Sussex matches and watching players like Box, Mynn,

Wisden and Lillywhite. Alexander was an exceptionally bright pupil and would have benefitted from a traditional public school education but that was not to be. After leaving Brighton in 1844, he endured a succession of private tutors, mostly Church of England curates, including more than a year spent with his mentor, the Reverend William Thomson at the theological college in Cuddesdon, Oxford. Alexander described his schooling as a farce and himself, aged seventeen, as "about as ignorant a boy as could be met with".

With much diligence and cramming he matriculated at University College, Oxford in March 1849, and three months later his father died at Woodhill, which had been the family home since 1840. Woodhill was a large country house with a thirty-acre garden and park near Send. It was here that Alexander developed his love of country pursuits, fishing, and hunting. And it was also here that, quite by chance, Alexander became linked to the county of Somerset. He had formed a close friendship with Francis Wheat Newton who shared his love of fishing, the countryside and cricket. Francis, stood to inherit Barton Grange in Pitminster but often stayed with family and friends near Woodhill. Francis and Alexander would fish and play cricket together. Francis was an average cricketer, and it is much more likely that his real interest lay in an affection for Alexander's sister, Catherine. When the Newton inheritance came through, Francis married Catherine in January 1849. Months later, Alexander's mother Margaret followed her daughter to the West Country where she resided at Lowlands in Wilton (now Wilton Close, Taunton). This is where Alexander would spend his time when down from the University either with his mother in Wilton or at 'Barton', 3 miles along the Trull Road. In due course, Francis and Catherine would produce a nephew for Alexander, one of Somerset's finest early cricketers, A.E. Newton **[63]**.

Alexander played cricket for his college XI but was never good enough to be considered for the University XI. He would later comment that sport came a poor second to his studies which he estimated lasted ten to eleven hours a day. His efforts were rewarded with a first-class honours degree in mathematics. Six months travelling with his college friends followed, through Europe, Asia, and North Africa, after which time he settled down to reading for deacon's orders. He was ordained to the curacy of Sopworth (Wiltshire) at Bristol Cathedral on 18 December 1853. A year later the priesthood of Corfe became vacant, and with a good word from Francis Newton, he became Corfe's priest in December 1854.

It is at Corfe where Alexander's drive, enthusiasm and organisational skills become apparent. During his fifteen years there, he enlarged the church, built a new tower, built a new school (his mother supplying much of the funds) and enlarged the vicarage to include stables and a coach house. At the same time, he set up various societies and unions and served as an examiner in mathematics for the Oxford Local Examinations Board. He lectured on his travels, especially his time in Palestine and the Sinai desert, and he produced pamphlets on various matters close to his heart such as *A FEW WORDS about INDIA, and the INDIAN MUTINIES* (1857) which sold for two pence and went to several reprints. And he still had the energy to indulge his passion for mechanical engineering, building a one-twelfth size steam engine called "Phoenix" which he demonstrated at local agricultural societies.

Alexander married a cousin of Francis Newton, whom he had first met at Woodhill when she was fifteen years old. Alexander and Catherine Susan Sadler married on 4 January 1855 and went on to have ten children, all born at Corfe, two of whom died in infancy. As for his cricket, in the absence of any decent cricket in Taunton, he founded Taunton Cricket Club, which played in Vivary Park but according to Alexander, the men were not very desirable adding that "on the whole I never enjoyed cricket less". The club folded with Alexander having to settle the club's debts comprised mainly of invoices for the champagne consumed at the club's matches! He then took membership of the Tiverton club and played matches there. Undeterred by previous experience of founding a club, he then set up the Corfe Cricket Club and persuaded his brother-in-law to provide a cricket field at Barton Grange.

The first match played by Corfe CC was against Taunton College School on 8 September 1859. Corfe won the toss and chose to bowl with Alexander and Myers Dallas Malden (M.D. Malden played one match for Gentlemen of Somerset in 1866) taking all the wickets that fell to a bowler. Alexander scored 28 of his team's innings of 67 and his dominance in the match indicates that both sides still had a lot to learn about the noble art. The *Taunton Courier* of 9 September 1859 reported 'On an excellent piece of ground, provided for their use by the kindness of F.W. Newton Esq, of Barton Grange, the members of the club have throughout the past summer assiduously devoted their evening hours to acquiring the mysteries of bowling and fielding, and to the practice of the abstruse art of batting'.

Judging by the scores and high number of extras, more assiduous practice was needed. Alexander would in future years strengthen the team with the likes of his son-in-law G.E.F. Peake **[59]**, F.T. Welman **[4]**, the Reed brothers from Fullands and his brother William, shortly to return from India. Perhaps Alexander enjoyed being a big fish in a small pond at Corfe and they certainly needed him. Alexander played his first match for Gentlemen of Somerset in 1861. It was a two-day match against Devon beginning 1 August 1861 and played on Martock CC's ground. Devon, batting first, were all out for 34, and Somerset scored 71 in reply, thanks to a top score of 20 from S.C. Voules **[VOL.5, page 36]** and the next highest score of 11 from extras. Devon managed just 65 in their second innings (20 of them in extras). The contribution from extras throughout the match says something about the standard of wicketkeeping, or perhaps more likely, the state of the Martock pitch. Somerset, needing 28 runs for victory, achieved it for the loss of one wicket with Alexander scoring the winning runs in his 16 not out. All considered, it was a decent debut for Alexander.

Other matches for the Gentlemen followed including the one against a Gloucestershire team in 1863 at Sydenham Field in Bath which contained W.G., E.M., Henry and Alfred Grace. Gloucestershire won by a comfortable margin, but Alexander managed scores of 20 and 8 in his two innings and took three catches. He made his last appearance for the Gentlemen in 1870. Alexander therefore had no reason to be at Sidmouth in 1875 having moved to Henstridge in the meantime. It seems likely that his supper invitation was specifically to chair the meeting which agreed to form the new county club and draw on his renowned organisational skills and influential contacts.

The move to Henstridge, in 1871, had been orchestrated by his interest in school boards and the Education Bill in parliament. His pamphlet *Notes on the Education Act* sold rapidly and so impressed the Bishop of Bath & Wells that he offered him the sadly neglected vicarage of Henstridge at a considerable higher stipend. Alexander, relishing a fresh challenge, immediately set about improving the lot of his 1300 parishioners and, over the twelve years he was there, the church was extended and improved, a new school built, and the 'wretched' vicarage updated. His years at Henstridge were not entirely happy due to illness and death in the family. He himself had bouts of illness, his wife caught diphtheria attributable to the miserably damp conditions in the vicarage, his mother had died at Wilton in 1873, and in February 1880 his dear son 'Alick' (his first-born son Alexander William Ainslie) was pronounced lost

at sea. He went down with three hundred other Royal Navy trainees on board *HMS Atlanta* in mysterious circumstances somewhere in the North Atlantic, a victim, not of the Bermuda triangle, but of poor planning and seamanship.
A second son, Cecil Colvin Ainslie, died in 1883, aged eighteen, but none of these tragedies seem to have affected his career. Additional responsibility was heaped upon him. In 1874, he was elected to the Lower House of Convocation, the synodical assemblies of bishops and clergy, and became an expert in the history and procedures of ecclesiastical law. He had further spells as the vicar of Langport (1888-1891) and Over Stowey (1891-1895) when he was given the living by Edward Stanley of Quantock Lodge, the father of the Somerset cricketer H.T. Stanley **[86]**. And then in December 1895 he accepted the canonry of Wells.
Further spells of illness followed, including being incapacitated by gout, but it did not stop him being appointed as Archdeacon of Taunton in 1896. He was based in Wells where he died, after a short illness, on 5 June 1903, aged seventy-two. He was laid to rest in the shade of Wells cathedral where a window was dedicated to him in 1905. A window in Corfe Church was also commissioned in his memory and dedicated in 1904.
Alexander Colvin Ainslie had led an exceptionally full life. Among the many eulogies, the Reverend Fish, secretary to the Diocesan Society, described him as 'vigorous in intellect, emphatic in his views, decisive in his methods, and possessed of a gentle and generous heart.' The Bishop of Bath and Wales praised his long service, calm judgement, and untiring work over forty years and said that the gap caused by his death would be "long felt and lamented". They might have also added that he was a born organiser, for that surely led to him lending his name to Somerset cricket history.

CYRIL JAMES WILSON [VOL.5, page 33]

Cyril was born in London on 21 August 1850 the son of Robert Wilson, an Anglican vicar in West Sussex who converted to the Roman Catholic church in 1858. It was described in the *Brighton Gazette* as a 'perversion to Romanism'. Cyril was brought up in that faith and completed his education at the English College in Rome. He was described as a chancer in VOL.5, and after various businesses ended in failure, he tried his luck in New York. He moved there

in 1881, aged thirty, and his wife Frances, the sister of F.T. Welman **[4]**, and their three young daughters joined him in the United States a year later. Two more daughters were born there.

VOL.5 referred to Cyril captaining Devon at rugby, but this is wrong. It was H.C. Wilson who captained Exeter and Devon during the 1870s. Cyril was a founder member and captain of Emeriti CC and he played for Somerset between 1876 and 1880. In his final match of that season, he scored 71 for Somerset in the innings defeat of Devon. His batting was very hit and miss and there is a clue to this in his score of 71. It contained 8 fours and 3 sixes. He would surely have played first-class cricket for Somerset had he not moved to New York.

He started playing for the Staten Island Cricket and Baseball Club in 1881. The club was founded in 1872, and with American cricket in its infancy and Cyril's experience as a county cricketer he very quickly established himself as the 1st XI opener before accepting the club captaincy in 1884. W. Massey **[13]**, his friend from their Somerset days, joined Cyril in 1886 and they played in the inaugural match at Staten Island's new ground at Livingstone. They can both be seen in the photograph that commemorated this match shown on page 20. Cyril and William also found time that year to play for Staten Island against the West Indians and a touring English XI captained by E.J. 'Ned' Sanders (of Devon CC and Exeter RFC). Cyril's brother-in-law, Tristram Welman **[4]**, kept wicket on the Sanders' tour.

Cyril headed the 1st XI batting averages in 1887 and won a silver cup for excellence in the field. His last season in 1888 was his best, again topping the batting averages with 35.20 with a top score of 108. It prompted the *New York*

Times to state that Cyril was 'without doubt the best and safest batsman on the team'. He also found time just before returning to England that September to play for an All New York XI against the Gentlemen of Ireland.

His business dealings were no more successful on his return, but he enjoyed a better time of it employed in the Special Intelligence Service based in Egypt during the First World War, attaining the brevet rank of major. Cyril died in Marylebone on 6 February 1927, aged seventy-six.

HENRY BOURDILLON [VOL.5, page 44]

This photograph was taken by William Morley whose studio was based at 27 East Street, Taunton from 1876 to 1890. Although the carte de visite was not attributed to Henry, there is no mistaking him when compared with the image used in VOL.5, which was taken while he was at Oxford.

Henry was born in Wimbledon on 25 January 1853 and educated at Haileybury, where he represented the school at cricket and rugby. At Queen's College, Oxford, he had more success at rugby than cricket, playing for the University XX in 1873 and 1874 and the XV in 1875 when the number of players was reduced to fifteen. He would play for Somerset at cricket and rugby. At cricket, he played four times between 1876 and 1879 with little success. The Somerset qualification came from his family which owned the country estate, Poundisford Park, north of Pitminster. He died at Hove on 13 February 1940, aged eighty-seven.

Henry's older brother Edmund also played for Somerset and was by far the better cricketer. E. Bourdillon **[VOL.5, page 6]** was born in London on 10 November 1844, and educated at Brighton College. He played in Somerset's inaugural match against Dorset at Combe Park, Bath in 1876. He played in a further four principal matches between 1876 and 1879 and achieved a respectable batting average of 28.83, boosted by an unbeaten century against Emeriti in 1879. Cricketing ability clearly ran through the Bourdillon genes as two of Edmund's sons played for Sussex after the First World War, one of them representing Rhodesia, and a great-grandson Paul Bourdillon played first-class cricket for Mashonaland as recently as 1994. Edmund, a teacher, astronomer, inventor, farmer, and author led a full life which spanned ninety-six years. He died in Brighton, a year later than Henry, on 17 June 1941.

CLEMENT HENRY RAVENHILL STOCK [VOL.5, page 251]

Long Ashton in North Somerset has a rich archive of early Victorian photographs thanks mainly to William Ravenhill Stock. He lived at the 'Cottage' in Long Ashton, an imposing 18th century dwelling now known as *Ashover House*. William's father, William Spry Stock, was an importer of sugar from the West Indies and owned a large refinery in Old Market Street, Bristol under the name of W.S. Stock & Co. Sugar refining at that time was an extremely messy and dangerous process subject to fires and explosions; and involving heat, steam, and ingredients such as lime, blood, and animal charcoal. It was also not without financial risk given the volatile price of molasses. Nevertheless, William snr made his fortune out of the business, at least until the middle of the Nineteenth Century when modern refining processes were introduced. William snr had retired by the time of the 1871 census, but three of his sons living in Bristol were managing sugar refineries or were sugar brokers. William Ravenhill Stock and his family had moved out of the city by this time. They first moved to Wraxall which was where Clement Stock, always known as Harry, was born on 9 March 1867. But by the 1871 census they had taken up residence in Long Ashton with Harry's father describing himself as a colonial sugar broker.
It was at Long Ashton that William took an interest in photography and his

amateur work was good enough to feature in publications like *The Sketch, Country Life,* and *Tatler*. Several examples of his copyright photographs are held in the British Library.

This photograph of a young boy with bat in hand was taken by William in 1874. The house in the background is the 'Cottage' and the boy is Harry, aged seven years old. Seven years after this photograph was taken, Harry would feature in the 1881 Somerset team photograph taken by his father.

But more of that later. William's other pastime was cricket and there is enough evidence to show that he was involved with the cricket club soon after his move to Long Ashton. A report in *The Illustrated Sporting News* of June 1866 gives credit to William Stock for being among the organisers of Long Ashton CC's athletics meeting. There is a fascinating account of this meeting in which the brothers E.M. and W.G. Grace excelled in the track and field events. They won all the sprint races up to and including 800 yards. W.G.'s time for 400 yards was an impressive 48 seconds (by comparison, the Olympic gold medal for 440 yards at Athens thirty years later was won in a time of 54.6 secs).

William Stock was keen to ensure that Harry had every opportunity to make the most of his cricketing talents and, to this end, he employed the Somerset professional J. Green **[VOL.5, page 181]** as his footman and butler. It is to be regretted that the photograph of young Harry did not come up for sale before the publication of VOL.5 because it would have been apparent that the image included on page 252 of VOL.5 was not him. The image had been sourced from a photograph of the Lancing College 1st XI of 1882, part of which is shown overleaf, which Lesley Edwards, College Archivist, had kindly supplied.

Believing that Harry had captained the team in 1882 (he didn't until 1883), it was assumed that the young man in the traditional captain's position (shown here sporting a moustache) was Harry. But the young man who captained the Lancing First XI in 1882 was Thomas Pellatt and a close-up of his image was used in VOL.5 instead. A simple comparison with the image of Harry as a seven-year-old shown above would have confirmed Harry to be standing top right in this Lancing College photograph. By coincidence, Tom Pellatt played for the Gentlemen of Wiltshire against Somerset at the County Ground in 1889.

Comparison of Harry's Lancing College image with the photograph below, taken a year earlier, removes any possible doubt over identification. The Long Ashton photograph is shown here as it appeared in the Stock family album with its handwritten note and Harry picked out in the narrative:

As the handwritten caption explains, this photograph was taken on 10 August 1881, the first day of a two-day match. It was affected by rain on the second day leading to an inconclusive draw. By the end of the first day, Somerset had been bowled out for 135 with J.B. Challen **[41]** top scoring on 25. Long Ashton in reply were 39 for 7 wickets when stumps were drawn having struggled to cope with the fast bowling of Somerset's professional, A.J. Fothergill **[5]**. The following day, at times in heavy drizzle, the home team struggled to 76 all out, with Fothergill's figures recorded as 32.2 overs, 18 maidens, 28 runs, 7 wickets. Somerset scored 150 all out in their second innings (John Winter top-scoring with 21) before the heavens opened with Long Ashton on 8 for 2. Long Ashton CC were by no means disgraced by the scores. Their strike bowlers Gage and Ham accounted for eleven wickets and the hosts also had the services of Somerset men H.G.H. Hall **[10 now 43]**, see page 14, J. Green **[VOL.5, page 181]** and W.W.F. Pullen **[VOL.5, page 187]**.
Harry would have been home from Lancing College for the summer holidays when this match was played. This was his first and only appearance for Somerset in 1881 and he didn't play for Somerset during the initial period of first-class cricket, 1882 to1885, most probably because of needing to work for his father at the family's refinery in Bristol. He appears to have had little spare time for cricket beyond turning out for his old club side Clevedon CC on occasional weekends.
Harry had some decent performances for his local club and before long he was again attracting the attention of Somerset. He had a few Club & Ground matches in 1887 and 1888 before being invited to play against Staffordshire in June 1889. He was asked to open the innings with G.B. Nichols **[61]** and against some indifferent bowling on a good pitch in fine weather the pair made hay in the sunshine putting on 115 for the first wicket. He kept pace with his senior colleague and was first out with 56 to his name. Believing that a player of some promise had been found, Somerset kept him in the side for the following games against Warwickshire and the return against Staffordshire but in his four successive innings, batting in the middle order, he managed just 33 runs. He was not selected again in 1889, but he featured in most of the minor matches played by Somerset during the following season. It was not quite enough to break into the XI playing the principal county matches because the club had finally produced a competitive and settled team. It was so competitive that it went through the season unbeaten and forced the authorities to readmit

Somerset as a first-class county in 1891. Harry had just the one opportunity in 1890, in the match against Glamorgan at Cardiff, but he had little chance to impress. Now batting with the tailenders, he got a duck in his only innings. A photograph of the team that played this match has recently surfaced and it can be found on page 220.

Harry's presence in the Glamorgan match suggests that he would have played first-class cricket for Somerset had he remained in the county. But he moved to Oxfordshire in 1890 to try his hand as a farmer on land near Shotover in Oxford. It was here that he met his wife, Alice Birch. They had no children. After spells in Lancashire, they settled for life running a smallholding in Ottery St Mary but later moved to Bisley near Stroud. After Alice died there in 1931, he married Clare Luscombe in 1934 and set up home with her at 'Littlegarth' in Churchill. Like his old Somerset teammate J.A. Winter **[40]**, whose rant in the 1911 census was mentioned in VOL.1, Harry clearly had a disdain for census returns. In the 1939 census he gave his occupation as 'general work of all sorts'. He died at his home in Churchill on 29 May 1954, aged eighty-seven.

EDWARD ASHTON ST HILL [vol 5, page 275]

One final correction needs to be made to the cricketing career of E.T. Hill **[113]** referred to earlier on page 90. Eustace's career has been enhanced by the addition of MCC appearances previously attributed to Edward Roden Hill, but an adjustment needs to be made in the opposite direction. Eustace should *not* have been credited by CricketArchive with a non-first-class Somerset match played against Hampshire at Southampton on 26 June 1890. The original Somerset scorebook clearly shows that it was E.A. St Hill who played in this match. He was not related to the Hill brothers.

Edward was born in Kaiwharawhara, a suburb of Wellington, New Zealand on 2 February 1867. He was the son of Rev Henry Woodford St Hill and Mary Ann née Turner. His father was the headmaster of Kaiwharawhara Grammar School at the time and would go on to become Canon of Napier Cathedral. Edward was sent to school at Bath College, where an aunt, Elizabeth Tanner, who lived in Bathwick, acted as his guardian. He went on to study Classics at Trinity College, Oxford. In 1886 he was the senior scholar at Trinity (meaning that he topped the examination results), although he did not graduate until 1890.

Perhaps this was a consequence of his mother having died in 1888 at sea, of a haemorrhage, en route to England from New Zealand.

There followed a period between the completion of Edward's degree and his acceptance as a fellow of New College, Oxford, when he was a frequent visitor to Bath. He had been a decent cricketer at school and at Oxford playing for his college and putting in a good performance with the bat in the trial match of 1888. But he was never able to break into the University XI. He was invited to play in just the one match for Somerset in 1890 , he scored 20 and 0 in his two innings.

E. A. St Hill – a much-loved schoolmaster at Rugby School, 'blessed with the ability to command silence in the classroom with a raised eyebrow rather than a raised voice'

COURTESY OF TRINITY COLLEGE, OXFORD

Having opted initially for life in academia, he had to leave because only single men were allowed to be fellows. He was married to Sylvia Field, a direct descendant of Oliver Cromwell, and daughter of the professional painter, Walter Field, who enjoyed notable success during the Victorian era. Edward was appointed an assistant schoolmaster at Rugby School, and a housemaster at the school in 1910. Edward and Sylvia would oversee the boys in their care for a further seventeen years until his departure in 1927 at the age of sixty. Judging by his valediction, he had a saintly demeanour worthy of his name. He is described as possessing 'unfailing cheerfulness, an infectious and good-natured laugh, and a remarkable memory for names and faces'.

He and Sylvia would have four children but endured a triple tragedy in 1940 when a son and daughter were killed during an air raid while they were both in residence at Queensborough Terrace in London and, to add to their woes, another son died from a revolver shot to his head while at Sandhurst. The coroner decided that he could not state beyond reasonable doubt that Michael

St Hill had committed suicide. A colleague would write that Edward and his wife bore their loss 'with a fortitude sustained by a deep faith that could remove [sic] mountains'. He died on 30 August 1947 in Wandsworth, London, at the age of eighty. His obituary in *The Meteor* (the Rugby School magazine) affirms that Edward St Hill had 'never made an enemy and never lost a friend'.

HENRY MURRAY-ANDERDON [vol 5, page 279]

Henry was descended from an ecclesiastical line that included several bishops and he was the great, great grandson of Sir John Murray, 3rd Duke of Athol. He may never have left his native county Kent had it not been for the fact that he stood to inherit Henlade House, an imposing Georgian mansion near Ruishton, now the *Mount Somerset Hotel*. He owed his inheritance to his mother's side of the family, the Anderdons. They were extremely wealthy, their riches obtained from West Indian plantations and the slave trade. The family coat of arms had shackle bolts as their heraldic device! Henry moved into Henlade House in 1880, first as a tenant, and inherited the property on the death of his great-uncle in 1888.

Henry's life is well covered in VOL.5, but it did not have sufficient space to place on record his huge contribution in securing the County Ground which was in danger of being lost to cricket. It remains his permanent legacy. It is true, the ground was already being used by Somerset before he came on the scene, but by 1885, Somerset was about to lose its first-class status and was in danger of folding. And it is quite possible that the County Ground could have been lost to the club at this point because the Taunton Athletic Company which held the lease of the ground was near bankrupt with little prospect of turning matters around. The first honorary secretary, E. Western **[27]**, was not coping with the increasing demands of the job and resigned, citing pressures of work. Edward Western had earned his place in history for having set up the club, but his resignation, a decision which may not have been entirely voluntary, was the right way forward because he simply did not have the gravitas and influence around Taunton to solve the club's many issues. Henry had both in spades and would hold the position of honorary secretary from 1885 to 1911, only relinquishing the post because of ill health.

Henry was confirmed as honorary secretary of Somerset in 1885 and enthusiastically set about turning the club around. Earlier that year, Edward Western had talked of the club folding if funds were not found and there is little doubt that Henry helped the club with money from his own pocket before organising a membership campaign to rescue the club. But the need to secure the future of the County Ground was of the greatest concern. The Taunton Athletic Company, which held the lease of the ground, was only being kept afloat by subscriptions from members, most of whom were active cricketers from Taunton CC and Somerset.

Matters came to a head at the company's chaotic AGM in February 1886 with the president, W.G. Marshall, resigning and the secretary, T.G. Williams, stating his intention to resign. The cricketers then held their own meeting under Henry's chairmanship to discuss how they could secure the athletic ground for Somerset. Despite being told that the company would not sell the lease of the ground (still with 8 years to run) the cricketers resolved to take over its management and two days later met with the company directors. The *Taunton Courier* representative, who was present at this well-attended meeting, reported:

... we believe from the opinions expressed that it was the general wish of the directors to assume the position of landlords with regard to the field...that they were not in a position to raise money themselves...that it was felt by the directors that the grounds were far more likely to be a success under the management of the Somerset Cricket Club than by any other arrangement...that the directors had unanimously resolved that the grounds be let to the County Cricket Club at a rental of 100 guineas per annum; which amount would include £45 rent to be paid to the owner, Mr Winter...the management would be entirely in the hands of the County Cricket Club who would be responsible for arranging the use of the grounds by other athletic clubs...

The *Taunton Courier* reporter was in no doubt about the advantages of this arrangement to Somerset stating that:

...they would be provided with one of the best wickets in England, while at the same time the arrangement would be an advantageous one for Taunton, as being the headquarters for the County cricket club, and the result would be a large influx of members, and a greater interest in cricket generally.

It seems the Taunton Athletic Company directors still believed they could call the shots and remain landlords, but Henry had persuaded J.A. Winter **[40]**, to offer his £400 of shares in the company, one-third of its share capital, to Somerset. John Winter's offer was subject to the county club making the ground its headquarters which was exactly what Henry intended. It was a most generous gesture, and it effectively handed control of the company to Somerset as its major shareholder. The directors had nowhere to turn, and Somerset bought out the company for £1246.2s.3d, financed from a mixture of donations and £25 debentures. A new lease of the ground was agreed directly with John Winter in March 1887 before Somerset purchased the County Ground during the mid-1890s for £2,000 (equivalent to £280,000 today). Somerset's current balance sheet rather modestly values the County Ground at less than £2 million.

Henry remained the driving force behind Somerset cricket until failing health forced his resignation as secretary in 1911 at the age of sixty-three. Several good judges, including Sam Woods, would later remark that he had single-handedly ensured that Somerset remained a first-class county. His membership of the MCC Advisory Committee helped in that regard. He lived for another eleven years and appears not to have neglected his civic duties. He remained president of Somerset County Football Association, a position held since 1896, and was president of Somerset from 1915.

His health declined during the spring of 1922 but rallied during the summer with reports that he had made a full recovery. But there was only one outcome for a man suffering from the advanced stages of prostate cancer. He died at Henlade House on 9 December *not* 11 December 1922 as stated in VOL.5. The incorrect date is his universally recorded date of death, but it was noticed while referring to his obituary that newspapers mention Henry dying on Saturday evening. This was 9 December, and the ninth has been confirmed since by reference to Henry's registered death certificate.

New Discoveries – Other

FULLANDS - SOMERSET'S FIRST GROUND

It was believed that there was no image available of the Fullands ground and it was therefore of great interest to discover the following photograph:

It is a superb carte de visite, taken by William Morley the well-known Taunton photographer and is included here with the permission of Allan Collier, Phil Nichols, and Robin Ansell, the authors of *Secure the Shadow–Somerset Photographers 1839-1939* published by the Somerset and Dorset Family History Society in 2018. It is possibly one of the earliest photographs to feature a cricket match, as it is known to date to the mid-1870s if not earlier. It cannot be proved beyond doubt that this is the cricket pitch on which Somerset played their first home matches, but there are enough reasons to believe that this is the Fullands ground. It is clearly a school match, located in the Taunton area. And there were no other public schools in the vicinity around this time which mentioned cricket as a key part of its curriculum. Also, a carte de visite would be very appropriate promotion for a school which boasted in advertisements that its 'cricket ground and play fields were unsurpassed in excellence and beauty of position'. Furthermore, the building in the photograph bears a striking resemblance to the Fullands school photograph shown on page 19 of VOL.5 and maps around that time show that the cricket pitch, formerly known as Bowling Green Meadow, is in exactly the right position relative to the main school building. This evocative photograph may well provide a tantalising glimpse of the illusive Francis Reed **[19]**, still without an image, dispensing advice to his pupils in Latin as he was wont to do in the Somerset slips.

Agreeing to form a Somerset County Cricket Club after the Somerset and Devon match at Sidmouth on 19 August 1875 was the easy part. The hard part was handed to Edward Western, the appointed honorary secretary, who was given the challenging task of implementing the three resolutions laid down at the meeting and formally reported in the *Taunton Courier* of 8 September 1875. The third resolution was 'that the clubs which possess first-rate grounds in convenient locations be requested to allow the use of their grounds for county matches'.

Unsurprisingly, none of the leading clubs to the north of the county greeted the resolution with much enthusiasm and many openly questioned the newly formed club's entitlement to represent itself as the county team and base itself in Taunton. Furthermore, there were no 'first-rate grounds in convenient locations' beyond those in the north of the county other than the one at Fullands. At that time, Bridgwater CC had yet to acquire and develop The Parks, later leased from Henry Murray-Anderdon, and Taunton CC used various temporary and unsuitable grounds along the Wellington Road.

Somerset's first match, against the Gentlemen of Dorset, was played at Combe Park, the home ground of Lansdown CC. It was not an auspicious start for the new club. The *Somerset County Gazette* reported that confusion over the venue for the match (it seems Edward Western had intended to hold the match in Taunton) and overcast weather meant that there were very few spectators in attendance. Combe Park had previously been the regular venue for matches between the Gentlemen of Somerset and Dorset, but the well-used ground would not have been available for other county fixtures on a regular basis. Nor would it have advanced the idea that county fixtures would be played in a centralised location, such as the county town, to attract a wider support base. Somerset resorted to playing the three remaining 1876 fixtures at Fullands in the absence of alternative and convenient venues.

Somerset had good reason to use Fullands School for these home fixtures. There were few pitches in Somerset as good as Fullands and William Reed snr, the school's proprietor, was very sympathetic to Somerset's needs. Each one of his three sons would play for Somerset in due course and the best of these, the Rev F. Reed **[19]**, had already proved his worth as an outstanding bowler for Gentlemen of Somerset. He was in the team at Sidmouth in 1875 and had destroyed Devon's first innings (all out for 33) by taking 7 wickets for 18 runs. Somerset also had close contact with the school through Edward Western, whose day job was to teach at Fullands. But Fullands was always going to be a stopgap and if Somerset were ever going to become a credible first-class county it was imperative to find a home ground suitable for purpose. The *Somerset County Gazette* summed it up perfectly when reporting on Somerset's Cricket Week in August 1878:

Fullands is scarcely the place for a county match. A better ground for cricket we admit cannot possibly be chosen. The wicket is perfection and there is pretty good accommodation for visitors. The ground however is too far from town and the railway station. Taunton people in their present mood will not go a hundred yards to see a cricket match and it is not likely, therefore, that they will go a mile and a half.

It would be several years before a replacement ground materialised. Fullands continued to be used for Somerset's home matches although not according to CricketArchive.

The home match against MCC in 1879 was played at Fullands *not* the 'County Ground' which did not exist as a cricket ground at that time. Likewise, the four matches that were played during the August cricket week of 1880 were played at Fullands. As explained in Henry Murray-Anderdon's biography (page 214), the ground now known as the Cooper Associates County Ground had been acquired by the Taunton Athletic Company and it was always the intention that Somerset would use the ground at the proper time. But it was not quite ready for county cricket or any cricket for that matter. The ground was being tended by W. Underwood who was Somerset's first groundsman and professional ground bowler. He had been groundsman at Fullands School for over ten years and was a prolific wicket-taker in local cricket. He is credited with getting A.J. Fothergill **[5]** a place on the Lord's ground staff. Despite Underwood's best efforts, the County Ground was not used for Somerset's home fixtures in 1881 either. Fixtures against Gloucestershire, Kent, and Hampshire were played at Combe Park while the MCC match on 8 August 1881 was played at Fullands *not* the 'County Ground' as stated in CricketArchive. This was the last ever Somerset match played at Fullands.

SOMERSET v GLAMORGAN 1890

This photograph is of the Somerset team that played Glamorgan at Cardiff on the 25-27 July 1890. It is a rare and previously unpublished image:

Back row: R Humphrey (umpire), T.H. Knight (scorer), J.A. Gibbs, E.W. Ebdon, E.J. Lock, A.E. Clapp, J.H.J. Devey (umpire);
middle row: EJ. Tyler, H. Ross, H.T. Hewett, L.C.H. Palairet, C.H.R. Stock;
front row: V.T. Hill, G.B. Nichols

PHOTOGRAPH COURTESY OF THE LATE ROGER MANN

This is the nucleus of the side that remained unbeaten throughout the 1890 season, earning the club a return to first-class status and championship cricket. The team had remained largely unchanged throughout the season, but several players were rested as the Welsh club were considered weak opponents.
It was an assessment that proved correct with Somerset winning by an innings and 76 runs. It gave the likes of E.J. Lock **[70]** and C.H.R. Stock **[VOL.5, page 251]** an opportunity to play for this successful side. In Ted Lock's case he was there to make up the numbers, probably filling in for his good friend Sam Woods who was taking a well-earned rest. In Harry Stock's case, it could have been another chance to prove his worth to the side, having had little opportunity to do so, but he batted low in the order and scored a duck. His presence in the photograph opposite does however offer another glimpse of Harry Stock to compare with those on page 208. Ted Lock also has an entry in this book beginning on page 65.
This photograph is almost certainly the only copy that has survived and is not in the Cricket Museum's collection. It was originally contained within the album owned by Ted Lock which was sold at auction in 2000. The description of the auction lot confirms that it was present in the album, but when the album came back onto the market years later, this photograph was missing. It was one of several of the more valuable album pages that had been removed which is most unfortunate and sadly quite common. Although this is not the only image of the 1890 team (another can be found on page 10 of *Somerset Cricketers 1882-1914* and repeated on page 282 of VOL.5) it is a welcome addition to Somerset's rich photographic history.

SOMERSET v SUSSEX 1899

Somerset played Sussex at Hove on 25-27 May 1899. The hosts scored 479 in a single innings, and it was enough to beat Somerset by an innings and 49 runs. For once, it was not C.B. Fry or K.S. Ranjitsinhji that plundered the Somerset bowling. Ernest Killick scored a painstaking century in just under three hours and was finally out for 140 runs. He had been badly missed three times during his innings and Somerset had other chances to restrict Sussex's total. It was only George Gill of the eight bowlers used by Somerset, who troubled the Sussex batsmen, with figures of 7 for 117. (It was more of the same at Hove a years later with Sussex winning by ten wickets, Killick scoring another century and Ranjitsinhji scoring a double century).

The Somerset team was photographed during the course of the Sussex match and John Daniell kept a copy in a photograph album which he had started on going up to Cambridge. The album is in the Cricket Museum's collection. This is the photograph of the team that met Sussex at Hove in 1899:

Standing L-R: G.C. Gill, J. McAulay (scorer), E.J. Tyler, H.T. Stanley, J. Daniell, E. Robson;
seated L-R: C.S. Hickley, W.C. Hedley, S.M.J. Woods, A.E. Newton, W.Trask;
foreground G.B. Nichols

SOMERSET v DORSET 1900

This match was played at the County Ground on 14 and 15 August 1900. It is recorded in some official sources, including CricketArchive, as played by the Gentlemen of Somerset, even though such a team had not existed for twenty-five years. Interestingly, Somerset are called Gentlemen, but their opponents, all gentlemen, were plain Dorset.

It is an example of inconsistent naming derived from newspaper sources, which in some cases seem reluctant to move with the times, harking back to the good old days when only gentlemen played cricket. The newspapers could not even agree on what side turned out to play Dorset. It all depended on which was read. The *Somerset County Gazette* remarked that 'This match commenced at Taunton on Tuesday, the Somerset team not by any means being a representative one'. Perhaps this explains why this outdated title was used for the Somerset team. This is the team that played:

Back row L-R: A.E. Lewis (umpire), W.L. Price, J. Daniell, H.E. Murray-Anderdon, J.W. Ebdon, O. Mettam (umpire);*
middle row L-R: W.N. Roe, C.E. Dunlop, S.M.J. Woods, G. Fowler, W. Trask;
front row L-R: H.S. Poyntz, E..P Spurway, O.M. Samson
**J.W. Ebdon, not his brother EW Ebdon as stated in CricketArchive*

It is true that Somerset had rested the professionals, Gill, and Tyler, who returned for the match against Kent the next day, but it was surely done in deference to the weaker opposition rather than any intention to field a team of amateurs. And even without the professionals, the team cannot be described as 'unrepresentative' of a Somerset team. It was comprised entirely of first-class cricketers and three of Somerset's most accomplished cricketers - Messrs Fowler, Woods, and Daniell - played. Somerset overwhelmed Dorset by an innings and 191 runs. Fowler and Woods scored centuries, Daniell was fourteen runs short of his, in Somerset's innings total of 603 for 9 declared. Woods took 11 wickets and Fowler took 7 wickets in this comprehensive victory. By any logic, this team should be recorded as Somerset in the records and archives.

SOMERSET v YORKSHIRE 1900

Standing L-R: T. Mycroft, G.C. Gill, A.E. Lewis, E. Robson, L.C.H. Palairet, C.A. Bernard, A. Shaw;
seated L-R: A.E. Newton, H.E. Murray-Anderdon, S.M.J. Woods, E.J. Tyler, C.E. Dunlop;
in foreground L-R: B. Cranfield, J. Daniell

This fine photograph was never found among those held by the Cricket Museum and consequently was not used in the *Somerset Cricketers* series nor has it ever been published elsewhere. It was only discovered on the author's bat repair visit to Millichamp and Hall at the County Ground where it was found to be hanging on the walls of the bat maker's showroom. It seems that some years ago, the Cricket Museum, which is Millichamp and Hall's landlord, loaned some pictures to brighten up the walls and the photograph had subsequently been missed from the Cricket Museum's collection records. This has since been rectified. It is a rare image which deserves to be seen.
This was the side that played Yorkshire on 20-22 August 1900. Yorkshire were victorious, as was often the case, winning by an innings and 120 runs. The photograph is unique because it is believed to be the only pre-First World War team photograph that was not taken with the old pavilion or the Priory barn as a backdrop. It is taken from the eastern side of the ground and offers the only known view of this undeveloped side of the ground as it would have looked in the early 1900s. The row of houses shown behind the players and umpires was known as Denmark Place which would have had access to St James Street from Coal Orchard between the old Taunton swimming baths and *The Ring of Bells*. The Council purchased the entire row of terraced houses from private ownership for £290 in 1937, but it is not clear when the houses were demolished.

SOMERSET v YORKSHIRE 1901

This was the famous defeat of Yorkshire which is talked of to this day. Somerset were the only county to beat the county champions in the fifty-six matches played by Yorkshire during the two seasons 1900 and 1901 and when the match began on 15 July no-one could have predicted a Somerset victory. Somerset had just been beaten comprehensively by Lancashire (by ten wickets) on the northern tour and morale must have been at a low ebb as the team travelled across the Pennines. The Yorkshire match began badly for Somerset when Sam Woods won the toss and decided to bat on a rain-affected wicket. They were skittled out before lunch for 87 and by the time that they were required to bat again they needed 238 to avoid an innings defeat. In a remarkable turnaround Somerset made 630 in the second innings with a first-wicket partnership of

272 between Lionel Palairet and Len Braund followed by a century from Frank Phillips and two half-centuries from Sam Woods and Vernon Hill. The mighty Yorkshire team, shell-shocked by the events of the second day, fell apart and were all out for 113, losing by 279 runs. A rare copy of the souvenir scorecard printed in 1902 is shown here:

Yorkshire County Cricket Ground,

Leeds, July 15th, 16th and 17th, 1901.

SOMERSET v. YORKSHIRE.

Yorkshire's Two Years' Record Beaten.

Last Year's Unbeaten Champions Defeated by Somerset.

	SOMERSET.	FIRST INNINGS.		SECOND INNINGS.	
1	L. C. H. Palairet	b Hirst	0	c & b Brown	173
2	Braund	b Rhodes	0	b Haigh	107
3	Lewis	c Tunnicliffe b Rhodes	10	b Rhodes	12
4	F. A. Phillips	b Hirst	12	b Wainwright	122
5	S. M. J. Woods	c Hunter b Haigh	46	c Tunnicliffe b Hirst	66
6	V. T. Hill	run out	0	c Hirst b Rhodes	53
7	Robson	c Hunter b Rhodes	0	c Tunnicliffe b Rhodes	40
8	Gill	c Hunter b Rhodes	4	st. Hunter b Rhodes	14
9	A. E. Newton	b Haigh	0	c Taylor b Rhodes	4
10	G. Burrington	c Brown b Rhodes	11	st. Hunter b Rhodes	15
11	Cranfield	not out	1	not out	5
		b2, l-b1, w, n-b,	3	b16, l-b, w, n-b3,	19
		Total...	87	Total..	630

Fall of the Wickets.

1-0	2-0	3-16	4-32	5-38	6-38	7-64	8-65	9-86	10-87
1-222	2-244	3-441	4-466	5-522	6-570	7-597	8-604	9-609	10-630

BOWLING ANALYSIS.

	First Innings.						Second Innings.					
Name.	O.	M.	R.	W.	Wd.	N-b.	O.	M.	R.	W.	Wd.	N-b.
Hirst	12	5	36	2	..	..	37	1	189	1	..	..
Rhodes	16	8	39	5	..	..	46'5	12	145	6	..	..
Haigh	4	0	9	2	..	.	20	4	78	1	..	..
Wainwright	..	..	..	..	..	..	34	3	107	1	..	..
Brown	.	..	..	..	..	..	18	1	92	1	..	..
....	..	..	..	..	..	..	..	..	..	..	..	..

	YORKSHIRE.	FIRST INNINGS.		SECOND INNINGS.	
1	Brown	c Braund b Cranfield	24	c sub. b Gill	5
2	Tunnicliffe	c Newton b Gill	9	c Palairet b Braund	44
3	Denton	c Woods b Gill	12	b Braund	16
4	T. L. Taylor	b Cranfield	1	absent hurt	0
5	F. Mitchell	b Gill	4	b Braund	21
6	Hirst	c Robson b Cranfield	61	l-b-w b Braund	6
7	Wainwright	b Gill	9	c Lewis b Cranfield	1
8	Lord Hawke	b Robson	37	c Barrington b Cranfield	4
9	Haigh	c Robson b Cranfield	96	not out	2
10	Rhodes	c Lewis b Robson	44	st. Newton b Cranfield	0
11	Hunter	not out	10	c Woods b Cranfield	0
		b13, l-b, w5, n-b,	18	b12, l-b, w, n-b2,	14
		Total...	325	Total...	113

Fall of the Wickets.

1-13	2-33	3-44	4-51	5-55	6-86	7-142	8-167	9-285	10-325
1-14	2-57	3-97	4-99	5-104	6-109	7-109	8-109	9-113	10-113

BOWLING ANALYSIS.

	First Innings.						Second Innings.					
Name.	O.	M.	R.	W.	Wd.	N-b.	O.	M.	R.	W.	Wd.	N-b.
Cranfield	27	5	113	4	..	..	18	5	35	4	..	..
Gill	23	2	105	4	..	..	4	1	23	1	..	..
Braund	5	0	33	0	..	..	15	3	41	4	..	.
Robson	10	1	35	2	..	..	..	.	..	..	..	..
Woods	5	1	21	0	..	..	..	..	..	..	..	..
Palairet	1	1	0	0	..	..	..	..	..	..	..	..

Umpires—Wright and Mycroft.

Wisden described the match as the most sensational of the whole season and stated that the victory could furnish few parallels in cricket history. There is a popular photograph of the victorious team which has been well-used in various publications down the years (it can be viewed on page 38 of *A Photographic History 1891-1991* or in *From Sammy to Jimmy*). It has also appeared in the *Somerset County Gazette* from time to time when Yorkshire are in town. But it has always been a mystery why the photograph was taken at Taunton and not Headingley as might be expected. This recently discovered team photograph provides the explanation:

Back row L-R: G.C. Gill, E. Robson, ***J. Daniell****, L.C. Braund, G. Burrington,* ***A.P. Wickham, S. McAulay*** *(scorer); middle row L-R: F.A. Phillips, A.E. Newton, S.M.J. Woods, L.C.H. Palairet, V.T. Hill; front row L-R: B. Cranfield, A.E. Lewis*

This photograph was taken during the match against Hampshire on 22-24

August 1901. It contains the eleven that played against Yorkshire a few weeks earlier and the three that did not play are shown in bold type in the above caption.
The popular photograph of the victorious eleven has each one of them in identical attire and position to the photograph above. When Montague Cooper turned up at the County Ground to take the usual end-of-season photograph against the wall of the Priory Barn, he must have thought it was his lucky day. Having taken the one shown above and scenting a profitable image on his hands, he must have uttered words along the lines: "Right now, you three out of the picture, shuffle up at the back and let's be having the ones that took Yorkshire apart"!

SOMERSET v SURREY 1903

This photograph was taken by Montague Cooper during the last championship match of the season played at Taunton, against Surrey on 20-22 August 1903. It is another that has never been published before:

Standing L-R: S .Brown (umpire), F.M. Lee, H.E. Murray-Anderdon, P.R. Johnson, A.E. Lewis, E. Robson, W. Richards (umpire);
seated L-R: FA. Phillips, L.C.H. Palairet, S.M.J. Woods, L.C. Braund, J. Daniell;
on ground L-R: B. Cranfield, O.M. Samson

Less than an hour's play was possible on the first day of the match which ended in a draw.

SOMERSET v SURREY 1904

This photograph was taken by Montague Cooper during the penultimate championship match of the season played at Taunton, against Surrey on 22-24 August 1904. It is another that has never been published before:

Standing L-R: E. Robson, A.E. Lewis, H.S. Poyntz, P.R. Johnson; seated L-R: H. Martyn, L.C.H. Palairet, S.M.J. Woods, L.C. Braund, J. Daniell; on ground L-R: F.M. Lee, B. Cranfield

As in the previous year against the same opposition, the match was affected by rain on the first day, this time preventing any play at all. Talbot Lewis and Len Braund were the difference between the two sides. Lewis took 5 for 60 in

Surrey's first innings and Braund took 6 for 62 in the second. And with Somerset needing 243 to win. Talbot hit an unbeaten 118 not out to see Somerset home for the loss of three wickets. The photograph below can be dated specifically to the last day of the match because while Montague Cooper was in the ground, he chose to create this magnificent photograph of the game in progress:

The steeplejacks had a splendid view from the top of the chimney. Judging by the batsman's posture at the pavilion end, Talbot Lewis is facing the bowling with John Daniell at the river end. The pair put on 141 for the first wicket which is no doubt why John included this photograph in his album.

THE WESTON FESTIVAL 1921

After many years of deliberation within the club and years of discussion with the Weston-super-Mare Urban District Council, the Pleasure Gardens Committee agreed in August 1913 to recommend the council to agree to lending Clarence Park for a week in 1914. It was subject to the council being reimbursed with the cost of adapting the park, reinstating fencing etc., not to exceed £100. The recommendation was agreed and a local festival committee set up to organise the event. Two three-day championship matches were proposed, against Yorkshire and Essex, for the week commencing 27 August 1914. The local committee were very successful in promoting the cricket week and introduced an inovative season ticket for the expected works holiday crowds. The one problem on the horizon was the possibility of war between Britain and Germany which was eventually announced on the 3 August. There were many objections to the festival taking place, the objectors suggesting that the cricketers should be fighting at the front, but it did go ahead albeit with depleted teams as some had already volunteered their services. In Somerset's case it meant the loss of P.R. Johnson **[133]**, H.S. Poyntz **[160]** and R.E. Hancock **[183]**. Ralph Hancock DSO would not reurn. He died at Festubert within two months of the festival ending.

Somerset sufferred resounding defeats against both counties but off the field the festival was a commercial success and it was no surprise to see it repeated in 1919. This photograph was taken during the 1921 festival and conjures memories of glorious summer days spent on the Clarence Park ground:

It is a wonderfully evocative photograph taken immediately after lunch on the second and final day of the match against Hampshire on 8 August 1921. Watching the death throes of Somerset's second innings are, from left to

right, J. Daniell **[114]**, M.D. Lyon **[237]**, J.C.W. MacBryan **[208]** and R.C. Robertson-Glasgow **[246]**. The overweight gentlemen in whites and jacket, enjoying Somerset's kamikaze batting (there were five run outs in this match), is Lord Tennyson who was taking a break from a heavy lunch and from his exertions during the morning session when he took the decisive wicket of Jack MacBryan from the last ball before lunch. Jack was out for 101. It was Tennyson's only over of the match and broke Somerset's attempts to set Hampshire a reasonable target. Hampshire, set just 78 runs to win the match, achieved this for the loss of two wickets.
The August holiday festival at the seaside town, extending to nine days and three championship matches in its heyday, continued until 1996 by which time the 'festival' had dwindled to a single championship match.

SOMERSET GENTLEMEN v SOUTH AMERICANS 1932

Mention has already been made of the use of the outdated team title, 'Gentlemen of Somerset', which was inappropriately applied to the team that played Dorset in 1900 (page 223). It was used again to describe the Somerset team that played a one-day match against the Gentlemen of Philadelphia at Taunton in 1903. Its use in this match can be quickly discounted as Somerset fielded their two professionals, E.J. Tyler **[62]** and F.P. Hardy **[138]**, which by the conventions of the time, would have precluded the team being called Gentlemen. There is therefore no plausible reason for it being called a Gentlemen of Somerset match except possibly to add symmetry to the fixture title or to appease the Philadelphians' sensibilities.
There has been one further use of the outdated term. It was applied to the team that played the touring South Americans in 1932. The term 'Gentlemen of Somerset' was used in all the media announcements and reports on the match. But the yearbooks name the team as the 'Somerset Gentlemen' and the official scorebook records the team as Somerset. All these official sources imply that the club authorities were never resolved to resurrect Somerset's predecessor of the nineteenth century; they had merely chosen to rest its professionals to match the strength of the opposition.
The name given to this team might be deemed inconsequential, and indeed Keith Walmsley, in his excellent book *THE ABC TOUR The South American Tour to*

Britain 1932 (ACS Publications 2022), describes it as an 'angels on a pinhead debate'. But it could be argued that it affected the way this match was treated by MCC which met soon afterwards to decide the status of the tour matches. As a result, there is an argument for stating that MCC deprived Somerset of a first-class match with consequential impact on first-class statistics.

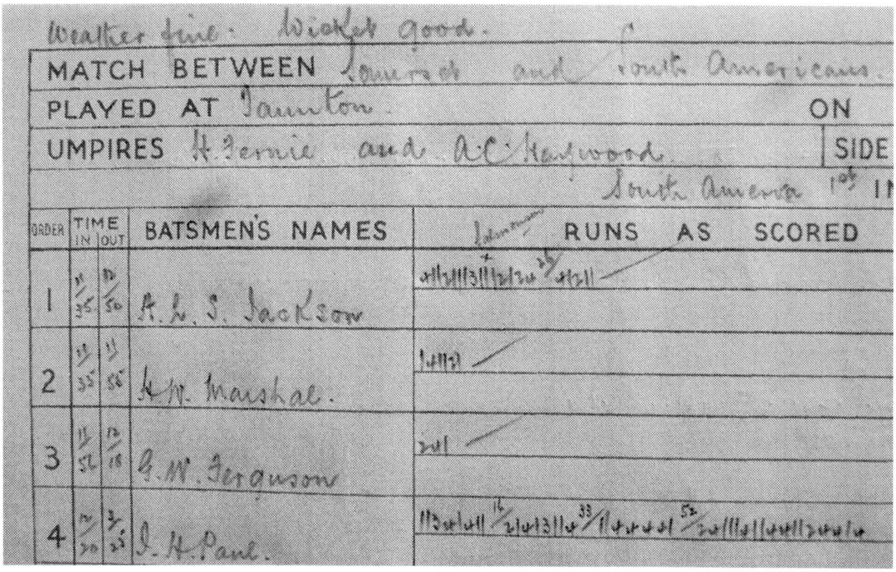

Weather fine. Wicket good.

MATCH BETWEEN Somerset and South Americans.

PLAYED AT Taunton. ON

UMPIRES H. Fernie and A.C. Haywood. SIDE

South Americ 1st IN

ORDER	TIME IN	TIME OUT	BATSMEN'S NAMES	RUNS AS SCORED
1			A. L. S. Jackson	
2			K.W. Marshal.	
3			G.W. Ferguson	
4			J. H. Paul.	

There was no doubt in the mind of Reg Trump, the scorer, that this was match played by Somerset

When the tour was announced in 1931 it was clearly stated that the South Americans would play the amateur teams of Somerset, Leicestershire, Surrey, and Sussex, as part of their nineteen-match tour. When the matches came to be played, Leicestershire and Sussex chose to field full county teams, although the latter county did rest two of their professionals, Bowley and Tate. These two matches were given first-class status. Surrey chose to field a truly gentlemanly group of players none of whom were selected to play in the championship match that followed immediately afterwards. The Surrey match was rightly deemed as non-first-class. Somerset also adhered to the tour's original intention, fielding an amateur side, and leaving out their five professionals. However, the team still comprised nine first-class cricketers that in time could boast 1,265 appearances between them. The team included the captain, Reggie Ingle, and five other regular members of the 1932 championship side: Messrs Northway, Case, White, Bennett and Hawkins. But the match was not awarded first-class status as might have been the case if the club had not added the word 'Gentlemen' to the name of the team. The club, and the staunchly amateur secretary John Daniell in particular, have only themselves to blame.

The MCC decision could not have been based on the strength of the team alone because the Somerset team was as strong as, if not stronger than, others awarded first-class status. For example, one of the six first class matches (a seventh against Worcestershire was abandoned to rain) was against the Army which fielded five players who would have only moderate acquaintance with first-class county cricket and five other players who only have this one first-class appearance to their name. Only J.W.A. Stephenson of this team could be regarded as a genuine first-class cricketer. Another of the first-class matches involved a weak Oxford University team, depleted because of examinations and injury with five of its players never awarded a blue. The University lost the match by ten wickets, one of only two wins for the tourists.

The other tour victory came against Sir Julien Cahn's XI, also given first-class status, and this team was also of moderate quality, except for the South African Test player D.P.B. Morkel (who scored a double century and was still on the losing side) and the fifty-six-year-old John Gunn. Cahn's team fielded five players making their first-class debut, including Sir Julien himself. Stephen Chalke has recently written that 'No English first-class cricketer of the 20th century can have had less ability than Cahn'. The 1932 UK tour followed Sir Julien's tour of South America in 1929/30, and according to Arthur Gilligan, it was Cahn who made the arrangements for this reciprocal tour. It raises the possibility that the MCC decision was Cahn's reward for his involvement in organising the tour as well as for his generosity in sponsoring this and other cricket tours.

If team strength was not the MCC's single consideration, match duration might have been a criterion in deciding which of the tour matches deserved first-class status. All seven first-class matches were of three-day duration whereas the other twelve were planned for, or lasted, one or two days. Pure coincidence? It is entirely possible that MCC were mistaken in believing the Somerset match was a two-day fixture. But it was always planned to be played on 8, 9 and 10 June 1932. The third day was not needed as the South Americans lost by eight

wickets within the first two days.
There are clearly good reasons to suggest that MCC made a wrong decision in Somerset's case. There is zero possibility that the status of this match will ever be reviewed but spare a thought for the eleven Somerset players who were denied a first-class match. A. MacDonald-Watson **[314]** took 7 wickets in the match which would have reduced his first-class bowling average from 27.37 to 21.12, and Jack White would have added another 8 wickets to his career total of 2,355. And Messrs Harvey and Illingworth, the two cricketers on the fringe of selection for Somerset, would have been credited with a first-class appearance for the county. As they came very close to joining Somerset's band of first-class players included in VOL.2, it is worth recording some detail about these two men if only to wonder how these two very talented cricketers ever slipped through Somerset's net.

Kenneth Gordon Harvey

In Ken's case, he was already on Somerset's radar before the match against the South Americans having appeared in a Somerset trial match a month earlier (see page 182). He was eighteen years old and was well-known to the club having played for Somerset Stragglers while still at school. Ken was from a well-known Bristol family. His grandfather, Herbert Harvey, was the managing director of the Ashton Gate Brewery and his father, Major Sidney Lancelot Harvey D.S.O., M.C., was a Bristol solicitor. He was born in Long Ashton on 12 August 1913 and would have no memory of his highly decorated father who survived the First World War with honour but died in Russia soon after while supporting the White Russian forces against the Bolsheviks. Ken was educated at Blundell's School. He played his club cricket for Bristol Bohemians CC and his rugby for Clifton RFC throughout the 1930s, captaining the 1st XV in 1938. He represented both Somerset and Gloucestershire at Rugby.

A faded close-up of Ken, captaining Clifton RFC in 1938 from the Clifton RFC website

He was regarded as one of the finest wicketkeepers in the Bristol area and was an excellent bat. In 1938, he played for Gloucestershire 2nd XI but a year later he left the area to further a business opportunity in Bournemouth. During the war he played a good deal of cricket with Denis Compton who described him as one of the best amateur wicketkeepers in the country. After the war he returned to Bristol Bohemians, regularly topping the batting averages and assuming the 1st XI captaincy in 1950. Ken died in North Somerset in February 2001.

Ron Illingworth

Ron was also on Somerset's radar and, as a Taunton CC regular, was well-known to the Somerset players. He was a very talented allrounder; a hard-hitting, top-order batsman, useful medium-pace bowler, and excellent fielder. Somerset had two hours left of day two to wrap up victory against the South Americans and avoid taking the match into the third day. When Ron went in first wicket down Somerset still needed 131 runs to win. An hour and twenty minutes later, the match was over. Ron had hit powerfully all around the wicket giving no chances and his 82 not out included eleven fours.

Born in Leeds on 27 July 1908 (no relation to Ray of Yorkshire and England), Ron played cricket and football for Yorkshire Schools and gained a diploma in teaching at Leeds University in 1930. His first teaching engagement was as a geography teacher at Huish's Grammar School. He played cricket for Taunton CC where he had several good knocks in 1932 including a century for Taunton Thursday. In 1934, he almost achieved 1,000 runs for Taunton but an enforced absence of two matches robbed him of this rare achievement. He finished the season with a batting average of 60.

Ron was also a fine rugby player, captaining Taunton RFC at centre and playing at three-quarters for Somerset throughout the time he was in the county. Somerset lost a fine all-round sportsman when he left the area in 1936 to further his teaching career at Burton-on-Trent Grammar School, but he often returned to guest for Taunton RFC in the late 1930s to team up with F.M. McRae **[343]** creating a formidable partnership in the centre. After leaving Taunton he played club cricket for Ealing Dean where he scored 1,000 runs in

1937 as well as achieving the best bowling figures of the season with 9 wickets for 40. Thereafter it was cricket and rugby for Burton. At the end of the war, he played for a Services XI against an Empire XI which included five Test cricketers, including Constantine, Achong and Gover, and scored 174 against them. Ron was at Burton Grammar school for thirty-seven years retiring in 1973. He died on 11 June 1992, aged eighty-three.

Both these men were good enough to play for Somerset and better cricketers than many that did. Neither has a first-class appearance to their name but arguably, they should have done following this appearance against the South Americans.

Appendix 1
The Long Ashton match 1881

Three of the twelve players featured in the 1881 Long Ashton photograph only played in this one minor match and are therefore not covered elsewhere in the *Somerset Cricketers* series. As this photograph is of historic importance, so are the men in it. Biographies of these three players are provided below:

Joseph John Cross

Joseph was one of two players in the Long Ashton photograph who stubbornly refused to give up their identities. The other was J.A. Winter **[40]**. Neither had any known image to assist with identification. It was more important to get Winter's image correctly identified because, as explained in John's additional biography (page 37), he had a significant impact on Somerset cricket off the field of play. The breakthrough came when it was discovered that one of the two mystery cricketers, the player standing far left in the photograph, was wearing an Uppingham Rovers blazer and cap and that could only point to one man, Joseph Cross.

Joseph was born on 23 February 1849 in Merriott, the son of the Rev Joseph

Cross, a minor canon at Bristol Cathedral. He was educated at Crewkerne School initially before he was sent to Uppingham School in 1865 at the age of sixteen. He was in the rugby 1st XV in 1866 but never made the cricket XI. He never made the University XI either while at Brasenose College, Oxford, but he did turn out for Clifton CC while he was home for the summer. The link with W.G. Grace's local club will account for his two matches played for Gloucestershire in 1870 when his two first-class matches yielded 5 runs.
Joseph played for Uppingham Rovers; a cricket club established in 1863 by former members of the school 1st XI. Election to the club was usually restricted to 1st XI cricketers but an exception was made for Joseph who was elected in 1871. He continued to play occasionally until 1883. Hedley Stroud, the Rovers' honorary secretary has kindly given permission to copy the page shown here, taken from volume one of the Rovers' historic archives entitled *The doings of the Uppingham Rovers*. The photograph shown here is of the Rovers team that played Hampshire at Southampton in August 1883. Joseph is seated far left, wearing the same blazer he wore in the Long Ashton photograph.

On graduating from Oxford, he taught Greek and classical studies at Newton College in Newton Abbott. He was also housemaster at The Hall, the college's prep school, a position he held for twenty-eight years. He played cricket for Sidmouth CC and Devon in the late 1870s and early 1880s including the Devon v Somerset fixture of 1879. He also appeared for Devon against Somerset at rugby. At Weston-super-Mare in December 1876, he played in the Devon three quarters under the captaincy of W. Massey **[13]** and against the half back pairing of Henry Bourdillon and

Julius Willmott who were also playing cricket for Somerset at the time.
Joseph was thus well known to Somerset cricketers, playing with and against them at both sports. And he would have had the chance to renew some of those acquaintanceships when turning up to play for MCC against Somerset at the County Ground in a two-day match ending the day before the Long Ashton match of 1881. His rugby captain William Massey was in opposition playing for a strong Somerset team. Three days after the Long Ashton match, he turned out for MCC again, this time against Lansdown at Combe Park.

Joseph continued to play cricket well into his forties playing for Uppingham Rovers, Newton College, and Newton Blues. He married Helen Philippa George in 1898 when he was forty-nine and Helen, a spinster, was forty-three. Helen was born, lived, and married in Westbury-on-Trym, and when Joseph retired from Newton College in December 1904, the couple returned to Westbury before a final move to Bath in 1915. He had continued to do some part-time tutoring, including giving some temporary assistance at Gresham's School, Holt. But when war broke out, he came out of retirement to cover for a schoolteacher at Sherborne School called away to fight.

He was at Sherborne for eight terms but a serious illness in the midsummer term of 1917 forced him to stop teaching. He was clearly well respected at Sherborne. The headmaster talked of 'his hearty willingness, which endeared him to all alike' and the *Sherburnian* would later recall that 'His absolute sincerity, manliness, cheerfulness, and humour, endeared him to old and young alike. He had been a keen cricketer and still was a keen sportsman with gun and rod. He was apt somewhat to overtax his strength in his love of outdoor exercise'.

Joseph never fully recovered from the illness, and he died at his home in Bath on 2 November 1918, aged sixty-nine.

Herbert George Fuller

Herbert was born in Bath on 4 October 1856. He was one of seven children born to Frances Jane née Pooley and Stephen Leedham Fuller, a coach builder. The firm of 'S and A Fuller' had been based in Bath since the early eighteenth century and Stephen was the fourth generation of Fullers running the business from Kingsmead Street and employing about fifty men and boys. When the motor car began to replace the carriage in the 1890s, the family was the first in Bath to move with the times and provide its customers with the modern form of transport.

Herbert was the youngest of four boys and showing early academic promise was sent to Christ's College, Finchley, where he excelled at several sports and was school captain. From there he went up to Peterhouse, Cambridge, and was awarded a second-class MA degree in mathematical tripos in 1880. Apart from a brief break around 1884 when he travelled abroad, Herbert spent the rest of his adult life studying, lecturing, and coaching at Cambridge. He was a senior scholar at his college and immersed himself in Cambridge life. He became pro-proctor at the University and held the University appointment as secretary of the Lodging House Syndicate.

Rugby was his main sport although one of the family's treasured mementos was an oar with which he rowed at 5 for his college eight in 1880. He played as a forward in six Varsity rugby matches for Cambridge, a record that stood for more than one hundred and thirty years. He had been captain of Bath RFC by the age of nineteen and led Somerset RFC (capped thirteen times). Herbert was the first Bath player to be capped by England. He played six times for his country, the first on 6 February 1882, a friendly against Ireland at Lansdown, and the last on 5 January 1884 against Wales in the home nations championship. Later he was secretary and president of the Rugby Football Union (RFU) at Cambridge and a member of the RFU committee. Prematurely bald, he is reputed to have invented the skull cap.

The 1881 Long Ashton match was Herbert's only cricket appearance for Somerset, but like J.J. Cross, he played in the MCC match that followed, in his case playing for Lansdown. Tragically, for such a gifted sportsman, he started to suffer from headaches and loss of balance during his late-thirties. Never married, he was looked after at his brother's house in Streatham during the closing stages of his illness. His brain tumour ended his life there on 2 January 1896, aged thirty-nine. His body was interred in the family grave at Lansdown Cemetery, joining his father Stephen who had died six months previously. The funeral was attended by hundreds of mourners which included his six siblings and their families, the secretary of the RFU, and by H. Fox **[8]** representing Somerset RFU. A memorial brass plaque was installed by his friends in Peterhouse College's chapel

Thomas Uttermore Cross

Thomas was the younger brother of J.J. Cross. Thomas, or 'Tory' as he was known by his school nickname, was born on 14 March 1851 in Merriott. He was educated at Blundell's School and Exeter College, Oxford. On graduating in 1873 he taught briefly at Wellington College before becoming a master at Blundell's. He never left, working tirelessly for the school and did much to enrich the relationship between the school and the local community in Tiverton. He played cricket for the school and organised an annual fixture against the Tiverton townsfolk. The Long Ashton match was his only appearance for Somerset and apart from his school matches there is no record of him playing any university or higher standard of cricket. It seems likely that his brother had brought him along for a game and it may explain why Somerset fielded twelve players. He batted at twelve and scored 4 and 11 not out.

As for his personal life, the Lord Bishop of Exeter was a close friend and Thomas was ordained by the Bishop at Exeter Cathedral in 1877. Thomas married Isabella

Hadow in 1883, the daughter of a local rector, and they had a daughter Anna in 1888. He took on increasing amounts of responsibility at school as well as in the community. His duties were conscientiously performed, but the weight of these tasks began to take their toll. In the spring of 1892, he broke down under the stress of it all and was given time to recuperate. Six months later after there was no improvement in his condition, he was advised by his doctors to take a trip to Madeira. He died en route on 7 December 1892, aged forty-one, having fallen overboard, most likely having taken his own life.

A small volume of work entitled *Blundell's Worthies* was published in 1904 to celebrate Blundell's tercentenary. It contained chapters on twenty-five noted Blundelians from the past three hundred years, ranging from the founder Sir John Popham, who as Attorney-General prosecuted Mary Queen of Scots and as Lord Chief Justice sentenced Guy Fawkes, to Samuel Wesley, brother of John, and to Bamfylde Moore Carew, the King of the Gypsies. Such was the high regard held for the Rev Thomas Uttermore Cross that he is among this august company of men.

Appendix 2
In memoriam

The following first-class cricketers have died since the publication of VOL.4:

2019

John Henry Harris **[385]**, 28 March, Sidmouth, aged eighty-three.

Dennis Raoul Whitehall Silk **[412]**, 20 June, Langport, aged eighty-seven.

Michael Antony Sutton **[370]**, 28 June, Teignmouth, aged ninety-eight.

2020

Roy Smith **[373]**, 20 September, Weston-super-Mare, aged ninety.

2021

Lewis Pickles **[405]**, 11 June, Skelmanthorpe, aged eighty-eight.

Clive Frederick Davey **[393]**, 3 August, Taunton, aged eighty nine.

2022

James Michael Parks **[471]**, 31 May, Worthing, aged ninety.

Frank Terence Willetts **[441]**, 24 October, Truro, aged eighty-two.

Jeremy Lloyds **[486]**, 22 November, Moreton-in-Marsh, aged sixty-eight.

2023

Cleveland Vincent Lindo **[438]**, 6 January, Stoke-on-Trent, aged eighty-six.

The oldest surviving Somerset cricketer at the time of writing is presumed to be J.D. Stenton **[391]** who, if alive, would have been ninety-eight on 26 October 2022. His family have refused to engage with the author as to whether John Stenton is still alive. Next oldest is Michael Hanna **[380]** who was born on 6 June 1926 and first played for Somerset seventy-two years ago. Michael is very much alive and in good health for his age.

Michael Hill

Michael never played for Somerset, but he was one of the most influential figures in recent Somerset history. He died on 27 December 2022. Michael was born at Stockland Lovell, near Bridgwater in 1934 and was educated at King's Canterbury. On leaving school he worked on the family farm, but always got to watch one day's cricket a year, which was normally Somerset against the tourists in Taunton. Michael obtained life membership in 1965, in return for writing off a £60 loan he had given the club five years previously and then took a more active interest in the club. He was voted in as one of the nine appointed vice president members. This was the beginning of a long association with Somerset, serving as chairman of cricket, then chairman of the club and later president, finally stepping down in 2003. During his time with Somerset, he was responsible for the re-introduction of the yearbook in 1979, editing it from 1987 until 2003.

Michael was a true gentleman who despite the pressures of running a highly successful farming business was a familiar figure at home and away matches during the season.

Michael at the Shepton Mallet EGM in 1986 during his time as chairman. He was the steadying hand and remained calm throughout this difficult time in Somerset's history